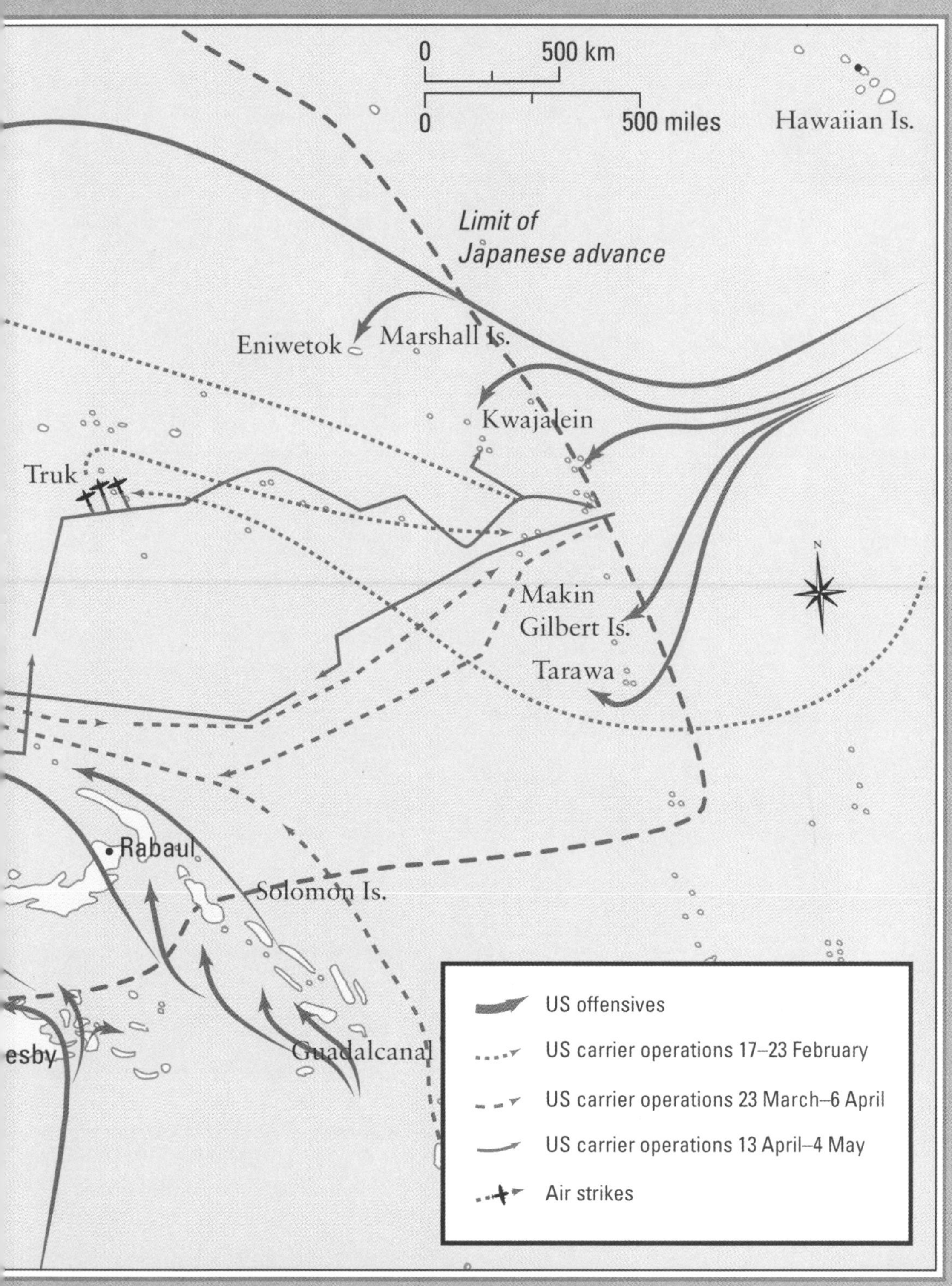
0
500 km
0
500 miles
Hawaiian Is.
Limit of
Japanese advance
Eniwetok
Marshall Is.
Kwajalein
Truk
Makin
Gilbert Is.
Tarawa
Rabaul
Solomon Is.
esby
Guadalcanal
US offensives
US carrier operations 17–23 February
US carrier operations 23 March–6 April
US carrier operations 13 April–4 May
Air strikes

THE MARINES IN WORLD WAR II

THE MARINES IN WORLD WAR II

MICHAEL E. HASKEW

THOMAS DUNNE BOOKS
ST. MARTIN'S PRESS NEW YORK

THOMAS DUNNE BOOKS
An imprint of St. Martin's Press

The Marines in World War II.

For information, address St. Martin's Press, 175 Fifth Avenue,
New York, N.Y. 10010.

www.thomasdunnebooks.com
www.stmartins.com

Library of Congress Cataloging-in-Publication Data
on file at the Library of Congress

ISBN: 978-1-250-10116-7 (hardcover)
ISBN: 978-1-250-10117-4 (e-book)

Editorial and design by
Amber Books Ltd
74–77 White Lion Street
London N1 9PF
United Kingdom
www.amberbooks.co.uk

Project Editor: Michael Spilling
Designer: Jerry Williams
Picture Research: Terry Forshaw

Printed in China

First U.S. Edition: December 2016
10 9 8 7 6 5 4 3 2 1

PICTURE CREDITS
Unless listed below all images are courtesy of the United States Marine Corps History Division.

Alamy: 8 (Stocktrek Images), 85 (Philip Game)
Art Collection, National Museum of the Marine Corps, Triangle, Virginia: 18, 48
Art-Tech: 25, 71 both, 84, 89, 109, 137, 180, 188, 212
Cody Images: 36, 44, 46, 49, 57, 75, 78, 88, 105, 146, 150, 158, 162
Mary Evans Picture Library/Illustrated London News: 27
Getty Images/Time Life: 67
Ronald Grant Archive: 26
Library of Congress: 10
US Department of Defense: 15, 76/77, 79, 131, 160/161, 178, 179, 183, 190, 210

Contents

INTRODUCTION

The United States Marine Corps traces its history to November 10, 1775, seven months before the 13 American colonies declared their independence from the British Crown. Since then, the role of the Marine Corps has evolved during two-and-a-half centuries of war and peace.

Initially conceived as shipboard infantry that would find among their primary tasks the maintenance of security between officers and crewmen—effectively a deterrent to mutiny—and the armed contingent that would board an enemy vessel in close combat, the Marines were also to be capable of fighting on land.

During its history, the Marine Corps has deployed to hotspots around the world, from Latin America to Southeast Asia, and from the Mediterranean coast of Africa to the continent of Europe. Its sternest test, however, occurred during World War II as the Marines served as the primary ground force during the offensive that traversed the Central and South Pacific through a series of bloody encounters against determined Japanese defenders, carrying the fight to the very doorstep of the Home Islands.

Opposite: A Marine aims his M1 Garand rifle on Puruata Island during landing operations in Empress Augusta Bay, Bougainville, November 1943.

In the process, the Marines made otherwise obscure and practically worthless spits of land—Tarawa, Peleliu, Iwo Jima, Okinawa, and others—household words. Amphibious warfare—transport across a vast expanse of ocean and then landing on hostile beaches and advancing inland to take control of enemy-occupied territory—became the hallmark of the modern Marine Corps. From 1942 to 1945, the Marines experienced some of the harshest combat in modern military history. They suffered horrific casualties, often perfecting processes and tactics as they advanced, and refused to accept anything short of the ultimate victory.

The emergence of the Marine role in modern amphibious warfare emanated from the realization that safeguarding American interests in Europe and the Pacific, particularly in light of the nation's overseas possessions gained following the Spanish-American War, required an expeditionary force that could be transported and deployed by naval vessels and capable of establishing advance bases and conducting sustained offensive or defensive operations.

Initial conceptualization of such a force was decidedly defensive in nature, and in 1913 the Advance Base Force was established. Comprised of two regiments, including infantry and field artillery for mobile defense and coast artillery, engineers, and other specialists for static defense, the fledgling force numbered 1750 officers and men. The following year, an aviation detachment was included with the Advance Base Force. Established in the spring of 1912, when Lieutenant Alfred A. Cunningham was detailed for flight training and later designated Naval Aviator No. 5 and Marine Aviator No. 1, Marine aviation was in its infancy.

Anticipating Threats

Despite the defensive orientation, a few visionary Marine staff officers recognized the possibility

Marine Recruit Training

Marine Corps recruit training was formally established in 1911 under Major General William P. Biddle, Commandant of the Marine Corps. Biddle mandated two months of training for recruits at four original depots—Philadelphia; Norfolk, Virginia; Puget Sound, Washington; and Mare Island, California. A year later, Mare Island became the lone West Coast recruit depot, and in 1915 the East Coast recruit depot was relocated to Parris Island, South Carolina.

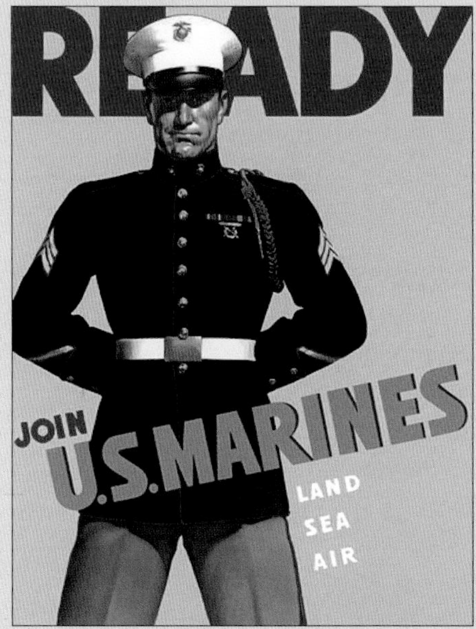

This World War II-era recruitment poster exhorts potential recruits to join up. At this time, the Marine Corps was made up mainly of volunteers.

During World War II, nearly 500,000 Marine recruits were trained stateside. Each received seven to eight weeks of training following an experiment that had shortened the period to a single month, which proved wholly inadequate. A third recruit depot was established at Montford Point, adjacent to the major Marine base at Camp Lejeune, North Carolina. Montford Point was exclusively for African-American recruits, and 20,000 graduated from the facility. Camp Lejeune and Camp Pendleton, near San Diego, California, were established in 1941 and 1942 during the early months of preparation for World War II. Active Marine units trained at these facilities, and as the strength of the Corps increased during the war years, new units were established and staged for deployment overseas.

As the Marine role expanded in the Pacific, the Corps maintained training facilities on the Hawaiian island of Oahu and at forward bases in Australia and New Zealand. Marine units that had experienced combat were also routinely pulled back to these bases for further training and to assimilate replacements.

of military conflict with Imperial Japan nearly three decades before it actually occurred. One of these officers, Major Earl Ellis, understood that the successful prosecution of a war with Japan would require the establishment of several bases at strategic locations across the Pacific, including Hawaii, Guam, Wake Island, and the Philippines. The United States would also be tasked with seizing territory occupied by the Japanese. The only way to accomplish such missions would be offensive projection of forces into enemy-held territory.

The Expeditionary Force

The seizure of Vera Cruz in Mexico in 1914 and unrest two years later in Haiti and Santa Domingo required the deployment of Marines to Central America and temporarily shifted the focus of Marine strategists from the Advanced Base concept. The Marine Corps grew to a peak strength of 73,000 during World War I, and the Advance Base Force was augmented to nearly 6300 personnel. By 1921, the Advance Base Force had been renamed the Expeditionary Force and was considered capable of establishing an advance base or dealing with unrest in the Caribbean. Postwar manpower constraints delayed the establishment of a similar force on the West Coast.

When the terms of the Treaty of Versailles were concluded in June 1919, a number of former German colonial possessions in the Pacific were mandated to Japan. In effect, the Japanese had extended their potential zone of defense significantly, and if these islands were fortified and in turn supported by a strong Japanese navy, they would present significant obstacles to an American offensive.

Once again, Major Ellis was uncanny in his discernment of the character of future warfare in the Pacific. In 1921, he completed a modified version of his earlier advance base ideas. In Operations Plan 712, also known as *Advanced Base Operations in Micronesia*, Ellis actually predicted the necessity of capturing islands in such now-familiar archipelagos as the Marshalls and the Marianas, naming several of the islands that the Marines took by storm a generation later.

Ellis was not alone. High-ranking Marine officers agreed with his perspective, and among them was Major General John A. Lejeune, then Commandant of the Marine Corps. In 1923, Lejeune told a gathering at the Naval War College: "The seizure and occupation or destruction of enemy bases is another important function of the expeditionary force. On both flanks of a fleet crossing the Pacific are numerous islands suitable for submarine and air bases. All should be mopped up as progress is made... The maintenance, equipping, and training of its expeditionary force so that it will be in instant readiness to support the Fleet in the event of war I deem to be the most important Marine Corps duty in time of peace."

After World War I, defense appropriations in Congress were curtailed substantially, and during the 1920s the Navy establishment emphasized preparedness for traditional ship-versus-ship confrontations and the role of naval aviation in future wars. Landing exercises were conducted only on a limited scale.

Nevertheless, in 1927 the Joint Board of the Army and Navy issued a directive titled *Joint Action of the Army and Navy*, which stated that the Marine Corps would bear primary responsibility "for land operations in support of the fleet for the initial seizure and defense of advanced bases and for such limited auxiliary land operations as are essential to the prosecution of the naval campaign."

The document went on to clearly delineate the role of the Marine Corps in establishing and maintaining the readiness of a landing force, stating: "Marines organized as landing forces perform the same functions as above stated for the Army, and because of the constant association

Above: Marine recruits march during a training exercise, Parris Island, South Carolina, May 1942.

with naval units will be given special training in the conduct of landing operations."

Following the clear definition of the Marine Corps' role in amphibious warfare, it became necessary to designate a force specifically assigned to train and develop amphibious tactics. In 1933, the Fleet Marine Force was created. Secretary of the Navy Claude A. Swanson issued General Order 241, specifying command responsibilities. By the summer of 1934, the necessary doctrine and practical application were taking shape in a "textbook" that was eventually published with the title *Tentative Landing Operations Manual*. In 1938, the Department of the Navy officially adopted the manual under the title *Fleet Training Publication 167*, while the Army incorporated it as *Field Manual 31-5*. The text addressed situations unique to amphibious warfare such as the coordination of naval gunfire, air support, ship-to-shore movement, loading combat units aboard transport ships, and the conduct of shore parties. In effect, the template for Marine amphibious operations in World War II had been laid down.

The World at War

At the same time that the structure and charge of the Fleet Marine Force were being clearly defined, the rise of totalitarian regimes in Europe and Asia foreshadowed the coming global conflict. On September 8, 1939, a week after Nazi Germany invaded Poland and ignited World War II in Europe, President Franklin D. Roosevelt proclaimed a state of limited national emergency. On May 27, 1941, the condition was heightened to an unlimited national emergency. Marine Corps manpower increased steadily throughout the period.

During the months preceding the Pearl Harbor attack, recruiting maintained a pace of about 2000 personnel per month. In July 1941, the Corps' total strength stood at 53,886. By the end of the year, the impetus of Pearl Harbor had increased total enlistment to 143,388, and enlistments averaged 20,000 per month.

When the Marine Corps reached its peak strength from 1941–1945, it had grown from a small expeditionary force of two brigades to two full corps comprised of six divisions, five air wings with 132 squadrons, 20 defense battalions, and a parachute battalion with a total complement of 475,000 personnel.

As World War II progressed, Marines on air, land, and sea served in a variety of roles and in every theater of the conflict. They were stationed aboard ships of the U.S. Navy, performed garrison and security duties, flew countless air missions, and participated in covert operations and training.

However, the Marines are best remembered as the gritty, determined combat force that matured rapidly, learned hard lessons, took on the powerful defenders of the Empire of Japan, crossed the Pacific Ocean island by island, and fought, bled, died—and won.

Marine Corps Base Quantico

Perhaps the best known permanent facility operated by the United States Marine Corps is Marine Corps Base Quantico, located in northern Virginia near Washington, D.C. Established as Marine Barracks Quantico in the spring of 1917, the facility served as a training base for thousands of Marines during World War I. In response to the growing prospects of a war in the Pacific during the 1920s, Quantico became a center for the development of the equipment and tactics needed to prosecute such a conflict.

Marine officers based at Quantico were largely responsible for the development of Marine amphibious warfare doctrine during the years between the world wars. Equipment was designed and tested there, while direct assault tactics were perfected and close air support techniques were refined. More than 15,000 officers received training in amphibious warfare at Quantico during the period.

Concurrent with the establishment of the Fleet Marine Force in 1933, officers stationed at Quantico organized the emerging Marine Corps amphibious doctrine into a publication titled *Tentative Manual for Landing Operations*. All aspects of amphibious assault were addressed, including logistics, air support, naval fire support, and the functionality of the beachhead. In 1938, the initial document was adopted as *Fleet Training Publication 167*, and it became the template for all Marine Corps amphibious operations conducted during World War II.

Quantico served as headquarters for the Fleet Marine Force until 1941, and with its departure the base embarked on a future devoted to the training of individual Marines. Today, Marine Corps Base Quantico is home to numerous commands and schools that provide educational experiences to enhance the career paths of Marine personnel.

CHAPTER 1

FIERY AWAKENING

In the opening phases of the war, U.S. Marines played a major part in defending Pearl Harbor and at the Battle of Midway, setting the scene for the amphibious operations that were to follow.

Standing at attention on the stern of the battleship USS *Arizona*, moored at Quay F-7 on Battleship Row in Pearl Harbor, Hawaii, a U.S. Marine honor guard prepared to raise the flag of the United States. The time was just before 8.00 a.m. on Sunday, December 7, 1941.

Two hours earlier, from a position 230 miles (370km) north of the island of Oahu, six aircraft carriers of the Imperial Japanese Navy, *Akagi*, *Kaga*, *Soryu*, *Hiryu*, *Shokaku*, and *Zuikaku*, turned into the wind to launch a powerful aerial striking force of 353 planes in two waves. The target of the First Air Fleet was the anchorage of the U.S. Navy's Pacific Fleet at Pearl Harbor. Other installations of the U.S. Navy and the Army, including Hickam Field, Wheeler Field, Bellows Field, the naval air stations at Kaneohe and on Ford Island in the heart of Pearl Harbor, and Ewa Marine Corps Air Station (also known as Ewa Mooring Mast Field) to the west were to be attacked as well. Other Japanese forces were to strike the Philippines, Wake Island, Midway Atoll, Guam, and Malaya.

Opposite: On alert for a renewal of the Japanese attack of December 7, 1941, American anti-aircraft gunners scan the skies from a .50-caliber machine-gun emplacement.

Years of diplomatic dialogue, charges, countercharges, provocations, and embargoes had come to an end. Imperial Japan had girded for war, and preemptive strikes against the U.S. military in Asia and the Pacific were expected to herald the defeat of the United States, shocking the Americans so profoundly that they would sue for peace and allow Japan to fulfill its territorial ambitions across the region without restraint. Successful attacks against Pearl Harbor and other installations would render the United States military impotent.

The architect of the Japanese attack on Pearl Harbor and other military targets on Oahu was 57-year-old Admiral Isoroku Yamamoto, Commander-in-Chief of the Combined Fleet of the

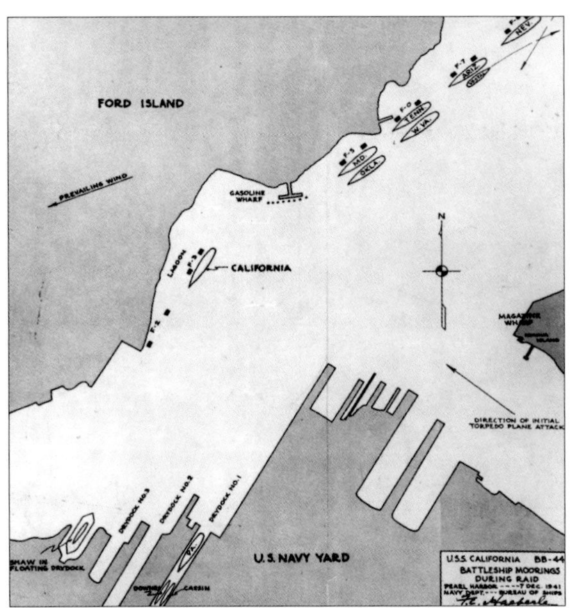

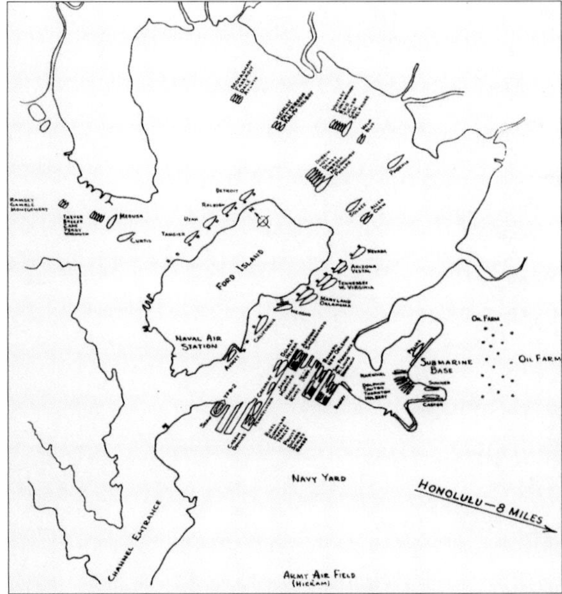

Above: Eight big battleships of the U.S. Pacific Fleet were at Pearl Harbor on Sunday, December 7, 1941. Six of them were moored along Battleship Row at the eastern end of Ford Island.

Imperial Japanese Navy. Yamamoto reasoned that the risky operation offered the best opportunity for a rapid Japanese victory in a war with the United States that most of Japan's civilian and military leadership had deemed inevitable.

Battleship Row

Moored along Pearl Harbor's Battleship Row at the eastern end of Ford Island that fateful Sunday morning were the battleships *Maryland* inboard of the *Oklahoma*, *Tennessee* inboard of *West Virginia*, *Arizona* inboard of the repair ship *Vestal* 200ft (61m) from the stern of *Tennessee*, and *Nevada* astern of *Arizona*. Just to the west lay the battleship *California*. The *Pennsylvania* was in Drydock 1 along with the destroyers *Cassin* and *Downes*. On the western side of Ford Island were moored the old target battleship *Utah*, the light cruisers *Detroit* and *Raleigh*, and the seaplane tender *Tangier*. Altogether, 96 warships of the U.S. Navy were present in Pearl Harbor.

The primary Japanese targets, the aircraft carriers of the Pacific Fleet, were at sea. *Lexington* was headed to Midway Atoll to deliver a squadron of Marine bombers. Delayed by a storm, *Enterprise* was returning to Pearl Harbor after delivering supplies to Wake Island. The third carrier, *Saratoga*, was steaming into the harbor at San Diego, California, as the Pearl Harbor attack got underway.

True to one of their original reasons for existence, Marines continued to serve aboard many ships of the U.S. Navy during the years between the world wars. On the morning of December 7, Marines were aboard 15 ships in the harbor, including eight battleships, two heavy cruisers, four light cruisers, and a support vessel. They provided shipboard security and often manned anti-aircraft guns.

The Marines of the honor guard on the stern of the *Arizona* heard the crump of the first

Opposite: Moored outboard of the battleship USS *Tennessee*, the battleship USS *West Virginia* was struck by several Japanese aerial torpedoes. In this photo, sailors aboard a motor launch pull a wounded seaman from the water as the *West Virginia* blazes.

Japanese bombs falling around the seaplane hangar on Ford Island. They glimpsed aircraft on strafing, bombing, and torpedo runs, hurriedly completed the raising of the flag, and then ran to battle stations. On Ford Island, the three Marine privates set to render honors to the flag completed the task, but not to the recorded tune of "Colors". Instead, "General Quarters" blared over the loudspeakers as Old Glory was raised.

Mitsubishi A6M Zero fighters under Lieutenant Commander Shigeru Itaya actually opened the Japanese attack, strafing Kaneohe Naval Air Station at 7.48 a.m. Marines assigned to Kaneohe were the only Americans there who had ready access to weapons, and they began firing back at the low-flying planes immediately. Seven minutes later, Ford Island and Hickam Field were under attack by Aichi D3A Val dive-bombers. At 7.57 a.m., the first Nakajima B5N1 Kate torpedo planes loosed their weapons. Level bombers attacked the harbor at 8.05 a.m.

Kates under Lieutenant Jinchi Goto, flying as low as 50ft (15m), lined up on the *Oklahoma* and slammed three torpedoes into her port side. Almost immediately, the battleship began to list to 45 degrees. Two more torpedoes found their mark and the great vessel rolled over and capsized. The *West Virginia* was struck by a total of seven torpedoes and also began to list; however, alert counterflooding allowed the ship to settle to the bottom of the harbor on an even keel. On the other side of Ford Island, the *Utah* took two torpedoes and capsized. A third torpedo hit the *Raleigh* below the bridge, flooding its forward engine room.

A catastrophic explosion ripped apart the 32,500 ton (29,483 tonne) *Arizona*. Several Japanese bombers had attacked the battleship, scoring two hits. The first bomb damaged air intakes and caused a shaft of smoke to rise from the stack. The second bomb struck the ship slightly aft of Turret No.2, passing through the main and second decks, crew quarters below, and exploding on the third deck directly above the powder magazines for the 14in (35.5cm) main batteries. In a flash more than 1100 men were killed or mortally wounded aboard the *Arizona*, 72 of them Marines.

Aboard the broken and sinking battleship, Major Alan Shapley, slated to leave the *Arizona* shortly for reassignment to the 2nd Marine Division in San Diego, encountered Lieutenant Commander Samuel G. Fuqua, the ranking officer aboard at the time. Fuqua told Shapley that he had given the order to abandon ship. Shapley and Corporal Earl C. Nightingale were near the mooring quay when a secondary explosion blew them into the water. Shocked by the concussion, Nightingale began swimming toward a pipeline some 450ft (140m) away. However, his strength began to wane.

Shapley swam to Nightingale, grabbed his shirt, and took him in tow. Then Shapley, too, became exhausted. Nightingale told the officer to let go and save himself. Shapley refused, and the two struggled on together. Miraculously, they reached safety. Later, Nightingale praised Shapley: "I would have drowned but for the major."

As the *Oklahoma* began to heel over to port, hundreds of sailors and Marines were trapped inside the hull. Second Lieutenant Harry H. Gaver, Jr. went to his knees while trying to close a watertight hatch on the port side of the battleship near the barbette of Turret No.1. His friend Ensign Paul H. Backus hurried past on his way from his quarters to his battle station on the signal bridge. Backus remembered the young Marine's heroic but futile effort to help with damage control and never saw Gaver alive again.

Casualties at Oshu

Chaos reigned across the island of Oahu, and everywhere Marines assisted in rescue efforts, fired at the attackers, and did what they could for the wounded. At Hickam Field, 35 men were killed while they were eating breakfast when a Japanese bomb smashed the mess hall. More than 20 others were killed as they readied bombers for training flights. At Wheeler Field, where most of the island of Oahu's fighter strength was stationed, 25 Val dive-bombers, followed by strafing Zeros, destroyed most of the 140 aircraft parked in neat rows.

The 36 Consolidated PBY Catalina seaplanes at Kaneohe were shredded by a dozen Zeros in an attack that lasted only eight minutes. Only three planes at Kaneohe escaped damage. Bellows Field was strafed by a single Zero about 8.30 a.m., following a warning from one enlisted man that Kaneohe had been "blown to hell!"

Ewa Marine Corps Air Station included a 5000ft (1524m) airstrip and a mooring mast for airships near the operations and intelligence buildings. Elsewhere, tents and wooden structures housing the motor pool, supply depot, and shops were scattered across the installation. Captain Leonard Ashwell, the officer of the day on that Sunday morning, was exiting the officers' mess at 7.53 a.m. He checked his watch and looked skyward as a flight of 18 Kates roared toward Pearl Harbor. At the same time, Ashwell realized

Below: Thick black smoke rises in the distance as ships of the U.S. Pacific Fleet and shore installations burn furiously after the Japanese attack. This view of the parade ground at the Pearl Harbor Marine Barracks was taken between 9.30 and 11.30 a.m. on that fateful morning.

that Ewa was under attack. He ducked back into the officer's mess and yelled: "Air Raid! Air Raid! Pass the word!"

Most of the 48 planes at the Marine base were Douglas SBD Dauntless dive-bombers and Grumman F4F Wildcat fighters, comprising three squadrons of the 21st Marine Aircraft Group. As at other airfields, the planes were lined up neatly in rows to protect against sabotage. They made easy targets, and 29 were riddled by a flight of 21 Zeros from the carriers *Akagi* and *Kaga* that strafed for more than 20 minutes.

Flames came dangerously close to the hospital and adjacent buildings where medical supplies were stored. Firemen leaped into the open to protect the structures. Another Marine jumped into a fire truck and headed across the runway toward several burning aircraft. The Japanese fighters shot out the rear tires, and the fireman took cover behind stacked crates.

Lieutenant Colonel Claude A. "Sheriff" Larkin, the base commander, was driving to Ewa from Honolulu in his 1930 Plymouth when the attack began. A single Zero peeled off and began peppering .303in (7.7mm) machine gun bullets at Larkin's car. The Marine officer hit the brake, left the engine running, and dove for cover into a ditch. He was wounded by shrapnel, but escaped with his life. As the raider winged away, Larking ran back to his car and continued toward Ewa, just in time to be strafed again—this time he was wounded in the hand and leg. Ignoring the searing pain, he issued orders as best he could in defense of the base.

Below: This artist's interpretation of combat depicts Marines engaging Japanese aircraft at Pearl Harbor. The primary weapon the Marines are firing is the .30-caliber Browning M1917 water-cooled machine gun. The Browning machine gun was a mainstay of the Marines during World War II.

Above: Marines ready their M2 Browning water-cooled .50 caliber machine guns on three-legged pedestal mounts, an anti-aircraft configuration. This photograph was taken in 1942 at Ewa, after the attack on Pearl Harbor.

Minutes after the first Japanese fighters roared away from Ewa, at least a dozen more rolled in. These were from the carriers *Soryu* and *Hiryu*, spitting lead at targets of opportunity, including the Marines' personal automobiles parked near the center of the base. During the short respite between fighter attacks, the Marines grabbed what weapons and ammunition they could. They fired steadily at these latest attackers, and a bullet punctured the forward fuel tank of Petty Officer 1st Class Kazuo Muranaka's Zero. With that, the marauding fighters withdrew.

Preparing for the Second Wave

By the time the Japanese aircraft of the first wave headed back toward their carriers, most of the military installations on Oahu were a shambles. The attackers had lost only three fighters, a single dive-bomber, and five torpedo planes.

The 170 Japanese planes of the second wave were 45 minutes behind the first and reached Pearl Harbor just before 9.00 a.m. Eighty Vals, led by Lieutenant Commander Takeshige Egusa, attacked Pearl Harbor.

Finding the holocaust of Battleship Row shrouded in smoke, the second wave concentrated on the *Nevada*, the only battleship to get underway during the attack. She had sortied at 8.50 a.m., and as many as 15 bombs exploded near the ship, five scoring hits. The *Nevada* was also down by the bow from the torpedo hit suffered during the first wave, and the Japanese hoped to sink her and block the entrance to the harbor. Eventually, the battleship was beached at Hospital Point with 50 dead and 109 wounded.

One bomb blast nearly stripped Corporal Joe R. Driskell's entire uniform from his body,

A Fateful Photo Session

Above: **Ewa Marine Corps Air Station on Oahu sprawls before the camera lens prior to the Japanese attack. Marine Technical Sergeant Harry Anglin and his son, Hank, endured a harrowing experience during the unexpected attack.**

Technical Sergeant Henry H. Anglin rose early on Sunday morning December 7, 1941, and a short time later he left his home in Pearl City, near Honolulu, for the drive to Ewa Marine Corps Air Station, where he was responsible for the installation's photographic section. This day was special. Anglin brought along Hank, his three-year-old son, so that he could take a few pictures of the child to send to his grandparents.

As the sergeant prepared to snap his camera's shutter, he heard a disturbance that he remembered sounding like "the mingled noise of airplanes and machine guns." He stepped outside the photographer's tent and was shocked to see aircraft with the rising sun of Japan emblazoned on their wings strafing the edge of the airfield. While the father looked skyward, the son darted out of the tent toward the sound of the gunfire. When Sergeant Anglin realized that his son was in grave danger, he sprinted toward the boy and covered him.

As bullets sprayed dirt over their heads, the father crawled 100ft (30m) while protecting his son and reached the relative safety of a radio trailer as bullets tore into its door. The pair then scurried back to the photographic tent, where Anglin told Hank to stay put under a wooden bench. Remembering his job, the sergeant gathered equipment to begin taking photos of the attack but was wounded in the left arm. Holding his useless limb, he checked on his son and found Hank pointing at a Japanese bullet lying on the floor. The youngster advised, "Don't touch that, daddy! It's hot!"

During a lull in the strafing, Anglin took Hank to the Ewa stockade, where a woman offered to drive the boy home. Amid the chaos of the day, this was easier said than done. It would take a few hours to get the boy safely to his mother, who was understandably worried and had left home to find her son.

wounding him seriously in both legs. Driskell had been manning an anti-aircraft gun at the time. He refused medical treatment, looked for another gun to service, fought fires, and helped evacuate other wounded men. When water lines that cooled machine guns on the *Nevada's* foremast were ruptured and the barrels began to overheat, the crews under the command of Gunnery Sergeant Charles E. Douglas disregarded an order to evacuate and continued firing. Both Driskell and Douglas received the Navy Cross for their heroism.

The Kates and Zeros of the second wave attacked the air installations on Oahu again. At Hickam Field, Hangars 13 and 15 were heavily damaged by 550lb (250kg) bombs, and repair shops, armament buildings, and the steam plant were damaged. Kaneohe was hit by Kates that destroyed a hangar and four seaplanes. Fighters strafed the field twice more, and Japanese pilot Fusata Iida attempted to crash into the base armory when he realized his plane was hit and that he would not be able to return to his carrier. Instead, riddled with machine-gun fire, his Zero crashed into a hillside.

At 8.35 a.m., Vals from the carrier *Shokaku* appeared above Ewa and were met with a sustained volume of fire from rifles, machine guns, and even pistols. The Vals dropped bombs and maneuvered with wings over to allow their rear gunners to fire at ground targets. Technical Sergeant William Turnage had supervised the effort to get Ewa's machine guns into action. When the task was complete, he manned one of the weapons and stitched the underside of a Val, which began trailing smoke as its engine sputtered. Master Technical Sergeant Emil Peters and Private William Turner took up a firing position in a damaged Dauntless dive-bomber and were believed to have shot down two Vals before strafing wounded them both. Turner later died.

Across Oahu, the Japanese second wave had encountered substantial anti-aircraft fire from defenders on full alert and had to contend with a few American fighter planes that managed to get aloft. The raiders lost six Zeros and 14 Vals. A total of just 29 Japanese planes were shot down during the raid.

Corporal Joe R. Driskell was wounded in both legs by a bomb blast, but carried on fighting fires and evacuating wounded men from the burning USS *Nevada*.

The last of the Japanese aircraft turned toward their carriers around 10.00 a.m. The damage was widespread and horrific. The *Arizona* and *Oklahoma* were sunk, total losses. *California* and *West Virginia* were sunk but later repaired. *Nevada*, *Pennsylvania*, *Maryland* and *Tennessee* had suffered significant damage. The *Utah* was sunk and never salvaged. The destroyers *Cassin* and *Downes* were damaged beyond repair, while the *Shaw* was eventually returned to service. The cruisers *Raleigh*, *Honolulu*, and *Helena* were damaged but repaired. A total of 165 U.S. aircraft were lost.

A total of 2403 Americans had died and nearly 1200 were wounded. A total of 109 Marines were killed and 69 wounded aboard the naval vessels, at Ewa, and at other installations scattered across the ravaged island. The United States was at war with Japan, and the Marines were in the thick of it.

War Comes to Wake

Just over 2300 miles (3700km) west of Oahu and across the International Date Line, Major James P. S. Devereaux, a veteran of 18 years in the Marine Corps and commander of the Wake Detachment of the 1st Defense Battalion, received word of the attack on Pearl Harbor just after 7.00 a.m. on December 8, 1941. At the same time,

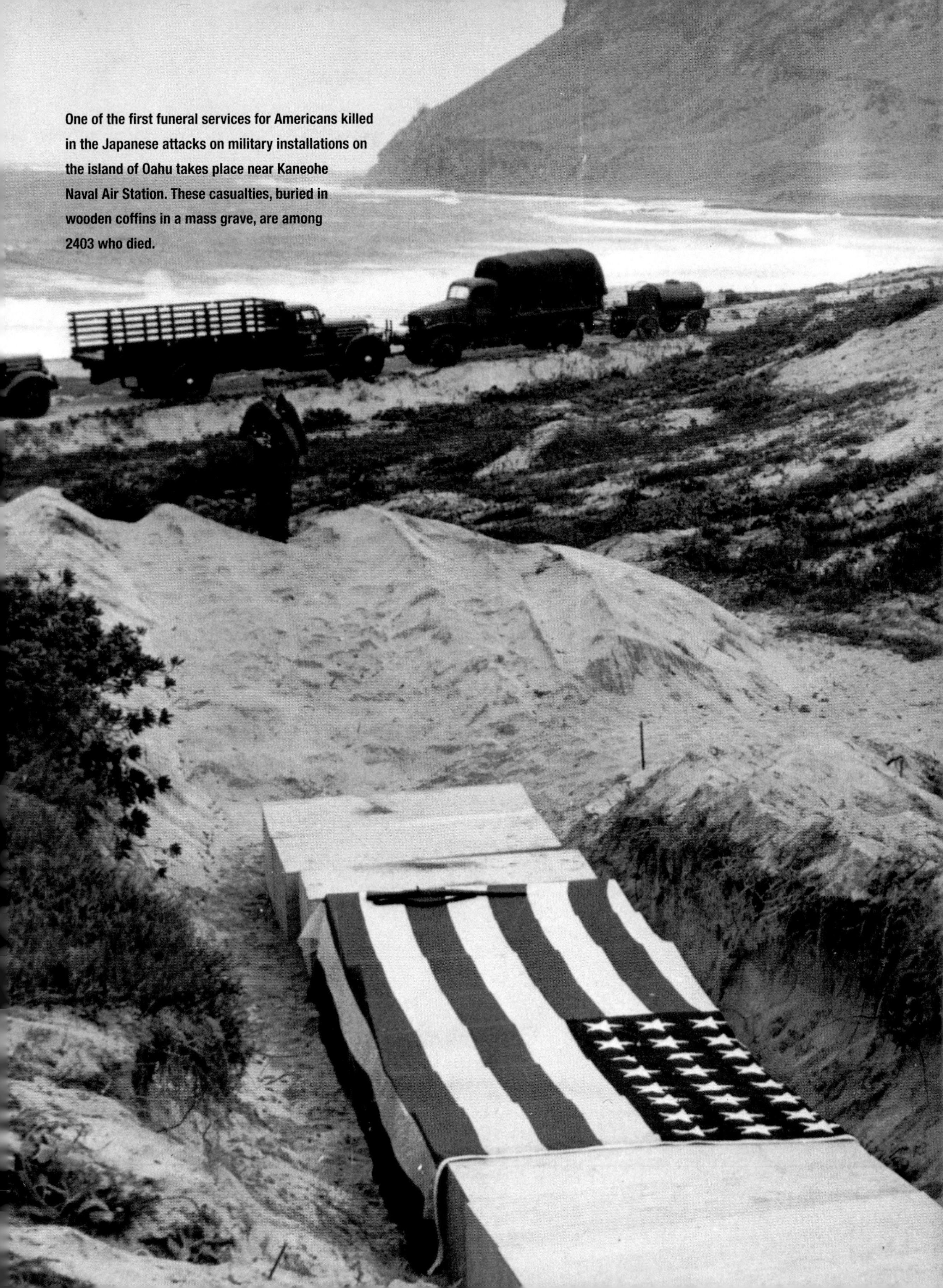

One of the first funeral services for Americans killed in the Japanese attacks on military installations on the island of Oahu takes place near Kaneohe Naval Air Station. These casualties, buried in wooden coffins in a mass grave, are among 2403 who died.

Above: These Grumman F4F Wildcat fighters of Marine Squadron VMF-211 were destroyed by the Japanese during the heroic defense of Wake Island. The Marine pilots who fought the Japanese in the air above Wake were under the command of Major Paul A. Putnam.

Navy Commander Winfield S. Cunningham, in overall command at Wake since November 28, ordered the Marine detachment to battle stations.

American commanders had known for some time that in the event of war with Japan, Wake Island (actually a coral atoll composed of three islets, Wake proper, Wilkes, and Peale) would be a prime target for Japanese offensive action. In January 1941, a military base was constructed at Wake, and by late summer about 450 Marines of the 1st Defense Battalion, along with 71 Navy personnel and more than 1100 civilian workers for contractor Morrison-Knudsen, were at Wake, while 45 Chamorros (the local indigenous people) were employed at the Pan American Airways station, a stop for the Pacific flights of the famed Pan Am Clipper aircraft that routinely transited the Pacific.

On December 4, a dozen F4F Wildcat fighter planes of Marine Squadron VMF-211 arrived at Wake under the command of Major Paul A. Putnam. The fighters were a welcome addition to the scant defenses. Along with their small arms, the defenders could muster only half a dozen 5in (12.7cm) guns, a dozen 3in (7.6cm) guns primarily used as anti-aircraft weapons, and 18 .50-calibre machine guns. The heavier guns were placed at the most advantageous positions around Wake, particularly in those areas that were considered most likely approaches for a Japanese amphibious landing.

Cunningham and Devereux knew that it was only a matter of time before the Japanese struck, and they did not have long to wait. Just after 7.00 a.m. on December 8, a force of 34 Japanese Mitsubishi G3M2 Nell bombers rose into the sky from their base on the island of Roi in the Marshalls. Just before noon, they arrived above

Wake and began discharging their cargoes of destruction from 1500ft (460m).

The raid was devastating. Eight of the VMF-211 fighters were destroyed on the ground, their protective revetments not yet completed. Putnam took a bullet in the shoulder, while 18 members of the squadron were killed and 15 men wounded, five of them pilots. Two of the squadron's Wildcats had been set to escort a flight of Pan Am's *Philippine Clipper*, scheduled to depart that morning. First Lieutenant George A. Graves and 2nd Lieutenant Robert "J." Conderman ran for their planes. Graves was killed while climbing into his cockpit as a Japanese bomb demolished the Wildcat, which erupted in a ball of fire. Conderman was seriously wounded and pinned under the wreckage of his fighter. More than 20 civilians were killed, and no Japanese planes were lost.

The next morning, 27 Japanese bombers returned. The Marines had worked to improve their gun emplacements, and the four remaining Wildcats from VMF-211 were on patrol when the enemy planes arrived shortly before noon. Pilots 2nd Lieutenant David D. Kliewer and Technical Sergeant William J. Hamilton teamed to shoot down one Japanese plane. The two 3in (7.6cm) guns of one Marine anti-aircraft battery fired 100 shells at the enemy and damaged 12 of the attackers.

The hospital was destroyed in the raid, killing one previously wounded man from VMF-211, while a metal shop and warehouse were seriously damaged. Three Marines who had been driving a gasoline truck died when a bomb struck the foxhole where they had taken shelter.

During the night of December 10, the submarine USS *Triton* and lookouts on Wake spotted flashes of light and the silhouette of what was undoubtedly a Japanese warship, the vanguard of the Japanese invasion force under Rear Admiral Sadamichi Kajioka that had departed Kwajalein in the Marshalls to the south on December 8. The powerful Japanese task force included three light cruisers, six destroyers, supporting vessels, and a contingent of troops from their Special Naval Landing Force to seize the atoll.

Marines Fight Back

In the predawn hours of December 11, the Marines braced for the Japanese attack. The four Wildcats of VMF-211 were armed with 100lb (45kg) bombs under each wing and took off shortly after 5.00 a.m. Minutes later, the first enemy naval shells began falling on Wake as the Japanese ships sailed westward and moved closer. The Marine gunners held their fire, following the enemy vessels until Cunningham remarked, "What

Right: This Marine is shown in combat gear similar to that worn by the Marines of the Wake Detachment, 1st Defense Battalion, at Wake Island. Early in World War II, the Springfield Model 1903 bolt-action rifle, World War I-era helmet, and leggings were standard issue.

WAKE ISLAND
America's Beach of Bayonets
Quotation from President Roosevelt's Message to the Congress
on the State of the Union, Jan. 6, 1942
"There were only some four hundred United States Marines, who in the heroic and historic defense of Wake Island, inflicted such great losses on the enemy. Some of these men were killed in action and others are now prisoners of war. When the survivors of that great fight are liberated and restored to their homes, they will learn that a hundred and thirty million of their fellow citizens have been inspired to render their own full share of Service and Sacrifice"
Paramount Pictures
Paramount Pictures

Left: This poster touts the release of the wartime feature film *Wake Island* (1942) starring Brian Donlevy, Robert Preston, and MacDonald Carey. The heroic Marine stand produced some of the first American heroes of World War II.

are we waiting for, open fire. Must be Jap ships all right."

At 6.10 a.m., the Marine guns barked. One 5in (12.7cm) battery on high ground near Wake's Peacock Point appeared to hit a Japanese cruiser, but exposed its own location. However, the return fire was woefully inaccurate. Another Marine battery damaged a Japanese transport.

On Wilkes islet, Battery L under the command of 1st Lieutenant John A. McAlister had been damaged during an earlier air raid, and its crew was having difficulty gauging the range to a growing number of offshore targets. Nevertheless, Battery L's 5-inchers were ordered into action. Swiftly, three salvoes hit the Japanese destroyer *Hayate*, which blew up and sank with its entire 167-man crew. Two more destroyers took hits from Battery L.

At the extreme tip of Peale islet, Battery B, commanded by 1st Lieutenant Woodrow M. Kessler, took on three Japanese destroyers and a pair of cruisers. One gun was disabled, and the crewmen shifted to assist with another that was still operational. A Japanese destroyer was hit and set afire, while 17 sailors were killed.

Compounding the Japanese difficulties, heavy seas swamped or overturned numerous landing boats, and Kajioka made the difficult decision to suspend the operation and retire out of range of the superb Marine gunnery. While they were contending with the shore batteries, however, the Japanese also came under attack from Major Putnam's four Wildcats, airborne since before daylight. Apparently, no Japanese planes were in the air that morning, and when the warships that had engaged Lieutenant Kessler's Battery B began to retire, the Wildcats dove on them from 20,000ft (6100m). Putnam, Captain Frank C. Tharin, and Captain Herbert C. Freuler raked the cruiser *Tenryu* with machine gun fire. Captain Henry T. Elrod dropped his bombs on the destroyer *Kisaragi*, starting a substantial fire. The crippled vessel limped off to the south and was later observed to explode and sink with all hands. Elrod's Wildcat took anti-aircraft fire, and although he managed to land on a rock-strewn beach on Wake, the plane was damaged beyond repair. Only three Wildcats remained airworthy, but these shuttled back and forth with fresh pilots, strafing and harassing the Japanese.

Second Lieutenant John F. Kinney and 2nd Lieutenant Carl R. Davidson took on 17 Nells that split into two groups, while Battery D on Peale islet fired at the enemy planes. Two of the bombers were shot down and 11 were damaged. Major Putnam credited each of the pilots with a kill.

Although the landing effort on December 11 was repulsed with embarrassing losses, the

Japanese were far from finished. Air raids on Wake continued, eroding the combat efficiency of the garrison and inflicting casualties. News of the heroic stand by the embattled Americans reached the home front, and broadcasters noted that when Wake's defenders were asked what they needed the reply was: "Send us more Japs!"

Plans were drawn up for the relief of the Wake garrison, but such an operation was eventually deemed too risky in the face of overwhelming Japanese naval power. As the realization that they were on their own became apparent, Lieutenant Kinney wrote: "We began to figure out that the U.S. was not going to reinforce us."

Wake proved a tough nut to crack, and the Japanese diverted the carriers *Soryu* and *Hiryu* and several escorts that were retiring from the Pearl Harbor raid to Wake on December 16. Japanese bombers continued to pound the Americans, and by the 20th VMF-211 was down to a single serviceable Wildcat fighter. When carrier-based planes hit Wake on the 21st, strafing Zeros kept Putnam from approaching the Wildcat while Vals pounded the airfield. When the Japanese turned back toward the *Soryu* and *Hiryu*, Putnam took off and tried to follow them but was unsuccessful.

The two other Wildcats were repaired and got back into action on December 22. Lieutenants Freuler and Davidson engaged a large formation of Kate bombers. Freuler shot down two before his Wildcat was heavily damaged and he sustained serious wounds. The same Zero pilot who hit Freuler then got behind Davidson and shot him down in flames.

Before dawn on December 23, a strengthened Japanese task force returned to Wake. Under cover of darkness, enemy troops landed and the last hours of resistance on the atoll began to tick

Below: These Marines, members of the Wake Detachment, 1st Defense Battalion, fought bravely at Wake Island against overwhelming odds and helped to develop the reputation of the Marine Corps as an elite combat force.

away. Marines had skillfully deployed machine guns around the three islets, and a mobile reserve was ready for action. Japanese *Patrol Boat No.33* brought troops ashore and beached at Wake islet. A short while later, 2nd Lieutenant Robert M. Hanna led a gun crew to a 3in (7.cm) mount near the airstrip.

Supported by Major Putnam's airmen, who had no planes to fly, Hanna's crew loaded the weapon, and since the gun had no sights the lieutenant directed its fire by looking directly down the bore. The first shot ripped through the bridge of *Patrol Boat No.33* and 14 more shells followed, and soon the vessel was burning furiously, with dead and wounded strewn about its deck. The firelight illuminated another Japanese craft, *Patrol Boat No.32*, beached nearby, and the Marines shelled it as well. Three Japanese naval infantrymen rushed the Marine gun position, and Hanna shot them dead with his pistol.

Commanding the mobile reserve, 1st Lieutenant Arthur Poindexter directed machine-gun fire against a pair of Japanese landing barges attempting to reach the shoreline east of Wilkes Channel. Then teams of volunteers worked their way toward the barges and attempted to lob grenades into them. One actually detonated inside a barge's hull, causing numerous casualties. Throughout the night and into the following afternoon, Poindexter commanded a spirited defense against overwhelming odds.

Everywhere on Wake, the Marines, Navy personnel, and civilians who had chosen to take up arms resisted the enemy. However, defeat at the hands of a superior force was a foregone conclusion. Covering the perimeter around Hanna's 3in gun, Putnam was wounded in the jaw. Blood stained the photographs of his young daughters that he carried in his pocket. Putnam held his line together and told his men resolutely, "This is as far as we go!"

Captain Elrod, whose bomb had shattered a Japanese destroyer days earlier, exposed himself to enemy fire while covering men that were keeping the Marine guns supplied with ammunition. As the first light of dawn tinged the sky, a rifle bullet killed Elrod at his post.

Individual acts of heroism delayed the Japanese, but Wilkes islet fell prior to sunrise. The Americans were being squeezed into isolated pockets of resistance, and by 6.30 a.m. Cunningham had conferred with Devereux and authorized arrangements for surrender. As the morning wore on, word of the capitulation was passed and Devereux walked in company with Japanese soldiers to convince a number of his hard-fighting Marines to lay down their arms.

All organized resistance ceased shortly after 1.00 p.m. The fight for Wake was over—49 Marines were dead and 32 wounded, while three Navy personnel had been killed and five wounded. An Army communications detachment of five soldiers surrendered intact. Since the beginning of the siege, 70 civilian workers had been killed and 12 injured. The Japanese suffered more than 800 dead and 300 wounded in the fighting on the atoll and aboard several naval vessels that were lost or damaged. The price of victory had been high.

The Marines fought heroically at Wake, boosting the morale of the American public at a time when good news from the Pacific was scarce. The epic defense of the atoll was soon immortalized in the feature film *Wake Island* that played to packed theaters across the United States, and the 15 days of fighting firmly established the reputation of the Marine Corps as a tough, dedicated combat force.

Guam and the Philippines

During the opening hours and days of World War II in the Pacific, Japanese forces also struck

Opposite: This makeshift plaque was dedicated to the Marines, U.S. Army personnel, and civilians who opposed the Japanese during the battle for Wake Island, December 8–23, 1941.

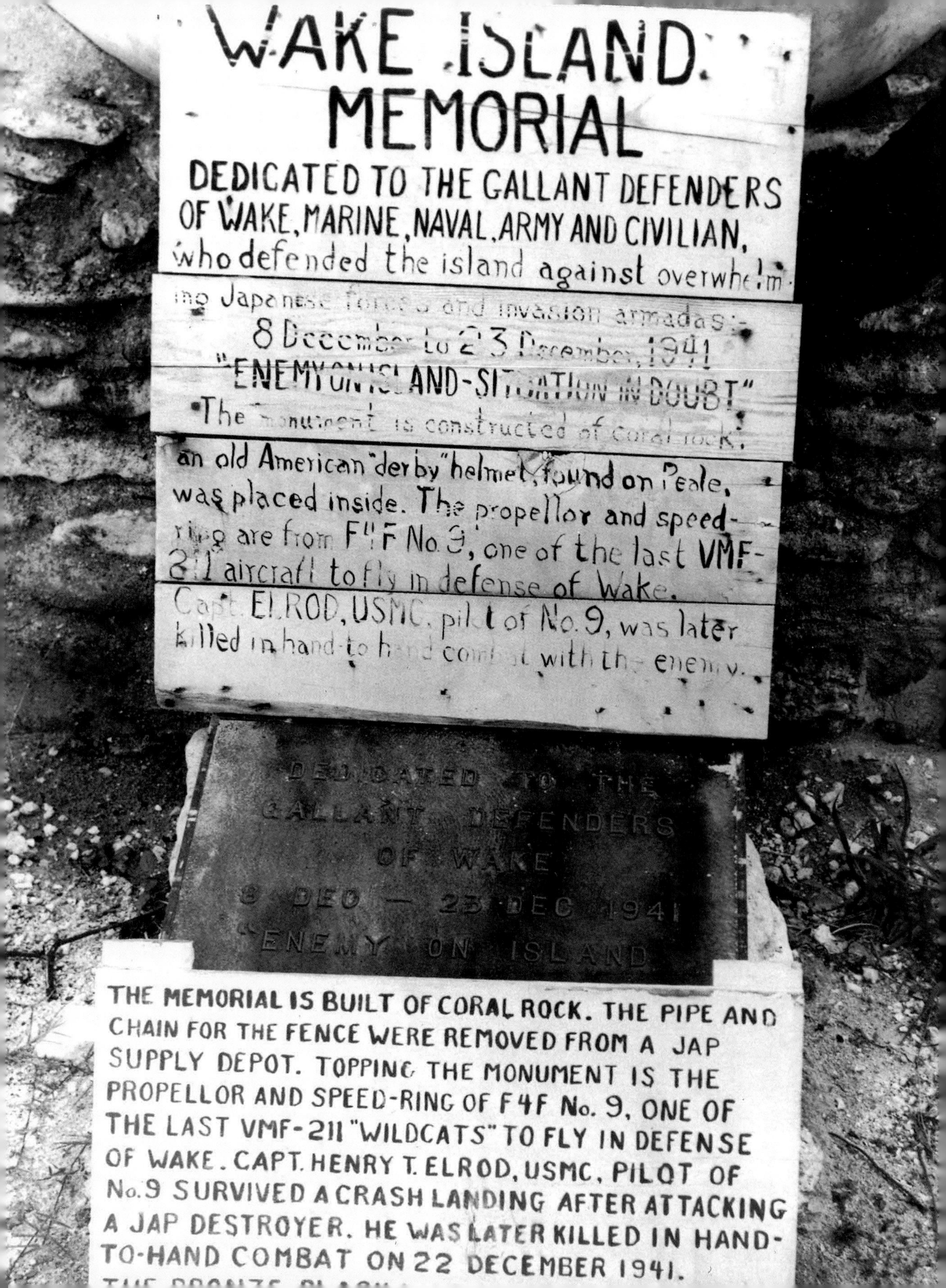

WAKE ISLAND MEMORIAL

DEDICATED TO THE GALLANT DEFENDERS OF WAKE, MARINE, NAVAL, ARMY AND CIVILIAN, who defended the island against overwhelming Japanese forces and invasion armadas:

8 December to 23 December, 1941

"ENEMY ON ISLAND-SITUATION IN DOUBT"

The monument is constructed of coral rock; an old American "derby" helmet, found on Peale, was placed inside. The propellor and speed-ring are from F4F No. 9, one of the last VMF-211 aircraft to fly in defense of Wake.

Capt. ELROD, USMC, pilot of No. 9, was later killed in hand-to hand combat with the enemy.

DEDICATED TO THE GALLANT DEFENDERS OF WAKE

8 DEC — 23 DEC 1941

"ENEMY ON ISLAND

THE MEMORIAL IS BUILT OF CORAL ROCK. THE PIPE AND CHAIN FOR THE FENCE WERE REMOVED FROM A JAP SUPPLY DEPOT. TOPPING THE MONUMENT IS THE PROPELLOR AND SPEED-RING OF F4F No. 9, ONE OF THE LAST VMF-211 "WILDCATS" TO FLY IN DEFENSE OF WAKE. CAPT. HENRY T. ELROD, USMC, PILOT OF No. 9 SURVIVED A CRASH LANDING AFTER ATTACKING A JAP DESTROYER. HE WAS LATER KILLED IN HAND-TO-HAND COMBAT ON 22 DECEMBER 1941.

From Wake Island to Congress

Among the Marines of the 1st Defense Battalion taken prisoner by the Japanese after the surrender of Wake Island was Major James Patrick Sinnott Devereux, the battalion commander. The son of an Army surgeon, Devereux was born in Cuba on February 20, 1903. He enlisted in the Marine Corps in 1923 and served in numerous capacities across the United States and in Nicaragua before assignment to Pearl Harbor in January 1941.

After the spirited defense of Wake against the Japanese invaders, Devereux suffered nearly four years as a prisoner of war in various locations, including 29 months at Kiangwan near the city of Shanghai, China. Shortly after his capture, his wife of nine years, Mary, whom he had met in the Philippines, died from complications of diabetes.

Devereux was liberated from a prison camp on Hokkaido, the northernmost of the Japanese Home Islands, on September 15, 1945. After the war, he received the Navy Cross for his leadership and heroism at Wake and served with the 1st Marine Division. In 1947, he published the book *Story of Wake Island*, and the following year he retired with the rank of brigadier general after 25 years of service. He settled in Maryland and served four terms in the U.S. Congress as the Republican representative of the state's 2nd District from 1951 to 1959. He made an unsuccessful bid for the Maryland governorship in 1958.

Devereux married two more times, worked in farming, raised horses, and served as the director of public safety for Baltimore County, Maryland, from 1962 to 1966. He died on August 5, 1988, at the age of 85.

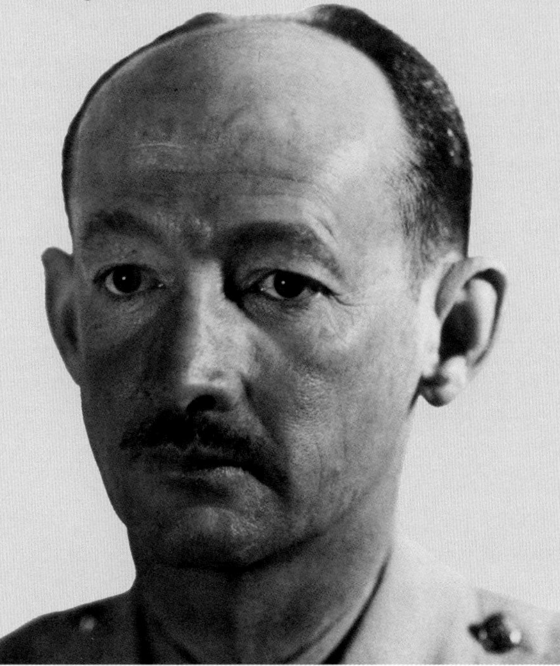

Right: Major James Patrick Sinnott Devereaux commanded the Marines 1st Defense Battalion on Wake Island. Among those taken prisoner by the Japanese, Devereux remained in confinement for nearly four years.

American outposts on the island of Guam in the Marianas and in the Philippines, while a pair of Imperial Navy destroyers shelled Midway Atoll approximately 1000 miles (1610km) west of Oahu.

Guam, the southernmost of the Marianas island group, had been a U.S. possession since the conclusion of the Spanish-American War. Other islands in the Marianas were territorial possessions of Imperial Germany until their administration was mandated to Japan after World War I. As tensions between Japan and the United States escalated in the 1930s, it became readily apparent that Guam, amid the growing presence and military strength of Japan, was an island in more ways than one.

For months prior to the opening of hostilities, Japanese reconnaissance planes had conducted flyovers of Guam, a peanut-shaped island with a territory of roughly 225 square miles (583 square km), 35 miles (56km) long and nine miles (14km) across at its widest point. The island's population numbered more than 20,000, but only 153 Marines, 271 Navy personnel, and about 80 soldiers of Guam's Insular Guard were detailed for its defense, while 134 civilian construction workers and Pan Am employees were present.

Navy Captain George J. McMillin, who also served as the island's governor, received the news of the Pearl Harbor attack at 4.45 a.m. on December 8, and quickly concluded that he would not be reinforced and that prolonged resistance was futile. The Japanese had estimated American defensive strength on Guam at roughly five times its actual number, and McMillin's command had no heavy weapons. The invaders assembled an overwhelming force of more than 5500 troops to take the island, and around 8.30 a.m. on the first morning of the Pacific War their bombers, flying from Saipan 150 miles (240km) away, struck installations on Guam and sank the minesweeper USS *Penguin*. The bombers returned the next day and inflicted further damage.

On the morning of December 10, approximately 400 Japanese troops of the Special Naval Landing Force came ashore. A brief but sharp clash occurred at Agana Plaza in the island's capital city, but the defenders soon realized that their cause was hopeless. McMillin surrendered the island that morning. In three days of fighting, 17 Americans had been killed and 35 wounded. Japanese casualties were light: one dead and six wounded.

For six arduous months, Marines assigned to Army General Douglas MacArthur's command in the Philippines fought the Japanese, withdrawing in an ever-tightening perimeter on the island of Luzon to the Bataan Peninsula and then to the island of Corregidor in Manila Bay. Approximately 80,000 American and Filipino military personnel surrendered on Bataan and later on the fortress island of Corregidor in Manila Bay, some of them enduring the infamous "Death March". The last organized resistance to the Japanese ended with the surrender of Corregidor on May 6, 1942. The Marines who fought in the Philippines upset the Japanese timetable of conquest and denied them the use of harbor facilities at Manila Bay for a while.

Veterans of the turmoil in China during the interwar years, the 4th Marine Regiment withdrew from the Asian mainland in November 1941 and played a major role in opposing the Japanese capture of the Philippines, particularly in defense against enemy landings on the beaches of Corregidor. In mid-December, the Marines were ordered to destroy facilities at the Olongapo Navy Yard. They subsequently withdrew to Corregidor, where they soon came under direct Japanese air attack. The Marines occupied fortifications constructed prior to World War I and worked to improve the small island's defenses.

The 4th Marine Regiment played a major role in opposing the Japanese capture of the Philippines, especially defending against enemy landings on the beaches of Corregidor.

On April 9, Bataan fell to the Japanese, who immediately intensified their preparations to assault Corregidor, where the 4th Marines, numbering approximately 1500 trained personnel, had also incorporated approximately 2500 more men from the Navy, the Army, and the Filipino military, along with some civilians who chose to resist the enemy. For nearly a month, the Japanese shelled Corregidor heavily and launched hundreds of air raids against the fortress island.

Assault on Corregidor

On the night of May 5, 1942, the Japanese began landing two battalions, numbering more than 1500 troops, on Corregidor. A preliminary artillery bombardment did not commence as planned, and strong currents caused some assault boats to drift from their assigned landing areas. Marine gunners tore into the enemy at the shoreline, and one Japanese observer described the scene as a "sheer massacre". Still, the Japanese came on in two waves. The second actually fared worse that the first, taking fire from fortifications on the island, machine-gun positions, and from the rifles of individual Marines crouched in foxholes.

Despite being roughly handled on the beach, the Japanese overwhelmed a Marine platoon and began moving inland toward the high ground of Malinta Hill. They captured a Marine anti-aircraft position whose guns had been rendered unserviceable and established a strong position to support a continued advance that eventually cut off some Marines on the eastern end of Corregidor. Colonel Samuel L. Howard, commander of the 4th Marines, ordered reinforcements to bolster the outnumbered troops that were trying to stem the Japanese tide, but enemy infiltrators were working their way behind Marine lines while snipers harassed the defenders incessantly.

Casualties were heavy, but the Marines mounted counterattacks where possible. Sergeant Major John H. Sweeney and Sergeant John E. Haskin moved up a slope that was crowned by a water tower to throw hand grenades at Japanese machine guns that were holding up an advance. Haskin was killed while passing grenades to Sweeney, who accounted for one enemy position before he, too, was cut down. Howard soon committed the last reserves of the 4th Marines.

At daylight on May 6, Japanese tanks were seen coming ashore. As the armored vehicles advanced, enemy artillery fire intensified. Marines

Below: After the surrender of Bataan on April 9, 1942, American prisoners, some of them carrying wounded comrades, begin the arduous trek to Camp O'Donnell. The prisoners were the victims of cruel treatment by their Japanese captors, and the trek later became known in infamy as "the Death March".

along the defensive perimeter were compelled to fall back. The Japanese closed to within a few hundred yards of Malinta Tunnel, where Army General Jonathan M. Wainwright, overall commander of American and Filipino forces, was headquartered and hundreds of wounded men had sought refuge.

Above: The heroic opposition of the 4th Marine Regiment and other Allied troops on the Bataan Peninsula and the fortress island of Corregidor in Manila Bay upset the Japanese timetable of conquest. However, approximately 80,000 Allied troops surrendered after the six-month defense of the Philippines. Many of these men died in captivity.

Wainwright gave the order to surrender. He later related that the appearance of the Japanese tanks convinced him of the correct decision. "It was the terror that is vested in a tank that was the deciding factor," he said. He could not bear the "thought of the havoc that even one of these could wreak if it nosed into the tunnel, where lay our helpless wounded."

In a last act of defiance, Colonel Howard ordered the 4th Marines' national and regimental colors to be burned to prevent them falling into the hands of the Japanese as war trophies. The 4th Marines virtually ceased to exist as a unit during the fighting on Corregidor. Although the amalgamation of other troops into the Marine formation makes determining overall casualties difficult, the actual roster of the 4th Marines included 315 men killed, 357 wounded, and 15 missing, a casualty rate of nearly 46 percent. The Japanese are believed to have lost as many as 4000 dead and wounded.

Like their comrades at other embattled Pacific locales, the Marines in the Philippines distinguished themselves in defeat. Although the Japanese seemed triumphant everywhere, as Admiral Yamamoto predicted, their string of victories would inevitably run its course. For now, though, they were just beginning to comprehend the character and fighting prowess of the U.S. Marines.

Marines at Midway

During the weeks that followed the outbreak of war, the garrison on Midway was steadily augmented. On December 17, the arrival of 17 Vought SB2U Vindicator dive-bombers of Marine Scout Bombing Squadron 231 (VMSB-231) arrived, completing the long flight from Hawaii. Within a couple of days more reinforcements were delivered. The 5in seacoast guns of Batteries A and C, 4th Defense Battalion came ashore. Hours later, 14 obsolete F2A-3 Brewster Buffalo aircraft, the vanguard of Marine Fighter Squadron 221 (VMF-221), landed at Midway. By the first week of June 1942, Midway was defended by 3652 men of the 6th Marine Defense Battalion supplemented by elements of the 3rd Marine Defense Battalion and the two companies of the 2nd Marine Raider Battalion. Its air group, under Lieutenant Colonel Kimes, included the six operational Wildcat and 21 Buffalo fighters of VMF-221 commanded by Major Floyd B. "Red" Parks, and the 18 Dauntlesses and 21 Vindicators of VMSB-241 (the squadron had split and been renamed) under Major Lofton R. Henderson.

Air Attacks

Until the moment that the enemy was sighted on June 4, 1942, the Americans defending Midway had been in the dark as to the grand design that was unfolding around them. The first Japanese attack included 108 bombers and dive-bombers, intent on destroying the runway at Midway and making the airfield inoperative.

Below: Marine Fighting Squadron 221 (VMF-221) pilots in front of a camouflaged building at Ewa Mooring Mast Field, Oahu, July 14, 1942. Most survived the Battle of Midway.

At 5.20 a.m., Midway reconnaissance sighted a Japanese aircraft carrier, and followed that with a report that enemy aircraft were approaching the atoll. Within minutes, every aircraft on Midway was sent aloft. Flying at 14,000ft (427m) roughly 30 miles (48km) distant from Midway, the pilots of VMF-221 spotted a large number of Japanese Vals flying in V-formations with accompanying Zeros. Major Parks' fighters were divided into two groups. Flying a Buffalo, Parks led the first group of eight F2As and five Wildcats. The second group, under the command of Captain Kirk Armistead, consisted of 12 Buffalo fighters and a single Wildcat. Parks led his fighters directly into the Japanese formations, while Armistead's group acted as a reserve.

Later, at 6.30 a.m., the Japanese force reached Midway. Bombs destroyed the seaplane hangar, and the fuel dump 1500ft (457m) was engulfed in flames. Major William Benson, in charge of the 6th Defense Battalion's Eastern Island command post, was killed when a direct hit demolished the position. In total, 24 Americans were killed and 18 wounded.

However, the Japanese paid a substantial price, as 11 attacking planes were either shot down or failed to return to their carriers and more than 40 were damaged, some of them beyond repair. The Marine anti-aircraft fire had been so accurate that it disrupted the Japanese attempts to crater the all-important airstrip. Only a couple of small holes had been made, and it remained functional.

When the Japanese planes were gone, the Midway air controller sent a message: "Fighters land. Refuel by divisions, 5th Division first." The only response was a crackle of dead air. The message went out several times, and finally a general recall was broadcast. With "All fighters land and reservice," only 10 VMF-221 planes came in. Of these just two remained airworthy.

With their location known, Kimes threw every available Midway-based aircraft at Nagumo's carriers. More than 50 planes without fighter escort mounted no fewer than five separate attacks against Nagumo's warships during a roughly 90-minute period from 7.05 a.m. to just after 8.30.

Captain James F. Collins led the four Army Air Corps Marauders, which mounted attacks on the Japanese carriers almost simultaneously with the six Navy TBF Avengers under Lieutenant Langdon K. Fieberling. No hits were scored. These were followed less than an hour later by the 16 Marine Corps Dauntless dive-bombers of VMSB-241. At 7.55 a.m., Major Henderson called out, "Attack two enemy CV on port bow!" Most of the Dauntless pilots were inexperienced, and Henderson elected a glide-bombing run rather than a steep dive-bombing attack. Quickly, the Zeros pounced on the squadron commander, whose plane was seen spiraling into the sea with one wing afire.

At approximately 8.20 a.m., 11 lumbering VMSB-241 Vindicators led by Major Benjamin W. Norris found the Japanese carriers. Norris knew that the nimble Zero fighters were likely to slaughter his obsolete dive-bombers and observed that the Japanese escort ships were putting up a veritable curtain of anti-aircraft fire. He elected to attack the closest targets, the enemy battleships, but without making any hits.

At least 19 American planes were shot down during the raids by Midway's planes, with only three Zeros downed. Although preliminary analysis might indicate that the gallant attacks were in vain, this is not the case. The Marine, Army, and Navy bomber pilots had stretched the Japanese combat air patrol resources to the limits of their pilots' endurance. More Zeros had to be launched, and those aloft needed to land to be rearmed and refueled.

CHAPTER 2

GUTS AND GLORY ON GUADALCANAL

Although the stunning defeat at Midway had thwarted their designs in the Central Pacific, the senior commanders of the Imperial Japanese armed forces remained firm in their intent to extend territorial control and influence to the south.

The major Allied bases in that region posed a threat to Japanese security and exploitation of the natural resources of the Dutch East Indies, which had been a pillar of the nation's decision to go to war in the beginning.

From their bases in Australia and elsewhere in the South Pacific, the Americans and their allies indeed threatened Japanese interests. Therefore, a decision to mount an assault against Port Moresby from the landward side on New Guinea was coupled with a renewed effort to secure the expansive defensive perimeter that included the Solomon Islands chain, 10 degrees below the equator, due west of New Guinea, northeast of Australia and New Zealand, and northwest of American bases in the New Hebrides.

Opposite: This photograph, taken during training exercises in March 1944, depicts Marines coming ashore from Higgins Boats on an uncontested beach. When the 1st Marine Division landed at Guadalcanal on August 7, 1942, the situation was similar. The Japanese were taken by surprise, and the landings were virtually unopposed.

Japanese Fortifications

In January 1942, the Japanese seized and began fortifying the major harbor of Rabaul on the island of New Britain in the Bismarck Archipelago. In conjunction with this security initiative, orders were given to build a seaplane base on the small island of Tulagi in the Solomons, and an airstrip at Lunga Point on the island of Guadalcanal, 22 miles (35km) to the south across Sealark Channel. In the months ahead, fighting would rage in the Solomons, and the melodic Sealark Channel would earn a new name—Ironbottom Sound—due to the number of ships sunk there.

Although their resounding triumph at Midway had evened the odds in the Pacific War and bought time for American forces to gain strength for the long road to Tokyo, the news that the Japanese were constructing facilities that could threaten communication and supply lines that were vital to their interests in the South Pacific prompted senior American commanders to act. If the Japanese were allowed to establish airstrips in the Solomons, American bases would be within range of their bombers and fighters.

In the summer of 1942, Operation Watchtower, initially aimed at Tulagi, but later expanded to include Guadalcanal and the islands of Gavutu and Tanambogo, was set in motion. True to their directive as first to fight, U.S. Marines were selected to undertake the first American ground offensive in the Pacific War. Vice Admiral Richard L. Ghormley commanded the South Pacific Area, while naval Task Force 61 was under the command of Vice Admiral Frank Jack Fletcher, the amphibious forces were led by Rear Admiral Richmond Kelly Turner, and the 1st Marine Division, commanded by Major General Alexander A. Vandegrift was slated to land at Guadalcanal and Tulagi.

The invasion force assembled near Fiji and set sail for the Solomons on July 31 after conducting a lackluster training exercise at Koro Island. August 7, 1942, was set as the landing date.

Although inexperienced, since many of its combat infantrymen had only enlisted in the military after Pearl Harbor, the 1st Marine Division was a powerful fighting force of 19,000 troops. Two Marine regiments, the 5th under Colonel Leroy P. Hunt and the 1st under Colonel Clifton B. Cates, were to seize the airstrip. The 11th Marines, commanded by Colonel Pedro A. del Valle, and the 3rd Defense Battalion were to provide support and exploit early gains. The total strength assigned to Guadalcanal amounted to just over 11,000 men. Across Sealark Channel, the 1st

Below: Men of the 1st Marine Division have placed a 75mm pack howitzer in a defensive position with a commanding view on high ground at Guadalcanal. Well fortified with sandbags, the position was initially constructed by the Japanese and then abandoned.

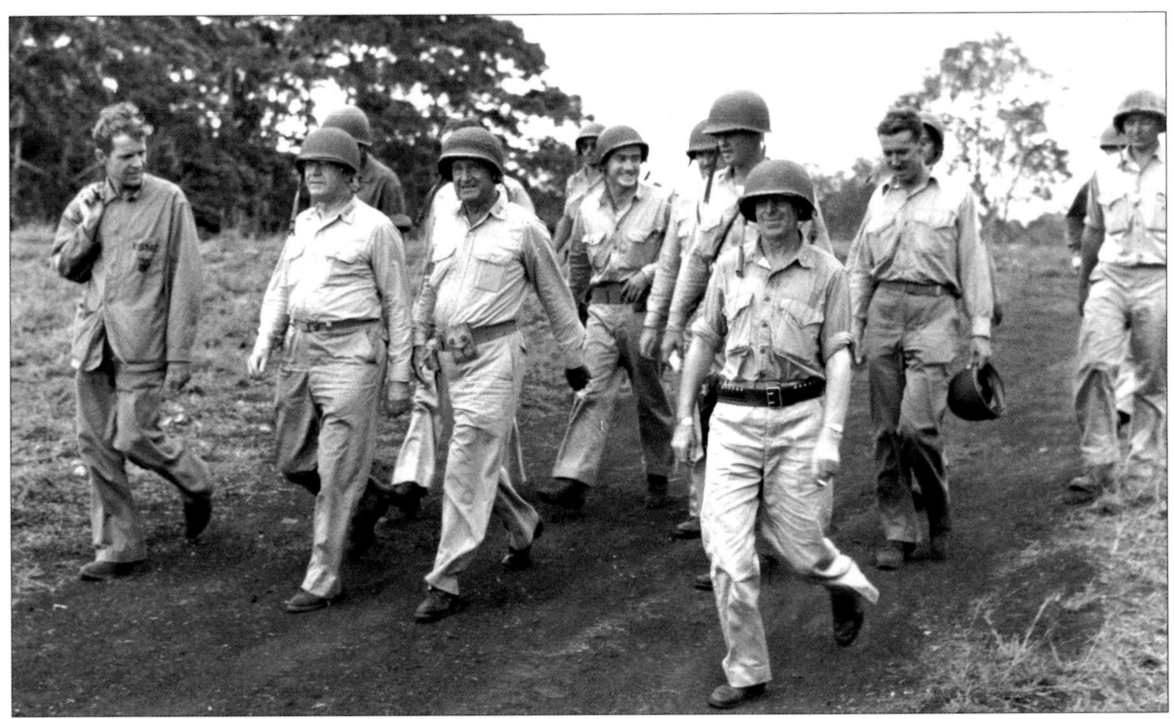

Above: Lieutenant General Thomas Holcomb (center), Commandant of the Marine Corps, makes an inspection on Guadalcanal. He is accompanied by Major General Alexander A. Vandegrift (left), commander of the 1st Marine Division, and other officers including Colonel Amor Sims, of the 7th Marine Regiment, and Colonel Julian N. Frisbie of the 1st Marine Regiment.

Marine Division's assistant commander, Brigadier General William H. Rupertus, commanded roughly 2400 Marines for the capture of Tulagi, Gavutu, and Tanambogo, including the 1st Raider Battalion under Lieutenant Colonel Merritt A. "Red Mike" Edson, the 2nd Battalion, 5th Marines under Lieutenant Colonel Harold E. Rosecrans, and the 1st Parachute Battalion commanded by Major Harold E. Williams.

For the Marines, the Solomons Campaign would present a new kind of war. Six months of savage fighting against the determined Japanese enemy loomed ahead—fetid jungles of an almost uninhabitable island and the ravages of malaria and other tropical diseases. As the date for the landings approached, Vandegrift wrote to his wife: "Tomorrow morning at dawn we land in our first major offensive of the war. Our plans have been made and God grant that our judgment has been sound... whatever happens you'll know I did my best. Let us hope that best will be good enough."

When the 5th Marines stormed ashore on Guadalcanal at 9.09 a.m. on August 7, to their surprise virtually no resistance was encountered. Only about 2500 Japanese troops and Korean laborers were present on the island, and they had melted into the jungle during the previous days' pre-invasion bombing and the morning's naval gunfire. Quickly, the Marines crossed the Ilu River and established a beachhead 6000ft (1829m) long and 1800ft (549m) deep. The following day, they advanced the last 3000ft (914m) and captured the airstrip.

Stiff Resistance

Meanwhile, the early going at Tulagi was anything but easy. The defenders there were few

Above: Marine Corps Aviation Douglas SBD Dauntless dive-bombers approach targets on Guadalcanal. The top priority for the Marines who landed on the island on August 7, 1942, was the capture of the airfield then under construction by the Japanese. The Americans finished the construction job and named the airstrip Henderson Field. Flying from this tactically vital location, Marine pilots provided air cover and ground support.

in number, only about 350 troops of the 3rd Kure Special Naval Landing Force and about 540 support personnel of the Yokohama Air Group, along with a handful of construction workers, but well entrenched and motivated. Nearly 1000 men of the Yokohama Air Group were on Gavutu and Tanambogo.

Tulagi was secured by the afternoon of August 8, but the Marines there endured heavy resistance, particularly as Edson's Raiders reached high ground overlooking the island's harbor. During the night of the 7th, the Japanese mounted several counterattacks, and the next morning Marine reinforcements assisted in the reduction of troublesome enemy machine-gun and mortar positions. More than 150 Marines were killed or wounded in the action, while the Japanese defenders were nearly wiped out. Only three prisoners were taken. Gavutu and Tanambogo were captured at a cost of 70 Marines killed and 87 wounded, while the Japanese suffered more than 500 dead.

The American landings in the Solomons took the Japanese high command by surprise, and in the days that followed the response to the offensive was piecemeal. Rather than the sledgehammer blow that they were capable of delivering against the Americans, the Japanese chose to commit only enough forces to deal with what they believed was a minor threat. Their failure to recognize the scale of the Solomons thrust contributed mightily to their eventual defeat. By the evening of August 8, the Marines were ashore on Guadalcanal along with artillery and supporting weapons. They numbered more than five times the strength that the Japanese had estimated during the early hours of the operation.

U.S. Losses at Sea

The initial enemy response to the Guadalcanal landings consisted of air attacks from Rabaul and naval retaliation. During the arduous campaign, several major engagements between warships of the U.S. Navy and the Imperial Japanese Navy swirled around the embattled southern Solomons. During the first of these on the night of August 8, a Japanese task force devastated Allied warships tasked with guarding the approaches to the beachhead. The U.S. cruisers *Quincy*, *Vincennes*, and *Astoria* were sunk, along with the Australian cruiser *Canberra*.

The disastrous Battle of Savo Island compelled Admiral Fletcher to inform Ghormley that his carriers were in peril. Offshore air support for the Marines could not be sustained. It followed that Turner had to pull his amphibious and supply vessels out as well. On August 9, the naval support began to withdraw, some of the transports with vital supplies still aboard. The Marines on Guadalcanal had only 17 days' rations available, and the headquarters element of the 2nd Marines was unable to get ashore on the island until the end of October.

Vandegrift and his subordinate commanders were flabbergasted, but the Marines proved resourceful. They scrounged abandoned Japanese food and materiel, conserved and rationed what they had, dug in along the Ilu River toward nearby high ground, and set about finishing the half-completed airstrip construction project begun by the Japanese. They named the airstrip in honor of Major Lofton Henderson, who had lost his life leading Marine squadron VMSB-241 during the recent Midway battle.

Within a week of the Marine landings, Henderson Field was operational. Control of the airstrip meant that fighters and bombers could defend against Japanese air attacks and possibly interdict the enemy delivery of supplies and reinforcements. It also meant that the Marines might expect some resupply of their own and that the wounded could be evacuated. In short, control of Henderson Field was the key to victory at Guadalcanal and in the Solomons.

When the Japanese Imperial General Headquarters in Tokyo began to stir in response to the Marine encroachment at Guadalcanal, the 17th Army under Lieutenant General Haruyoshi Hyakutake, already engaged heavily in the fighting on New Guinea, was tasked with eliminating the American lodgment. Hyakutake ordered the 35th Infantry Brigade, under Major General Kiyotake Kawaguchi, to action. Kawaguchi selected an elite unit then based at Guam, the 28th Infantry Regiment under Colonel Kiyono Ichiki, to land on the island and wipe out the Americans.

The captured airfield was named in honor of Major Lofton Henderson, who had died at Midway leading Marine Squadron VMSB-241.

By August 18, six destroyers had delivered Ichiki and nearly 1000 men to Guadalcanal. A Marine patrol got the drop on a Japanese reconnaissance party and brought back intelligence that confirmed what the Americans had known all along. A concerted Japanese attack was coming, and soon. Colonel Cates ordered his defensive lines lengthened along the Ilu River, incorrectly identified on Marine maps as the

Tenaru, which was actually further east. The 2nd Battalion, 1st Marines defended a perimeter that stretched 8100ft (469m) from the coast at Lunga to the river. Ichiki assembled his command and issued orders to hit the Marines between the Ilu and Lunga Point on the night of August 21. Once the Marine line was breached, the Japanese infantry would split, seizing Henderson Field and reducing the defensive position at Lunga Point.

Under the Cover of Darkness

Private John L. Joseph of Company G, 2nd Battalion, watched the river intently. He was startled to see the silhouette of a man seemingly rise directly out of the water. As the enemy soldier crept closer to Joseph's foxhole, the Marine shot him in the face. Soon the entire Marine line was alerted, spitting fire at Ichiki's soldiers as they made for a sandbar in the middle of the river. At about 2.00 a.m., a green flare lit the night with a sinister glow, illuminating clutches of Japanese troops that were making their way forward.

Marine machine guns and Springfield Model 1903 rifles chattered and barked. Artillerymen packed their 37mm anti-tank guns with canister rounds, effectively turning the weapons into oversized shotguns. When the canister rounds exploded, they spewed lead balls in every direction, tearing great swaths through the Japanese infantry. Despite horrific casualties, Ichiki's men were relentless, and the colonel committed the balance of his forces to the fight. Several Marine positions were overrun, but the line held.

Below: The Americans initially landed 19,000 Marines to capture Henderson Field on Guadalcanal. The Japanese responded by sending a naval force and sank an American cruiser and some other ships in the Battle of Savo Island on August 9, 1942.

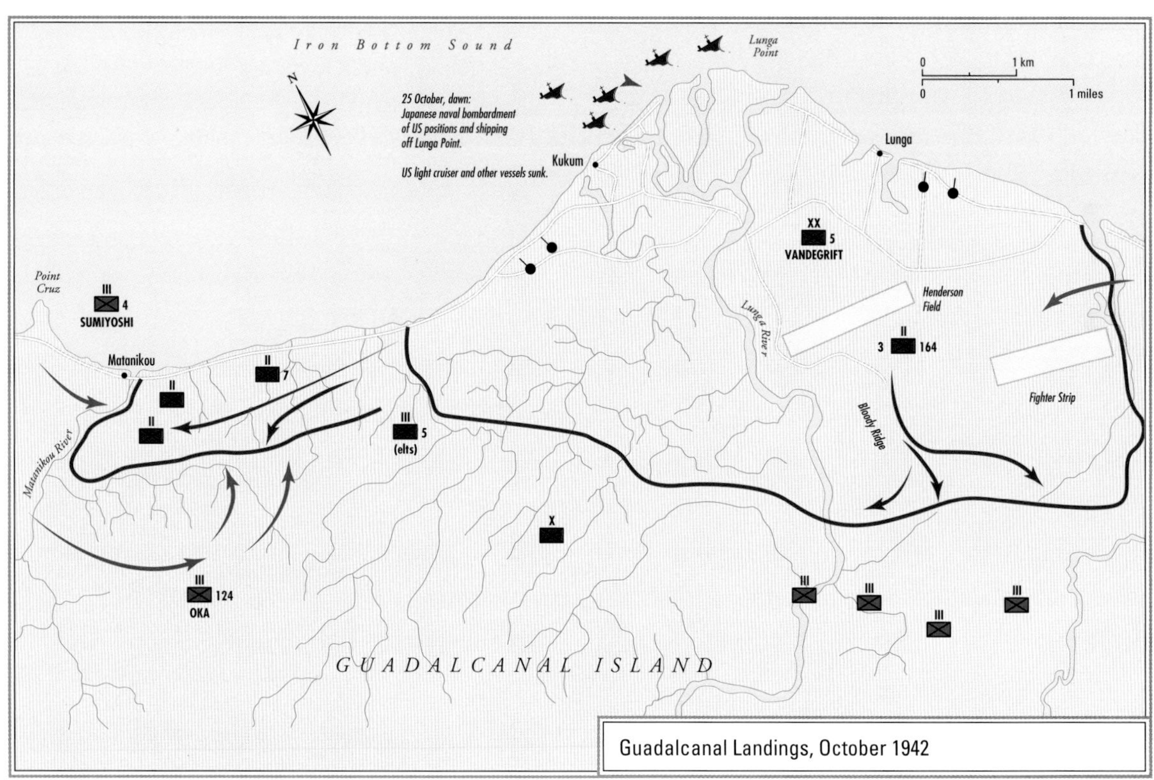

Guadalcanal Landings, October 1942

During the night, repeated Japanese thrusts were repulsed, and near dawn an effort to outflank the Marines was cut to ribbons by the concentrated fire of .30-caliber machine guns, rifles, and 75mm shells from the 3rd Battalion, 11th Marines artillery. The enemy force was pinned down, and as dawn broke, Colonel Cates and his subordinates held a hasty war council.

"We aren't about to let those people lay up there all day," groused the division operations officer Colonel Gerald C. Thomas. Cates replied, "We've got to get them out today!"

Lieutenant Colonel Lenard B. Cresswell's 1st Battalion, 1st Marines, crossed the Ilu upstream and then hit the enemy position from the north, rolling up the Japanese left flank. Joining in the assault was a platoon and five M3A1 Stuart light tanks under Lieutenant Leo Case of Company B, 1st Tank Battalion. Lieutenant Nick Stevenson led Company C, one of four Marine companies engaged in the flanking maneuver, chewed up a platoon of Japanese soldiers. The enemy force was squeezed into an ever-tightening triangular perimeter, and as the day wore on the tanks ravaged them, grinding some of the hapless Japanese soldiers beneath their treads and blasting others with 37mm shells and machine-gun fire.

Author Richard Tregaskis, whose book *Guadalcanal Diary* brought the story of the island battle home to millions of Americans, watched the tanks work through a stand of palm trees. "It was fascinating to see them bustling amongst the trees, pivoting, turning, spitting sheets of yellow flame... We had not realized

Below: The campaign to capture the Solomon Islands from the Japanese lasted from August 1942 to December 1943. The campaign was essential in denying the Japanese air bases for operations in New Guinea.

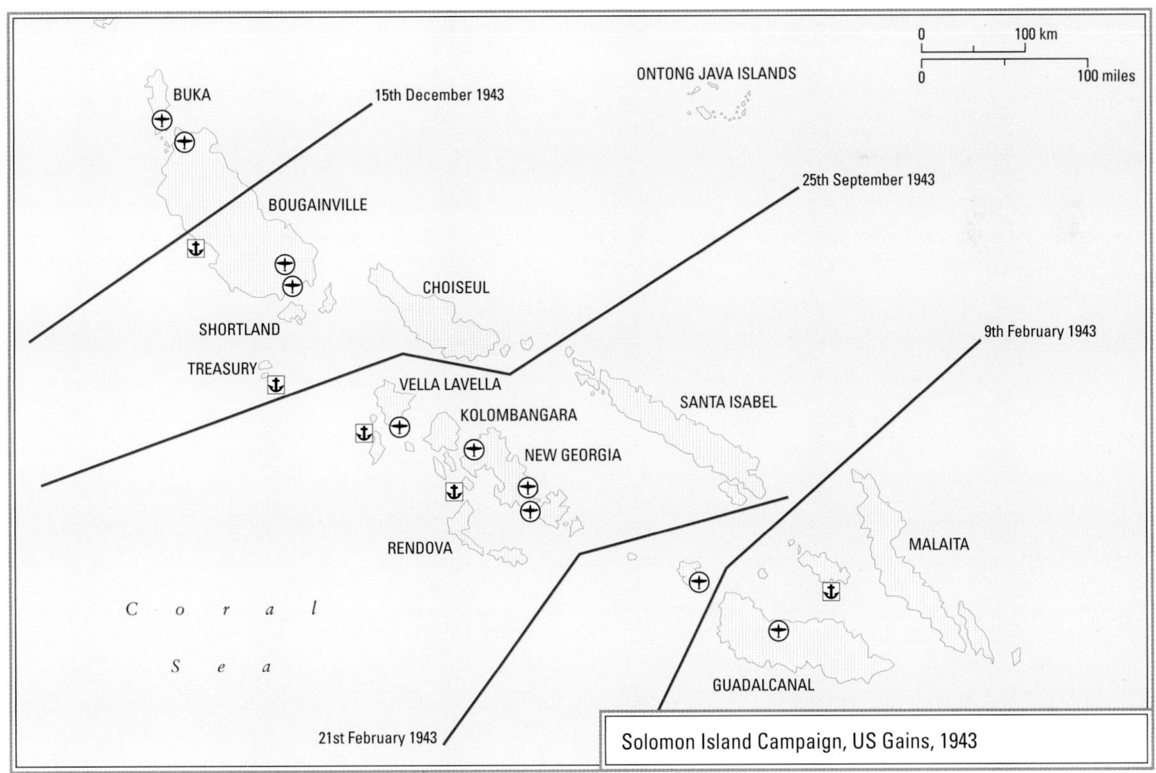

Solomon Island Campaign, US Gains, 1943

Above: This Marine M2A4 light tank was one of several that provided much-needed firepower on Guadalcanal. The M2A4 mounted a 37mm main weapon along with .30-caliber machine guns that devastated enemy troops, particularly during the pivotal battle at the Ilu River on August 21, 1942.

there were so many Japs in the grove. Group after group were flushed out and shot down by the tanks' canister shells."

When Cates became concerned that the tanks were too exposed, he ordered Case to pull back. The lieutenant's blood was up, and he responded tersely, "Leave us alone! We're too busy killing Japs!"

As the erroneously named Battle of the Tenaru River petered out, 800 Japanese soldiers were dead, while only 15 were taken prisoner. The Marines lost 34 killed and 75 wounded. Ichiki burned his regimental colors and shot himself.

During this period, the naval and air war off Guadalcanal intensified. The naval Battle of the Eastern Solomons was fought August 24–25, resulting in a tactical draw as the aircraft carrier USS *Enterprise* was damaged while the Japanese suffered damage to a light carrier and the loss of many planes and trained aircrews.

The Cactus Air Force

During the Battle of the Eastern Solomons, the pivotal role that Henderson Field was to play in the campaign came sharply into focus. The Allied codename for Guadalcanal was "Cactus", and on August 20 the first planes of Marine Air Group 23 (MAG-23) landed on the embattled island. These were the 19 Grumman F4F Wildcat fighters of Marine Squadron VMF-223 and the 12 Douglas SBD Dauntless dive-bombers of VMSB-232. At the end of the month, these planes were joined by two more squadrons, the fighters of VMF-224 and the bombers of VMSB-231. Along with Bell P-400 Airacobras of the Army's 67th

Fighter Squadron, these intrepid pilots and their planes came to be known as the Cactus Air Force.

The struggle for superiority in the air above Guadalcanal intensified, and the day after his arrival Captain John L. Smith, commander of VMF-223, shot down a Japanese Zero. Marine pilots quickly became proficient aerial duelers, and their number of kills climbed steadily. Cactus Air Force planes downed 16 enemy aircraft during a raid on September 24. During that twisting and diving dogfight, Captain Marion E. Carl shot down three enemy planes. Carl was one of only a few land-based fighter pilots who had flown during the Battle of Midway and lived through the ordeal. He went on to finish the war as one of the Marine Corps' top scoring aces with 18.5 victories.

During three days of aerial combat from August 29–31, Marine Wildcat pilots shot down 29 enemy planes. Nevertheless, Japanese raids seriously damaged Henderson Field and destroyed much-needed supplies of ammunition and aviation fuel. During the air melee on the 31st, four Wildcats were shot down.

The leading fighter ace of the early campaign in the Solomons was Marine Captain Joseph J. Foss of VMF-121, who received the Medal of Honor for his combat exploits. His citation read in part:

"For outstanding heroism and courage above and beyond the call of duty as executive officer of Marine Fighting Squadron 121, 1st Marine Aircraft Wing, at Guadalcanal. Engaging in almost daily combat with the enemy from October 9 to November 19, 1942, Captain Foss personally shot down 23 Japanese planes and

Below: Posing in front of one of their aircraft, these personnel of Marine Fighter Squadron VMF-212 were among those of the Cactus Air Force who flew countless missions from Henderson Field on Guadalcanal.

damaged others so severely that their destruction was extremely probable..."

Foss was said to have damaged at least another 14 Japanese planes, and doubtless some of these were shot down. He ended the war with 26 confirmed kills. Three other Marine fighter pilots, Captain Jefferson J. DeBlanc of VMF-112, Major Robert E. Galer of VMF-224, and Captain Smith of VMF-223, received the Medal of Honor. Collectively, these four pilots destroyed 67 Japanese aircraft.

Land-based Maneuvers

On the ground, General Vandegrift took the opportunity to consolidate his available infantry strength, transferring the Raider and Parachute battalions under Lieutenant Colonel Edson and the 2nd Battalion, 5th Marines, to Guadalcanal from Tulagi. At the same time, the Japanese had deemed the continuing daylight runs of troops to Guadalcanal as too hazardous due to the American air presence at Henderson Field. As an alternative, they undertook nocturnal supply and reinforcement missions down the narrow Solomons channel nicknamed "The Slot" and delivered thousands of troops to the embattled island. Japanese cruisers and destroyers also shelled Henderson Field and other Marine positions nightly. The Marines dubbed these supply runs under cover of darkness the "Tokyo Express".

Early in their deployment, the Marines had fortified positions along high ground facing west toward the Matanikau River, and Vandegrift fully expected a renewed Japanese effort to capture Henderson Field. He knew that the enemy was growing stronger, and by early September Kawaguchi's 35th Infantry Brigade was on Guadalcanal in force.

Opposite: The Marine 1st Raider Battalion and 1st Parachute Battalion, under the command of Lieutenant Colonel Merritt A. Edson, defended a ridge before Henderson Field on the night of September 12, 1942, against repeated Japanese attacks. From then on the high ground was known as "Bloody Ridge" or "Edson's Ridge".

Kawaguchi believed that the Marines had strengthened their flanks at the expense of the center of their line, and with 2000 troops he intended to attack straight into the belly of the Marine defenses directly at Henderson Field. Although the success of Kawaguchi's plan depended on Vandegrift being preoccupied with his flanks, the Marine commander was convinced that Henderson Field was Kawaguchi's objective. He told Edson to place his Raiders and Parachute troops along a ridge that stretched within a mile of the vital airstrip.

Edson, who later remarked that he was "firmly convinced that we were in the path of the next Jap attack," ordered his men to dig in on the forward slopes, and by the evening of September 10 they were in place. Two days later, a Japanese patrol brushed the defensive perimeter, and the Marines knew to a man that the big enemy push was only hours away.

At 9.00 p.m. on the 12th, the storm broke. Japanese soldiers rushed from the thick jungle foliage and assaulted Edson's left flank. They were repulsed but undeterred. Moments later a second charge hit the Marines' right flank. This time enemy troops got into some Marine foxholes, and the fighting was hand-to-hand before the attackers faded away. A third charge hit the tired Marines once again and failed. After five-and-a-half hours of combat, Edson radioed Vandegrift that the Marines would hold the line. No one, however, believed the fight was over.

Edson encouraged his troops and told them, "They were just testing. They'll be back." He added, "You men have done a great job, and I have just one more thing to ask of you. Hold out just one more night. I know we've been without sleep a long time. But we expect another attack from them tonight and they may come through here. I have every reason to believe that we will have reliefs here for all of us in the morning."

The following night, perhaps the most stirring defensive stand in the history of the Marine Corps took place along the high ground that has since been known as either "Bloody Ridge" or "Edson's Ridge" in honor of the gallant officer who seemed to be everywhere during the battle that saved Henderson Field, the American perimeter, and possibly the entire Allied initiative in the Pacific War.

Attack Waves

Edson's men braced themselves, and the 2nd Battalion, 5th Marines, came up to reinforce the network of foxholes and machine-gun nests. The Japanese came on in waves, overlapping forward Marine positions and engaging in close-quarter combat. Captain William J. McKennan remembered, "The Japanese attack was almost constant, like a rain that subsides for a moment and then pours the harder... When one wave was mowed down—and I mean mowed down—another followed it into death."

Three companies of Japanese infantry managed to skirt the Marine line and reached the edge of Henderson Field, but it was their high-water mark. A swift counterattack by Marine engineers threw them into retreat. Attacks lasted until approximately 4.00 a.m. on September 14, when two Japanese infantry companies struck the 3rd Battalion, 5th Marines, near the beach and were hurled back with great loss.

Throughout the savage fight for Bloody Ridge, Marine artillery was superb. "The 11th Marines' 105mm howitzers gave good account of themselves in the battle with the heaviest concentration of artillery fire Guadalcanal had

Below: In this highly colorful artistic imagining, Marines fight off the Japanese 36th Infantry Brigade during the Battle of Bloody Ridge, September 12, 1942.

seen so far," recalled one veteran of the action, "dropping well-placed barrages into enemy positions just 200 yards from the dug-in Marines. When it was over the Marines' 105 howitzers had fired 1992 rounds into the enemy's ranks. The 75s alone had unloaded more than 1000."

Above: Japanese dead lie in contorted positions where they fell during the furious fighting at Bloody Ridge on September 12, 1942. Courageous U.S. Marines under the command of Lt. Col. Merritt A. "Red Mike" Edson repulsed numerous Japanese attempts to breach the Marine defensive line and retake vital Henderson Field.

A forward observation post was maintained on top of the ridge, and the range to Japanese targets closed at times to a mere 4800ft (1463m). "The way it fell," said one observer, "it looked as if the artillery lads were trying to burn out their barrels, so fast and furiously did the shells go over the Raiders. Out of this barrage grew an apocryphal story: a Jap officer is supposed to have asked later, upon his capture, to see the 'automatic artillery' we used that night."

More than 800 Japanese soldiers were killed and 600 were wounded before the ferocious Marine defenders of Bloody Ridge broke the back of their repeated charges. The Marines lost 59 dead with nearly 200 wounded. Captain Kenneth Bailey of Company C, 1st Raider Battalion, received the Medal of Honor for conspicuous bravery. Suffering from a serious head wound, the company commander rallied his men during 10 hours of on-again, off-again hand-to-hand fighting. Bailey survived the hellish night, but was killed in action at the Matanikau River two weeks later. For his courage under fire and outstanding leadership, Edson also received the Medal of Honor.

Costly though it was, the victory at Bloody Ridge bolstered Marine morale and electrified the American public. The Marine Corps was fast earning its reputation as one of the world's premier land combat forces. Vandegrift had no time to revel in the newly found fame. While scores of sick and wounded Marines were evacuated, reinforcements came ashore. By late

Marine Raiders: The Noble Experiment

The 1st and 2nd Raider Battalions, U.S. Marine Corps, which fought so bravely under Lieutenant Colonel Merritt A. "Red Mike" Edson and Lieutenant Colonel Evans F. Carlson at Guadalcanal were the embodiment of a noble experiment that began in the early days of World War II. The short-lived Raider battalions, four of which were eventually formed, were sanctioned by Lieutenant General Thomas Holcomb, the Commandant of the Marine Corps, in February 1942.

Carlson was the catalyst for the Marine Raiders. A veteran of the Army, he joined the Corps in 1939 and then left the service to warn the American people that war with Imperial Japan loomed in the near future. When he returned to the Marines, he brought with him the experience of observing the Chinese Communist army of Mao Tse-tung. He was impressed with the esprit de corps that existed and the guerrilla tactics that the troops had honed to perfection. He also brought the mantra "Gung-ho!" which loosely translated into English as "Work together!"

During the 1930s, Carlson served with the Marine security detail at the Little White House in Warm Springs, Georgia, and he became friendly with President Franklin D. Roosevelt and his son James. After the U.S. entered World War II, Carlson approached the president for support for his Raider idea. The endorsement from the executive mansion and the fact that the president's son, James, had become a Carlson devotee, helped make the concept a reality. After a thorough selection process, prospective members of the Rangers underwent rigorous training.

On August 17–18, 1942, while the 1st Battalion was fighting in the Solomons, Carlson led elements of the 2nd Battalion on a daring raid against Makin Atoll in the Gilbert Islands. During the fight 19 Marines were killed, and a rumor circulated that Carlson contemplated surrender. However, serious losses were inflicted on the Japanese garrison, and some useful intelligence was obtained. Although the results of the raid remain controversial and are debated to this day, the Makin Raid was touted as a great victory in the American press. The people were in need of heroes, and the Raiders fit the bill.

While 1st Battalion fought with distinction at Guadalcanal, Carlson brought the 2nd Battalion to the island in November 1942. After landing at Aola Bay, 30 miles (48km) beyond the established Marine defensive perimeter, these Raiders embarked on a month-long operation behind Japanese lines while engineers determined the feasibility of building a second airfield on the island near their initial landing point. The foray has been remembered as the "Long Patrol". The Raiders killed or wounded more than 500 enemy troops and lost 16 of their own, with 18 wounded.

Although the Long Patrol was a resounding success, the days of the Marine Raiders were already numbered. While molding an effective fighting force, Carlson had engendered the enmity of numerous high-ranking Marine Corps' officers. They resented the existence of an elite force within the Corps—itself already elite in their eyes. They believed Carlson had breached military protocol by taking advantage of his relationship with President Roosevelt and circumventing the chain of command in getting the go-ahead to put the Raiders together. The rumor of his supposed surrender overture at Makin dogged him. Perhaps worst of all, some considered him an outright Communist for his admiration of the Chinese and their principles of tactical warfare.

After the Long Patrol, Carlson was sent home to be treated for malaria and to consult on movies

about the Raiders' exploits. Shunted to staff positions, he never again served with the Raiders. In November 1943, he was allowed to participate in the landings on Tarawa Atoll in the Gilberts as an observer. He fought bravely during the four-day battle, prompting Colonel David Shoup, commander of the 2nd Marines, to remark, "He may be Red, but he isn't Yellow."

Two additional Raider battalions were formed in the autumn of 1942, and later the Raider formations were reorganized into two regiments. By early 1944, however, the character of the war in the Pacific had changed. There seemed to be little need for light infantry to perform deep penetration missions, while the formation of new Marine combat divisions required all available manpower. The Raiders were summarily absorbed into other units, passing into history after a fleeting moment of glory.

Above: On September 30, 1942, Admiral Chester W. Nimitz, Commander-in-Chief, Pacific, awards Lt. Col. Evans F. Carlson, commander of the Marine 2nd Raider Battalion, a gold star to his Navy Cross medal for heroism. Carlson was an innovative and controversial proponent of the Marine Raider concept.

Evans Carlson went ashore with the Marines again at Saipan in 1944 and suffered a serious wound while saving the life of another man. He died of a heart attack at the age of 51 on May 27, 1947.

September, the Marines on Guadalcanal were up to division strength, more than 19,000. The reinforcements did not reach the island without a price, though. On November 15, the aircraft carrier *Wasp* was sunk by a Japanese submarine, while the same torpedo spread damaged the battleship *North Carolina* and a destroyer.

As their casualties mounted and airstrikes from Henderson Field sank several transport craft loaded with combat troops, the Japanese realized that the outcome of the battle for Guadalcanal would be critical to the course of the war. At least two divisions of Japanese troops were detailed to the island for a decisive struggle.

Vandegrift expanded his defensive perimeter toward the Matanikau River in the direction of the Japanese landing beaches. The 1st Battalion, 7th Marines, under the command of Lieutenant Colonel Lewis B. "Chesty" Puller and supported by the 5th Marines, now under Edson's leadership, conducted a reconnaissance in force near the heights of Mount Austen and beyond the Matanikau and encountered stiff resistance. It was readily apparent that any Marine movement westward on Guadalcanal would be hotly contested.

Jungle Combat

Although he knew the going would be rough, Vandegrift maintained an offensive initiative and sent forward another strike at the Japanese along the Matanikau. This advance was undertaken by five infantry battalions, and the tip of the spear was the Whaling Group, a force of riflemen that were familiar with jungle fighting and highly trained as scouts and snipers, led by Lieutenant Colonel William "Wild Bill" Whaling. Commanding his own men and the 3rd Battalion, 2nd Marines, Whaling plunged into the jungle to blaze the trail for the 1st and 2nd Battalions, 7th Marines, who would arc toward the coast and Edson's 2nd and 3rd Battalions, 5th Marines, that would attack directly across the river mouth.

A contingent of Japanese troops from the 4th Infantry Regiment had ventured across the Matanikau to establish artillery-firing positions. They offered stiff resistance to the Marine advance, but a reinforcing Raider company hit their flank, and in the ensuing near-encirclement the Japanese were routed. As Whaling wheeled toward the coastline on October 9, Puller's 7th Marines caught a concentration of enemy troops in a ravine and decimated them with small arms and mortar fire. Eventually, Whaling and Puller circled back toward Edson, and the combined Marine force cleared the mouth of the Matanikau. The action disrupted the Japanese timetable for their own offensive and cost them 700 dead and wounded against 65 Marines killed and 125 wounded.

General Hyakutake finally made landfall on Guadalcanal on October 7, just as the Whaling operation was getting started. Undeterred, he supervised the landing of more Japanese troops of the Sendai Division under Major General Masao Maruyama. The Japanese Navy offered support in a coordinated effort to bombard Henderson Field, continue reinforcement and resupply for the troops ashore, and draw the Cactus Air Force into battle, where Japanese planes would hopefully annihilate the Americans.

Four days after Hyukatake's arrival, a heavily escorted run of the Tokyo Express met U.S. Navy cruisers under Rear Admiral Norman Scott. Both sides suffered heavily during the nocturnal Battle of Cape Esperance, but the Japanese were able to land additional reinforcements. On October 13, the Japanese battleships *Kongo* and *Haruna* blasted Henderson Field, and the following day more than 4500 Japanese troops were landed on Guadalcanal as Hyakutake prepared a major push to capture Henderson Field.

On October 13, just in time to endure the bombardment from the Japanese battleships, the Army's 164th Infantry Regiment of the 23rd Division, popularly known as the Americal

Above: During a lull in the fighting on Guadalcanal, tired Marines rest in a field. They are armed mainly with M1 Garand rifles, the primary long arm of U.S. troops in World War II.

Division, came ashore. The Army troops were a federalized National Guard outfit, and they brought with them one of the true war-winning weapons of the global conflict, the M-1 Garand rifle, a dependable semiautomatic weapon that was capable of a considerably higher sustained rate of fire than the bolt-action Springfield that the Marines fielded. Perhaps as fiery as the M-1, Admiral William F. "Bull" Halsey took command of the Guadalcanal campaign, replacing Ghormley on October 18.

Hyakutake approved Maruyama's plan to move the bulk of nearly 7000 Japanese troops along an arduous jungle trail and across two rivers, the Matanikau and the Lunga, to attack the Marine perimeter from the south near the site of Edson's heroic stand nearly six weeks earlier. The long march sapped the strength of the soldiers, but the order to attack would not wait for them to recover. On October 20, the Japanese probed near the mouth of the Matanikau as Murayama's force advanced.

Three days later, nine Japanese tanks crossed the river. Immediately the 37mm anti-tank weapons of Lt. Col. William N. McKelvy, Jr.'s, 3rd Battalion, 1st Marines, swung into action, destroying eight of them. A single tank got across the river, and an intrepid Marine blew one of its treads off. A halftrack rolled up and blasted the stationary target with its 75mm gun. Once again,

Below: Marines move across a river at sunset as they embark on a hazardous nocturnal patrol on Guadalcanal.

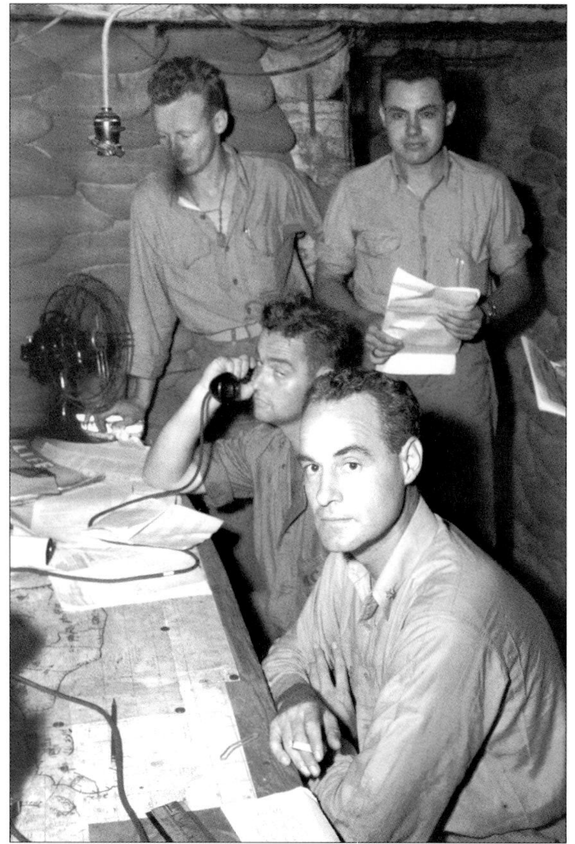

Left: Lieutenant Colonel Merill B. Twining, assistant chief of staff of the 1st Marine Division, and Lt. Col. Henry W. Buse, the division's assistant operations officer, work inside a Marine command post on Guadalcanal.

accurate artillery fire riddled the Japanese troop concentrations.

As Maruyama crept closer to his jumping-off positions, the 7th Marines held 7500ft (2286m) of frontage from Lunga to Edson's Ridge where they met the untested 164th Regiment, under Lieutenant Colonel Robert K. Hall, that held 19,800ft (6035m) of terrain running eastward from the base of the high ground. The action near the seacoast prompted Vandegrift to shift the 2nd Battalion, 7th Marines, east to a 12,000ft (3658m) gap in the defensive perimeter. The redeployment was fortuitous, placing the battalion squarely in front of one designated axis of the Japanese advance.

After daylight on October 24, a Japanese officer was seen observing the Marine perimeter through binoculars. A short time later, scout snipers sent forward to reconnoiter reported smoke from fires rising roughly two miles (3.2km) south of Lieutenant Colonel Puller's positions. Six battalions of the Sendai Division waited for darkness and then stepped off in the rain just before midnight, slipping around a reinforced Marine outpost that warned Puller that the enemy attack was underway.

Soon enough, Puller received another phone call. A company in the line reported that the Japanese were cutting through the barbed wire entanglements to its front. Puller called in the men from the outpost, 46 Marines of the 1st Battalion under Sergeant Ralph Briggs, telling them to move to the left and keep moving into the Marine line.

"Don't fail, and don't go in any other direction," Puller admonished. "I'll hold my fire as long as I can."

Curiously, some of the Japanese junior officers began to stand up, offering targets for Marine rifles. In moments, Puller passed the word to commence firing. The Marine perimeter lit up with a hail of bullets, and mortar shells whooshed from their tubes. One of the early heroes of the fight was Gunnery Sergeant John Basilone, a veteran of the Army who was familiar with the .30-caliber Browning machine gun and now as a Marine commanded of two sections of the water-cooled weapons.

Basilone was a proficient killing machine during the nocturnal brawl, and enemy dead piled up in front of his position, obscuring his line of fire until the bodies were cleared during a lull in the fighting. When he was able, Basilone went to the rear for ammunition and parts to keep his machine guns firing. After the Japanese renewed their attacks, he was still fighting hours later, firing his pistol at the enemy. He received the Medal of

Honor in May 1943, along with 2nd Lieutenant Mitchell Paige, who also commanded a machine-gun section during the battle.

Counterattacks eliminated a wedge the Japanese had driven into the line, but Puller was hard pressed and called for artillery fire from the reliable and accurate guns of the 11th Marines. He also sent for the 3rd Battalion, 164th Infantry Regiment. Puller met Hall and tersely informed him, "I don't know who's senior to who right now, and I don't give a damn. I'll be in command until daylight at least because I know what's going on here, and you don't." Hall readily agreed, responding, "I understand you. Let's go."

The two officers walked Puller's perimeter, feeding the Army troops into positions with Marines. The inexperienced soldiers of the 164th would soon become battle hardened beside the Marines. Repeated Japanese attacks rolled in, but the machine guns and 37mm guns of the 7th Marines' weapons company sliced into their flanks.

As the sun rose, Japanese bombers attacked the Marine positions while their artillery pounded the defensive line and a pair of destroyers fired a few rounds before 5in (12.7cm) Marine shore batteries drove them away. The muddy runway at Henderson Field dried out sufficiently for the Cactus Air Force to rise into the sky, promptly shooting down 22 enemy planes for the loss of three of their own.

Below: A destroyer of the U.S. Navy fires at targets ashore on Guadalcanal. Destroyers often braved return fire from hidden enemy positions on the island and dashed close to shore to hit enemy targets with their 5-inch main guns.

As daylight ebbed on October 25, Maruyama sent his depleted troops forward again. This time, the results were predictable. The 2nd Battalion, 7th Marines under Lieutenant Colonel Herman Hanneken withstood three charges from the remnants of the Sendai Division. The battalion executive officer, Major Odell M. Conoley, led a counterattack that patched a breach in the line.

Finally, Maruyama was spent. He had lost more than 3500 men and gained nothing. Combined losses among the Marines and Army troops amounted to 300 killed and wounded. General Vandegrift commended the 3rd Battalion, 164th Infantry saying his "division was proud to have served with another unit which had stood the test of battle."

Puller was less effusive. In his own way, he praised the Army troops with the comment: "They're almost as good as Marines."

Battle of the Santa Cruz Islands

While the combined Marine Corps and Army defense pushed the Japanese back from Henderson Field with heavy casualties, the struggle for naval supremacy continued. On October 26, U.S. and Japanese carrier forces clashed in the Battle of the Santa Cruz Islands. The carrier *Hornet* was sunk, and the *Enterprise* was badly damaged. Three Japanese carriers were damaged, and more than 100 of their planes were shot down. With the failure of Maruyama's land offensive, the Japanese fleet pulled back as well.

Vandegrift seized the moment and marshaled reinforcements. In early November, Marine squadrons VMSB-132 and VMF-211 joined the Cactus Air Force at Henderson Field, and the aircraft of MAG 11 were relocated to Espiritu Santo, a base closer to Guadalcanal. Another 4000 troops came ashore with the commitment

The Legendary "Chesty" Puller

Before the October 1942 fighting along the Matanikau River at Guadalcanal took place, Lieutenant Colonel Lewis B. "Chesty" Puller was already a famous figure in the U.S. Marine Corps. Puller was a combat veteran who had fought in dozens of engagements in Haiti during the Banana Wars of the 1920s. He had served in Nicaragua and received a pair of Navy Crosses by 1932. Before his career ended after 37 years of service, he became one of only two U.S. service personnel to receive the Navy Cross five times.

Puller was born in West Point, Virginia, on June 26, 1898. He enlisted in the Marine Corps during the waning days of World War I and received his commission as a 2nd lieutenant in 1924. He was nicknamed "Chesty" because of the girth of his barrel chest. In the late summer of 1941 he was given command of the 1st Battalion, 7th Marines. He led the unit with distinction through the thick of the fighting on Guadalcanal. He fought with the 7th Marines at Cape Gloucester on the island of New Britain and commanded the 1st Marine Regiment at Peleliu.

"Chesty" Puller was again in the field during the Korean War, receiving the Distinguished Service Cross and the Silver Star for heroism. After the Korean War, he commanded the 2nd Marine Division, and later served as deputy command of Camp Lejeune in North Carolina. He suffered a stroke and retired in 1955, one of the most highly decorated Marines in the history of the Corps, with the rank of lieutenant general and 14 personal combat decorations. He died at the age of 73 on October 11, 1971. In 2015, the U.S. Navy commissioned one of its mobile forward landing platform vessels the USNS *Lewis B. Puller*.

Above: The interior of this former Japanese barracks has been converted by the Marines into a hospital on Guadalcanal.

of the 8th Marine Regiment from New Caledonia and the artillery of the 1st Battalion, 10th Marines. In time, the remaining elements of the Americal Division, additional units of the 2nd Marine Division, and the Army's 25th Infantry Division would enter the battle.

In November, the Marines continued clearing Japanese resistance west of the Matanikau River and expanded their defensive perimeter. The Japanese were still full of fight and sent a regiment of the 38th Infantry Division to Guadalcanal to mount a two-pronged offensive against the American flanks. Both forays were beaten back with serious losses. At mid-month, one Japanese reinforcement effort was turned back during the Naval Battle of Guadalcanal, while a second succeeded in landing some troops. During four days of fighting, both sides took severe punishment. American planes sank seven Japanese troop transports, killing many enemy soldiers, while Imperial Navy destroyers rescued 5000 from the water.

Only about 3000 additional Japanese soldiers reached the island during the lengthy naval battle of Guadalcanal, but including other recent Tokyo Express missions up to 10,000 soldiers of the 38th Division managed to land. Even so, the cost was becoming too steep for the Japanese. The Tokyo Express had run its course, and this marginally successful operation marked the last large-scale Japanese reinforcement effort. By late November it was apparent that the resupply effort would tax their resources beyond capacity. Losses in ships and supplies could not readily be replaced. Starvation, disease, and the strengthening enemy relentlessly stalked the Japanese soldiers already ashore.

November proved to be the month of decision at Guadalcanal. The 1st Marine Division and attached units had held the line, sometimes just barely, and the Cactus Air Force had kept the Japanese at bay in the skies above the southern Solomons. In time, both were strengthened and

began to assert supremacy. While the Japanese effort to wrest control of the island had begun the long downward spiral toward failure, American losses could be replaced.

After four months of relentless fighting on the fetid island, ravaged by disease with more than 3000 cases of malaria, the 1st Marine Division was withdrawn from Guadalcanal in early December. In its place during the first week of December came the 132nd Infantry, the last regiment of the Americal Division, followed by the 6th Marine Regiment, which joined the other three regiments of the 2nd Marine Division, the 2nd, 8th, and 10th, already on Guadalcanal, and the Army's 25th Infantry Division.

Under extremely adverse conditions, Vandegrift had performed admirably. Army Major General Alexander M. Patch subsequently relieved him of command on Guadalcanal, and Vandegrift received both the Navy Cross and the Medal of Honor for his sterling service. Patch's command, 50,000 strong, was designated the XIV Corps. A new fighter strip was built at Henderson Field, and the aircraft of the 1st and 2nd Marine Air Wings were rapidly strengthened while three new Army fighter squadrons and a bomber squadron arrived. American air power made any Japanese transit of "The Slot" during daylight hours virtually impossible.

Attack and Destroy

In late December, Patch gave the order to mount the largest American offensive of the campaign to "attack and destroy the Japanese forces remaining on Guadalcanal". Combined Army and Marine advances isolated the Japanese troops dug in on Mount Austen and adjacent high ground that threatened any further movement westward. Japanese troops of the 38th Division and the remnants of the Sendai Division put up stiff resistance, but the Army's 27th and 35th Infantry Regiments drove west with the 1st Battalion, 2nd Marines, advancing on their left flank. The 8th, 2nd, and 6th Marines were heavily engaged.

Captain Henry P. Jim Crowe of the 8th Marines, who later distinguished himself during the fight for Tarawa in the Gilbert Islands, exhorted his men with: "You'll never get a Purple Heart hiding in a foxhole! Follow me!"

By late January, resistance was waning and disorganized. The ground gained sometimes exceeded 6000ft (1829m) per day. The reason for the more rapid advance was not clear at first. Patch had been warned of increasing Japanese movement of men and ships and initially believed that the enemy intended to renew its offensive effort on Guadalcanal. Actually, by the middle of December the Japanese Imperial General Headquarters had grudgingly acknowledged that Guadalcanal should be conceded to the Americans. About 11,000 Japanese soldiers were withdrawn from the island during early February.

On the 9th, American forces converging from the east and west linked up at Cape Esperance. The fight for Guadalcanal was over. The victory had been at a terrible cost, and the Marines had borne the brunt of the casualties. Nearly 1600 U.S. personnel had died, and more than 1150 were Marines. Of the 4709 wounded, 2799 were Marines. The Marine pilots of the Cactus Air Force suffered 147 dead and 127 wounded. In turn, the Japanese suffered 25,000 casualties, many of them from elite formations that would never again take the field as cohesive units.

Guadalcanal was the crossroads to victory for the United States in the Pacific War. Among the high-ranking Japanese officers who understood the gravity of the defeat, Kawaguchi of the 35th Infantry Brigade concluded: "Guadalcanal is no longer merely a name of an island in Japanese military history. It is the name of the graveyard of the Japanese Army."

Opposite: A Marine sits at a high vantage point on overwatch duties manning an M1917 Browning machine gun while his comrades bathe in a stream.

CHAPTER 3

BOUGAINVILLE AND THE NORTHERN SOLOMONS

The victory at Guadalcanal was a turning point of World War II in the Pacific. Nevertheless, more than three years of difficult, costly fighting lay ahead for the U.S. Marine Corps and the marshaled military might of the United States before the Japanese empire was vanquished.

The early action in the Solomon Islands was the initiation of a grand strategy that would accomplish three goals. First, the occupation of Guadalcanal, Tulagi, and the islands of the Santa Cruz group would provide a springboard for further operations up the Solomons chain. Second, the capture of the northeastern coast of New Guinea and the seizure of the islands in the Central Solomons would provide bases and logistical support for the most significant of the three objectives. The neutralization of the Japanese bastion at Rabaul on the eastern coast of the island of New Britain in the Bismarck Archipelago was essential to the success of future Allied operations.

The Japanese had landed on New Britain in February 1942 and immediately begun to establish their principal forward base in the region at Rabaul. Simpson Harbor provided a fine natural anchorage for Japanese naval vessels operating in the Solomons and elsewhere, while aircraft flying from bases at Rabaul threatened the Allies on Guadalcanal. Enemy planes were also positioned to interdict supply and troop convoys and possibly sever lines of communication with Australia and New Zealand.

Opposite: A Japanese air raid makes a direct hit on an American gas and oil dump at Empress Augusta Bay, Bougainville, where approximately 8000 drums were set afire.

Rabaul also served as a shield for the vast Japanese base at Truk in the Caroline Islands. As long as Rabaul remained operational and in Japanese hands, American progress toward the Philippines and the Central Pacific was impeded.

Operation Cartwheel

In the summer of 1942, the American Joint Chiefs of Staff issued a directive targeting Rabaul and outlining the three stages of the effective reduction of the base. Army General Douglas MacArthur, Commander-in-Chief, Southwest Pacific Area, had previously formulated the Elkton Plan as a strategic template for the neutralization of Rabaul.

Naval planners also offered a methodology, and eventually Elkton evolved into a strategic initiative codenamed Operation Cartwheel. With the capture of Guadalcanal, the remaining two phases of Cartwheel came under MacArthur's supervision. Naval and Marine forces in the region were directed by Admiral William F. "Bull" Halsey, to whom the task of reducing Rabaul devolved on a tactical level.

Halsey understood the importance of the coming Marine operations in the Solomons and said, "Rabaul, a Japanese naval and air stronghold, appeared at this time to be the logical objective towards whose seizure or neutralization all efforts of both the South and Southwest Pacific Forces would be directed. Until Rabaul was seized, or at least naval and air control of the New Britain area was established, the planned advance of the Southwest Pacific Forces along the New Guinea coast was impracticable."

Originally, the Cartwheel manifesto identified 13 distinct operations. However, on closer inspection it was determined that its goals could be accomplished with only 10. The direct seizure of three objectives, Kavieng at the northern tip of New Ireland, the island of Kolombangara, and Rabaul itself, were deemed too costly. These would be bypassed and left to literally wither on the vine as American forces advanced.

After Guadalcanal, senior American commanders wanted to sustain their momentum, and no time was wasted. The 3rd Raider Battalion and Army troops landed unopposed and took control of the Russell Islands at the end of February 1943. On June 30, the 1st and

Below: Marine Raiders in a rubber dinghy land on the Russell Islands in February 1943. The Marine in the bow of the boat is armed with a Browning Automatic Rifle (BAR), a squad automatic weapon that offered Marines mobile firepower.

4th Raider Battalions, the 9th Defense Battalion, a tank platoon of the 10th Defense Battalion, Marine Air Group 22 (MAG-22), and units of the Army's 43rd Infantry Division began landings and air operations against the Japanese on the island of New Georgia, 200 miles (322km) north of Guadalcanal.

The 12th Defense Battalion and Army units, including the 112th Cavalry Regiment and the 158th Regimental Combat Team, occupied the Trobriand and Woodlark islands in conjunction with landings on New Guinea.

The 4th Raider Battalion seized the Segi Point area on New Georgia and marched to secure Viru Harbor on July 1. Navy Seabees (Construction Battalions) moved in to build an airfield, and by the end of July Army and Navy fighter and bomber squadrons were operational. The primary objective of the New Georgia operation was the airfield at Munda, which fell to the Army troops and Marines on August 5 after six weeks of stubborn Japanese defense. The enemy barge base at Bairoko was attacked by the Raiders and elements of the 148th Infantry Regiment on July 20, but did not fall until the end of August when the Japanese finally decided to evacuate New Georgia.

Dogfights Over Rabaul

The island of Vella Lavella was captured by 25th Infantry Division troops and soldiers of the 3rd New Zealand Division on September 3, and 10,000 Japanese troops were cut off and bypassed on Kolombangara. Japanese efforts to evacuate their remaining forces in the Central Solomons were a difficult undertaking as the U.S. Navy sank a number of transports and contested the withdrawal. By the end of October, American air power was exerting daily pressure on Rabaul. Planes from Guadalcanal, New Georgia, and Vella Lavella began hammering the base, and dogfights involving large numbers of planes were daily occurrences.

Operating from Guadalcanal on April 7, 1943, 22-year-old VMF-221 pilot Lieutenant James E. Swett led a division of four Marine F4F Wildcat fighters on patrol over the Russell Islands in his first combat mission. Swett spotted a formation of 15 Japanese Val dive-bombers and swept in to attack. In short order he downed three of the enemy planes. He cleared the formation and attacked a second group of six Vals, flaming another and then damaging a fifth.

Eventually, Swett was credited with seven aerial victories during the mission and received the Medal of Honor. Both the rear gunners in the Vals and friendly anti-aircraft fire damaged his Wildcat, and Swett ditched in the water off Tulagi. He returned to duty and later qualified to fly a new fighter, the Vought F4U Corsair, meeting with further success as VMF-221 transitioned to the powerful aircraft. He finished the war with 15.5 confirmed kills and four probables, retired from the Marine Corps in 1970 with the rank of colonel, and died in 2009 at the age of 88.

VMF-221 pilot Lieutenant James E. Swett downed seven Japanese bombers while on patrol over the Russell Islands in his F4F Wildcat.

As the air war in the Solomons intensified, the Japanese committed at least 700 planes to the campaign during five months of fighting from June to October 1943, and many of these were shot down by proficient American pilots.

At this juncture, a failure of the Japanese command structure became apparent. Without unity of command, the Japanese Army and Navy failed to coordinate their efforts—now decidedly on the defensive—and in the end it was clear to Imperial General Headquarters that their defensive perimeter would inevitably contract. All efforts were to be made to slow the American

Boyington and the Black Sheep

One of the legendary fighting units to emerge from the Solomon Islands Campaign, and more broadly from World War II in the Pacific, was Marine Fighter Squadron 214 (VMF-214), popularly known as the Black Sheep Squadron. The commander of VMF-214, Major Gregory "Pappy" Boyington, gained lasting fame.

VMF-214 was formed on June 1, 1942, at Ewa Naval Air Station on the Hawaiian island of Oahu. Originally known as the Swashbucklers, the squadron completed a tour of duty based at Henderson Field on Guadalcanal and then disbanded. VMF-214 was reconstituted in August on the island of Espiritu Santo in the New Hebrides, and its 27 pilots came under Boyington's command at that time.

When he reached the Solomons, Boyington was already a combat veteran, having flown with the famed Flying Tigers of the American Volunteer Group in China, where he claimed six aerial victories. The pilots nicknamed Boyington "Pappy" because at the age of 31 he was a decade older than most of his subordinates. They also chose the name Black Sheep—not because of their somewhat mythical hijinks on the ground, but due to the circumstances under which the squadron had been formed. The Black Sheep flew from bases in the southern Solomons and then deployed to a forward airfield at Vella Lavella, amassing an impressive service record during a brief period from September 12, 1943, to January 3, 1944. During its first two weeks of operation and flying the Vought F4U Corsair fighter, VMF-214 shot down 23 Japanese planes and claimed another 11 probable victories while five of its own pilots were lost. Boyington was well on his way to becoming the top Marine Corps ace of World War II, ending the conflict with 28 victories.

The flamboyant Boyington instilled an aggressive attitude among the young pilots of VMF-214, and during 84 days of combat the squadron shot down 100 enemy aircraft and destroyed a like number on the ground. In October 1943, the pilots publicized an appeal to major league baseball teams, offering to shoot down a Japanese plane for every cap forwarded to them. The St. Louis Cardinals sent 20 caps, and the hotshot Marine pilots returned 20 stickers, each representing a kill.

Boyington became famous for his brash leadership style, and one incident recounts his leading 24 Corsairs in a sweep over the Japanese airfield at Kahili where 60 enemy fighters were based, goading them into the air. The Black Sheep shot down 20 of these Japanese planes and incurred no losses of their own, and Boyington received the Medal of Honor for the exploit. On October 4, 1943, Boyington and his Black Sheep Corsairs escorted a flight of Douglas SBD Dauntless dive-bombers on a mission over Bougainville. In the space of a single minute, he shot down three Zero fighters.

When Boyington was awarded the Medal of Honor, it was originally thought to be posthumous. On January 3, 1944, he shot down his 28th enemy plane and was himself downed. Pulled from the Pacific by a Japanese submarine crew, he spent the last 20 months of the war in a prison camp. Five days after he was shot down, the Black Sheep concluded their second combat tour in the Solomons and the squadron was disbanded. The pilots were assigned to other squadrons, and the legend of VMF-214 took on a life of its own.

Boyington retired from the Marines with the rank of colonel, and died at the age of 75 on January 11, 1988.

advance toward their obvious target, Bougainville in the northern Solomons, which lay astride the Allied axis of advance toward Rabaul. Japanese senior commanders were also painfully aware that the effectiveness of Rabaul as a forward base was eroding with each passing day.

Therefore, the focus of Japanese defense in the South and Central Pacific was modified with the American successes in the Solomons and New Guinea. The principal line in the late summer of 1943 became the Caroline and Mariana island groups. Thus, the Imperial Japanese Navy was not to commit major resources in further defensive efforts in the Solomons.

Below: Pilots of Marine Fighter Squadron VMF-214, the famed Black Sheep that flew under the command of Major Gregory "Pappy" Boyington, stand on the wings of the fighter plane that helped make them famous, the gull-winged Vought F4U Corsair.

In addition to its proximity to New Britain and Rabaul, Bougainville was also the center of Japanese troop strength in the northern Solomons, particularly since those troops evacuated from other islands during the previous months had concentrated there. Lieutenant General Haruyoshi Hyakutake, who had lost Guadalcanal to the Marines months earlier, commanded the 17th Army at Bougainville, including the 6th Division, his most effective combat troops. Peak Japanese troop strength on Bougainville was estimated at more than 45,000.

Operation Cherry Blossom

With the completion of ground operations in the central Solomons during the first week of October, Allied efforts then concentrated on the upcoming landings on Bougainville. The date for the invasion, code named Operation Cherry

Blossom, was set for November 1, 1943, and planning was modified several times during the weeks leading up to the landings. Empress Augusta Bay was chosen as the Marine landing site because of its distance from the bulk of the island's Japanese defenders, the nearest of whom were at least 25 miles (40km) away. The area also provided a good location for a radar station and PT-boat (patrol torpedo) base.

Senior American commanders deemed it unnecessary to capture all of Bougainville. The seizure of enough suitable ground for the construction of an airfield that could accommodate shorter-range light and medium bombers and fighters that were striking Rabaul would be sufficient.

While the landings on Bougainville were the primary thrust of the renewed offensive, supporting operations occurred in the Treasury Islands, the island of Choiseul southeast of Bougainville, and finally the Green Islands in February 1944. Combined with air superiority in the vicinity, these landings were intended not only as diversions to the main operation at Bougainville, but also to cut the supply lines to and from Rabaul and contribute to the containment of the garrison there until the end of the war.

Major General Alexander A. Vandegrift, who had performed brilliantly in command of the victorious forces on Guadalcanal, was to lead the I Marine Amphibious Corps (IMAC) in the effort in the northern Solomons. IMAC included the 3rd Marine Division, under Major General Allen H. Turnage, the 2nd Marine Raider Regiment, and

Below: Loaded with combat Marines, landing craft lie off the island of Bougainville. As the Pacific war progressed, the U.S. Marine Corps refined its amphibious warfare doctrine, utilizing pre-invasion naval and aerial bombardment, underwater demolition teams, and coordinated assaults to achieve victory.

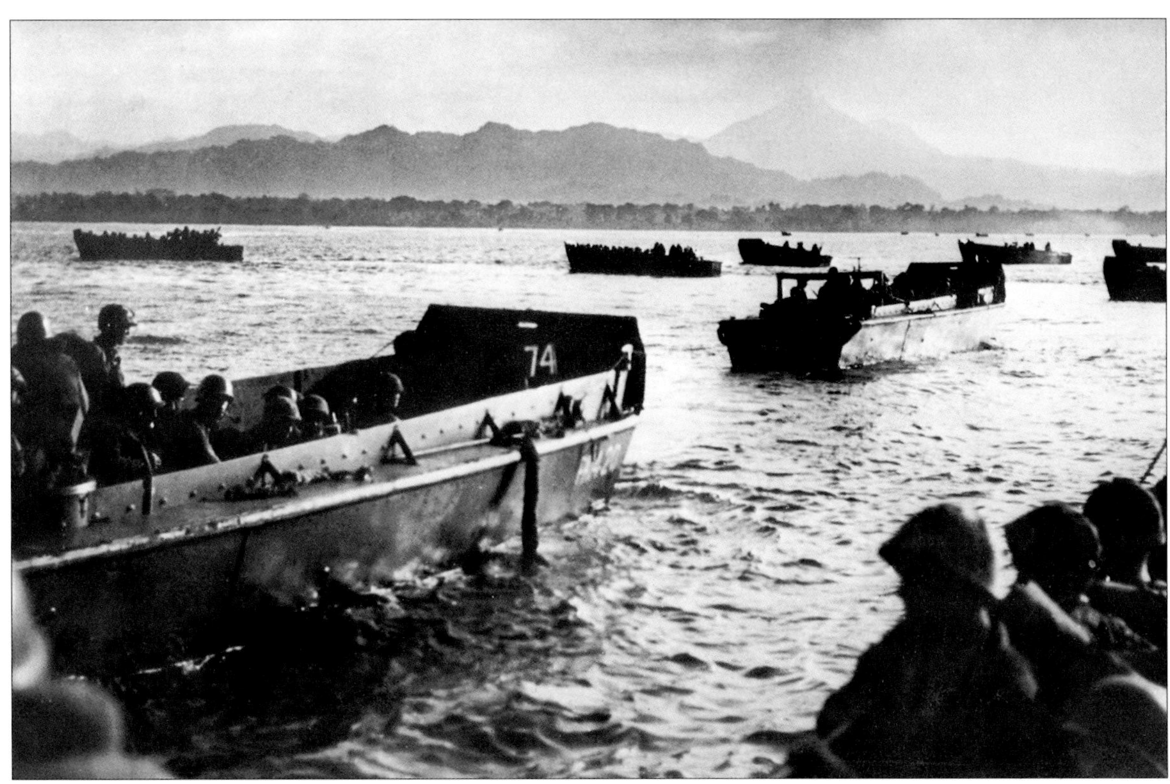

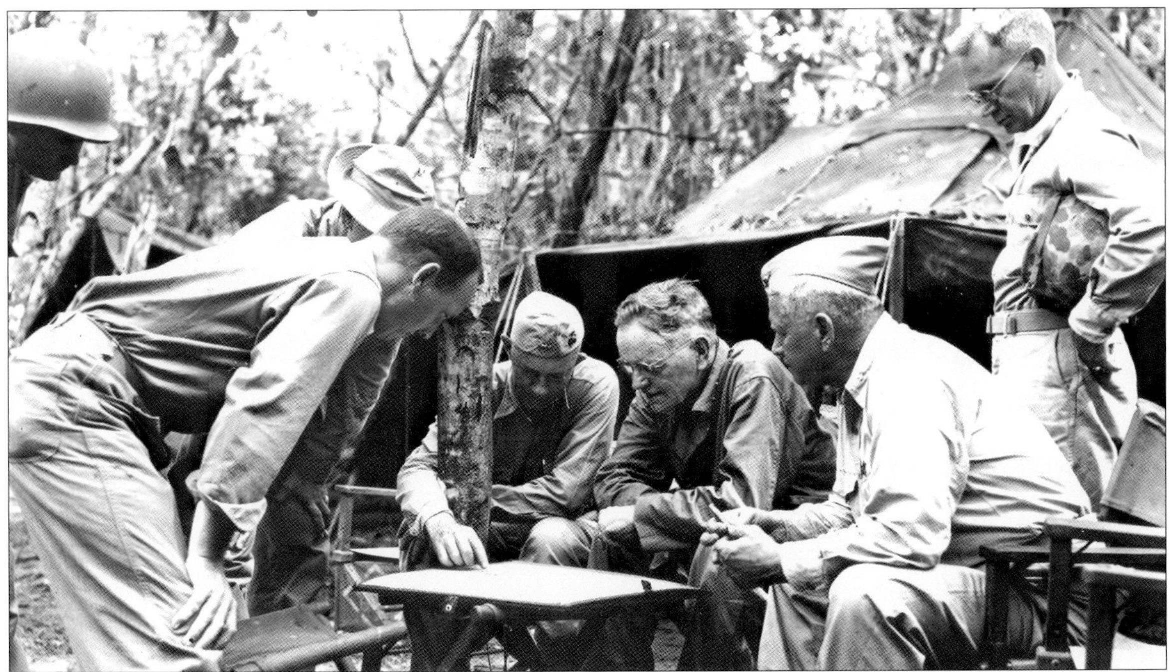

the 1st Marine Parachute Regiment. Its reserve element was the Army's 37th Infantry Division. Vandegrift had been on his way to Washington, D.C., to assume the post of Commandant of the Marine Corps when the sudden death of IMAC commander Major General Charles D. Barrett necessitated his return to the combat zone. Vandegrift held the IMAC command until November 9, when he was relieved by Major General Roy Geiger.

The landing beaches at Empress Augusta Bay stretched approximately 4.5 miles (7.3km) from Cape Torokina in the east to Koromokina Lagoon in the west. They were divided into 11 sections, each designated by a color. A 12th landing was to take place on nearby Puruata Island, a short distance offshore. The 9th Marines, commanded by Colonel Edward A. Craig, and Lieutenant Colonel Fred E. Bean's 3rd Raider Battalion were responsible for the five beaches on the left along with Puruata, while the 2nd Raider Regiment minus one battalion, under Colonel Alan Shapley, and the 3rd Marine Regiment, commanded by

Above: Vice Admiral William F. "Bull" Halsey (center), Major General Allen H. Turnage, commander of the 3rd Marine Division, and Major General Roy S. Geiger, commander of the I Marine Amphibious Corps, confer during operations on Bougainville.

Colonel George W. McHenry, would hit the six beaches to the right.

Well before dawn on November 1, naval gunfire heralded the beginning of the Marine effort to secure objectives on Bougainville. Shells screamed overhead as the men ate their breakfast and clambered to the decks of their transports. When the order was passed at 7.10 a.m., 7500 Marines began to clamber down nets and into waiting Higgins Boats (Landing Craft Vehicle, Personnel or LCVP) for the 2.8 mile (4.5km) run to the beaches.

Landing Difficulties

Despite heavy surf, the first wave of landing craft reached the shoreline slightly ahead of schedule. The following waves, however, encountered serious problems as the big swells tossed them

Above: A landing craft carrying Marines to the beach at Empress Augusta Bay on the island of Bougainville churns a heavy wake.

into one another and threw them off course. A number of boats were emptied on the wrong beaches, while three of the originally approved sites were abandoned as unusable. Amid the chaos that ensued, one company of the 3rd Marines ran a gauntlet of enemy fire and filtered through the zones of two other formations before reaching its assigned position.

The 9th Marines encountered little resistance, but the 3rd Marines encountered heavy fire from Japanese machine-gun and mortar positions, along with a single well-placed 75mm gun at Cape Torokina. A total of 14 landing craft were destroyed, and among the casualties were Major Leonard M. "Spike" Mason, commander of the 1st Battalion, 3rd Marines, and Lieutenant Colonel Joseph McCaffery, executive officer of the 2nd Raider Regiment.

For more than an hour, the Marines were pinned down on the beaches or holed up in shell craters along its edge. Then Sergeant Robert A. Owens, ignoring a serious wound, rose up and charged the bunker that housed the troublesome 75mm gun. He killed its crew, but was fatally shot down in an instant. Owens received a posthumous Medal of Honor for his act of courage. Elsewhere, individual Marines performed extraordinary acts of heroism to gain the upper hand. As they moved inland to their initial objectives up to 3000ft (914m) from the shore, it became apparent that the naval bombardment had inflicted little or no damage on the enemy strongpoints.

As the sun rose, the Marines unloaded supplies, and the guns of the 12th Marine Artillery came ashore. Japanese troops continued to harass the landing beaches, and enemy planes appeared overhead. An aerial melee resulted in the downing of 26 Japanese aircraft. Meanwhile, five Marines of a reinforced company of the 3rd Battalion, 2nd Raiders, were killed subduing stubborn Japanese resistance at Puruata Island, which was not secured until November 3.

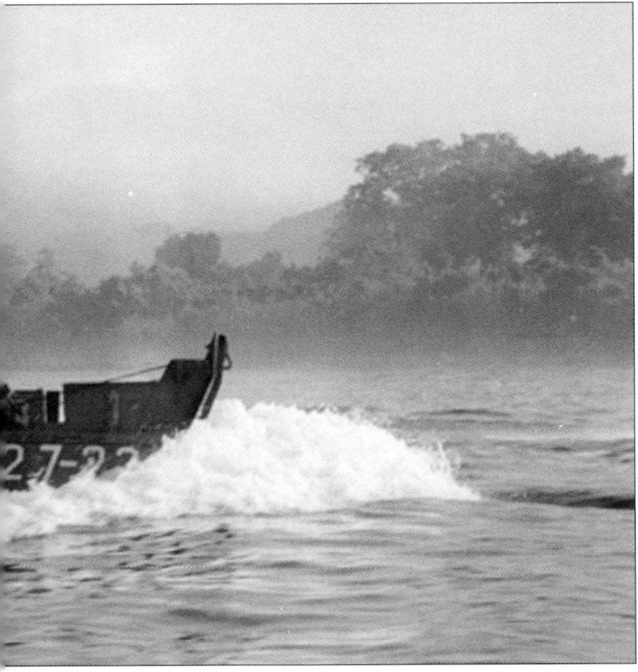

A Japanese naval force sailed from Simpson Harbor with orders to destroy the American ships off Bougainville, and during the night of November 1–2, the Battle of Empress Augusta Bay ended with a decisive American victory. The Japanese lost a light cruiser and a destroyer sunk, a heavy cruiser, light cruiser, and two destroyers damaged, and 25 aircraft shot down. The Americans suffered damage to a light cruiser and a destroyer.

Although their perimeter on Bougainville was becoming well established, the Marines were not immune from counterattack. They labored for a week and fought periodic skirmishes with the Japanese, and then, on November 7, a landing was spotted to the west between Koromokina Lagoon and the Laruma River. The landing craft were similar in construction to those used by the Americans, and one Marine anti-tank gun held its fire for a time as landing craft carrying 475 Japanese soldiers approached.

When the Japanese landing cut off a group of Marines, Pfc. John F. Perella swam 3000ft (914m) to retrieve a rescue boat that delivered his unit to safety. He later received the Silver Star. More than 30 Japanese soldiers were killed when Marines under Lieutenant Colonel Walter Asmuth, commander of the 3rd Battalion, 9th Marines,

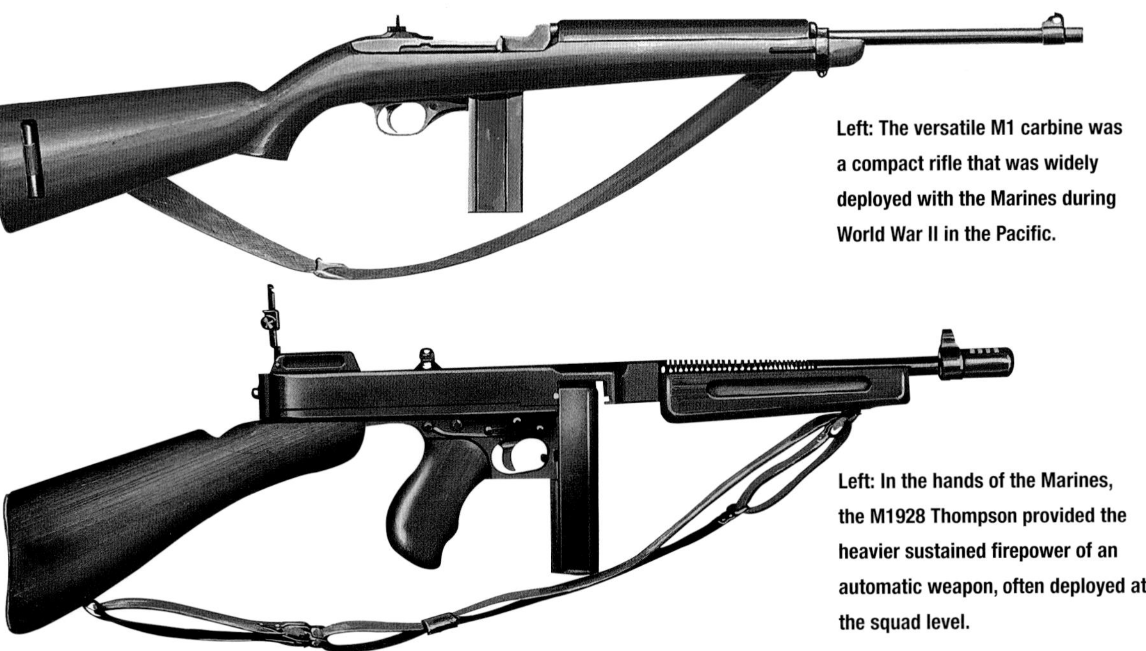

Left: The versatile M1 carbine was a compact rifle that was widely deployed with the Marines during World War II in the Pacific.

Left: In the hands of the Marines, the M1928 Thompson provided the heavier sustained firepower of an automatic weapon, often deployed at the squad level.

sent a company to assault the enemy and zeroed in howitzer fire from the 12th Marines artillery.

Medics Under Fire

The Japanese persisted, yelling "Marine, you die!" and the 1st Battalion, 9th Marines, relieved the beleaguered 3rd Battalion just after 1.00 p.m. During the night, enemy soldiers crept through the Marine perimeter and fired their rifles into the tents where doctors of the 3rd Medical Battalion were tending their wounded. Rear echelon Marines, including cooks and clerks, were pressed into security service, adding truth to the assertion that every Marine is a rifleman first.

Finally, on November 8 the leading elements of the 21st Marines were in position to take the offensive, and Lieutenant Colonel Ernest W. Fry's 1st Battalion stepped off with light tanks in support following a heavy artillery and mortar barrage. Fry unleashed his Marines in an area 900ft (274m) wide by 1800ft (549m) deep, and they advanced steadily against sporadic resistance. The preliminary fusillade of large-caliber munitions had literally shattered the Japanese, blowing some men to pieces and flinging bodies into nearby trees. The corpses of more than 250 enemy dead littered the area. During the desperate fighting of November 7–9, two Marines, Sergeant Herbert J. Thomas of the 3rd Marines and Pfc. Henry Gurke of the 3rd Raider Battalion, earned posthumous Medals of Honor by smothering live hand grenades with their own bodies to shield comrades.

At the same time, Marines of the 2nd Raider Regiment had established a roadblock along the Piva Trail. These Marines were reinforced by more Raiders and the weapons company of the 9th Marines. An order to advance to the junction of the Piva and Numa-Numa trails was issued, but before the Marines could move forward the Japanese struck. Hand-to-hand fighting and Marine artillery fire left 550 Japanese dead. By mid-November, the 129th, 145th, and 148th Infantry Regiments of the 37th Infantry Division, under the command of Major General Robert S. Beightler, were ashore on Bougainville along with three Army field artillery battalions with 105mm howitzers. On the 11th, a combined Marine-Army offensive went forward to seize a critical crossroads along the Numa-Numa Trail. When the Japanese sprang an ambush, the 21st Marines were locked in a vicious fight and called in air support from Marine bombers. The trail junction was secured in what became known as the Coconut Grove Battle, and the beachhead leaped forward another 4500ft (1372m) in some areas.

During the last week of November, the pivotal Battle of Piva Forks occurred, resulting in the destruction of an entire Japanese infantry regiment. Marine patrols discovered an enemy roadblock along the East-West Trail between the two forks of the Piva River, and when elements of the 3rd Battalion, 3rd Marines, had put its defenders to flight they established a roadblock of their own. A patrol was then sent to occupy the summit of a 400ft- (122m-) high ridge with commanding views of the surrounding terrain all the way to Empress Augusta Bay.

Holding the Ridge

During the next four days, 1st Lieutenant Steve J. Cibik and his handful of battle-hardened Marines endured repeated Japanese charges against the top of the ridge. The Marines held, and Cibik received the Silver Star along with having the high ground renamed in his honor as Cibik Ridge.

The rest of the 3rd Marines continued to advance against more Japanese positions. With Raiders and elements of the 21st Marines and the 37th Division in support, they encountered heavy resistance but refused to abandon the

Opposite: Heavy rain, swamps, and thick jungle slowed the advance of the Marines on Bougainville. Even tracked vehicles experienced difficulty negotiating the terrain, as dirt roads and pathways were turned to rivers of mud by frequent downpours.

initiative. After falling back briefly, one Marine unit positioned a machine gun to deter further Japanese attacks. The weapon cut down 74 of 75 enemy soldiers that approached to within 90ft (27m). Marine patrols got the drop on often unsuspecting Japanese troops, and one mowed down scores of the enemy as they milled about in a chow line.

The Marines fought the Japanese and the debilitating jungle conditions, repeatedly driving the defenders from objectives their commanders labeled with the phonetic alphabet, such as Dog, Easy, and Fox. By November 23, they detected a strong Japanese line of resistance with at least 1200 defenders in place. Artillery observers on Cibik Ridge registered their weapons, and an impressive array of heavy guns and howitzers was assembled as the Marines prepared to cross the Piva River for the assault.

At 8.35 a.m. the following morning, Thanksgiving Day, the artillery roared to life. These included 155mm, 105mm, and 90mm antiaircraft guns of both the Army and the 12th Marines. In addition 44 Marine machine guns began chattering. As the American heavy weapons fired 5600 rounds at the positions occupied by the Japanese 23rd Infantry Regiment, the enemy artillery replied.

Below: With the initial artillery support to land on Bougainville, the 12th Marines set up firing positions for 75mm pack howitzers just inland from Blue Beach 2.

Major Donald M. Schmuck, a company commander in the 3rd Marines, remembered: "For 500 yards, the Marines moved in a macabre world of splintered trees and burned-out brush. The very earth was a churned mass of mud and human bodies. The filthy, stinking streams were cesspools of blasted corpses. Over all hung the stench of decaying flesh and powder and smoke, which revolted the toughest. The first line of strong points with their grisly occupants was overrun and the 500-yard phase line was reached."

Schmuck continued, "The Japanese were not through. As the Marines moved forward a Nambu machine gun stuttered and the enemy artillery roared, raking the Marine line. A Japanese counterattack hit the Marines' left flank. It was hand-to-hand and tree-to-tree. One company alone suffered 50 casualties, including all its officers."

More Marine outfits joined the offensive, which steadily gained momentum. On November 25, elements of the 1st Battalion, 9th Marines, charged a small knoll that was known as Hand Grenade Hill from that day on. The Marines approached within 150ft (46m) of positions held by about 70 enemy soldiers, tenaciously refusing to retreat and flinging grenade after grenade at the Americans. That night, the enemy melted into the jungle.

Hill 1000 and Hellzapoppin Ridge

The limit of the previously established American defensive perimeter on Bougainville was in sight as November waned. Some 6000ft (1829m) distant, near the spot where the East-West Trail crossed the Torokina River, a group of hills had to be taken to consolidate the perimeter. Hill 1000, so named due to its height in meters, was the focus of the Marine attack spearheaded by the 1st Parachute Regiment. A spur of this high ground soon became known as Hellzapoppin Ridge. With the help of three

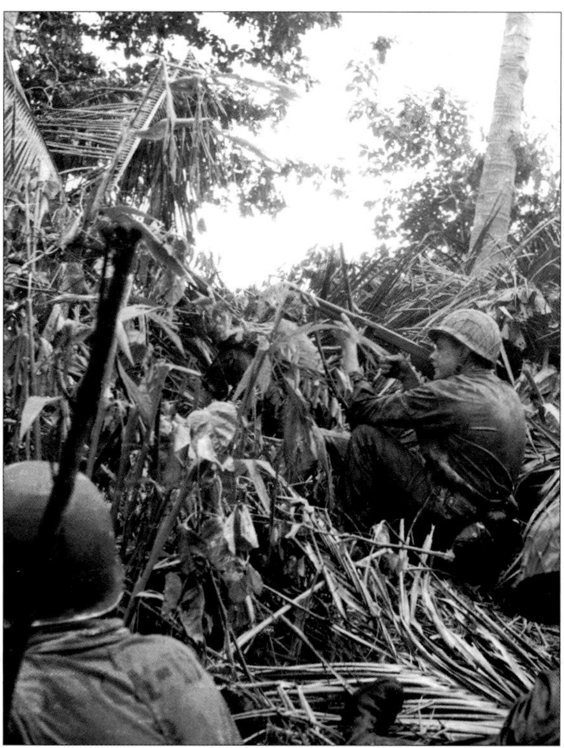

Above: Amid the dense jungle on the island of Bougainville, a Marine takes aim at a Japanese sniper. This Marine is armed with a Thompson submachine gun, which provided the Marines with automatic firepower at the squad level.

other Marine regiments, Major Robert Vance led his parachutists as ground troops and took Hill 1000 on December 5.

Vance attacked the spur on December 9 and made little headway. The next day two battalions of the 21st Marines and a supporting battalion of the 9th Marines renewed the attack. Brutal fighting raged for six more days, and dozens of Marines were killed or wounded. The bodies of the parachutists were constant reminders to the ground pounders of the tenacity of the enemy defenders.

While the battle swirled on Hellzapoppin Ridge, one of the primary objectives of the Marine presence on Bougainville began to bear fruit. Corsair fighters of VMF-216, the vanguard

A battle-hardened group of Marine Raiders poses for a photograph at the entrance to a Japanese dugout near Cape Torokina on the island of Bougainville. This photograph was taken in January 1944, shortly after these Marines have participated in the capture of the Japanese fortification.

of an aerial onslaught and the command known as Air Solomons that would ravage Rabaul, had reached the now operational airstrip at Torokina on December 10. Marine planes roared in on Hellzapoppin Ridge and dropped 100lb (45kg) bombs, some a scant 225ft (69m) from Marine positions. The Marine pilots flew repeated sorties over the next several days. The aerial bombardment was followed by a torrent of 155mm artillery shells from Army howitzers positioned near the mouth of the Torokina.

Finally, on December 18, two battalions of the 21st Marines advanced from Hill 1000 and executed a double envelopment of Hellzapoppin Ridge. Those enemy soldiers who had survived the heavy Marine pounding of the preceding days were too stunned to offer much resistance. A Marine combat correspondent observed, "No one knows how many Japs were killed. Some 30 bodies were found. Another dozen might have been put together from arms, legs, and torsos. The 21st suffered 12 killed and 23 wounded."

For another five days, the 3rd Marine Division fought to dislodge enemy defenders from the remaining high ground around Hill 1000. On Christmas Day, the Marines discovered that the Japanese had evacuated.

U.S. Troop Withdrawal

Their mission on Bougainville accomplished, tired Marines, some of whom had spent nearly two months in the line, were withdrawn from the island. The 3rd Marine Regiment departed on Christmas Day, followed by the 9th Marines on December 28, and the 21st Marines on January 9, 1944. Marine casualties on Bougainville amounted to 423 dead and 1418 wounded. Estimates of the casualties they inflicted on the Japanese run as high as 2500.

Below: Dead Japanese soldiers lie unburied on Bougainville following a mass suicide, or banzai, charge. Eventually, the Japanese reconsidered the tactics of such charges and adopted the concept of defense in depth.

The Navajo Code Talkers

The need for swift communication in the heat of battle was readily apparent during the Solomon Islands Campaign. Responding to Japanese attacks, calling in artillery support, and relaying orders to frontline units without allowing the enemy to read the radio traffic offered a distinct tactical advantage for the Marines on Guadalcanal, Bougainville, and elsewhere.

That advantage was provided by a small group of Native Americans who used a dialect of their own tongue, one that communicated with sounds that were sometimes reminiscent of gurgling water. These were the Navajo Code Talkers. Although the idea was not totally new—Native Americans had served in a similar capacity on a limited basis during World War I—the concept was revived early in World War II by Philip Johnston, the son of a Protestant missionary who had grown up on a Navajo reservation.

Johnston traveled to Camp Elliot near San Diego, California, and proposed a Code Talker unit to Lieutenant Colonel James E. Jones, the area signal officer. Jones was skeptical at first, but a demonstration message convinced him. The colonel admitted that it would have taken his own communications team two hours to encode and decode a message that Navajo recruits dispatched and delivered in the startlingly short span of two minutes.

Recruiters visited Navajo reservations, and soon 29 young men were in training. After the Marine landings on Guadalcanal, 27 of these Code Talkers were ordered to the island while two stayed in the United States as instructors. By the time the war ended, more than 400 Navajo had volunteered as Code Talkers. They rendered valuable service during Marine combat operations across the Pacific.

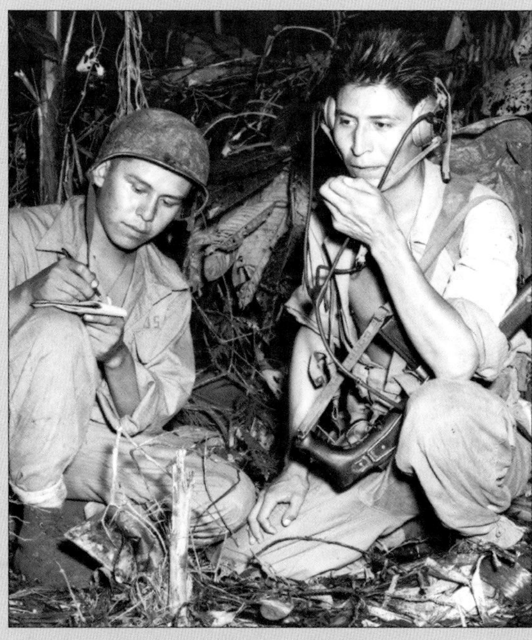

Above: The Navajo Code Talkers rendered valuable service on New Britain and elsewhere during the Pacific War. Two of the Code Talkers, Henry Bake and George Kirk, are shown plying their craft in this wartime image.

The existence of the Code Talker program remained secret until it was declassified in 1968. Afterward, the surviving Code Talkers received recognition that was long overdue. President Ronald Reagan proclaimed August 14, 1982, as National Code Talker Day. In 2000, a Congressional Gold Medal was awarded to the original 29 Code Talkers and Silver Medals were presented to others in the program.

In 2008, President George W. Bush signed the Code Talkers Recognition Act, saluting the Native American Code Talkers who served in both world wars. These included Cherokee and Choctaw military personnel.

After the withdrawal of the 3rd Marine Division, the Army's 37th and Americal Divisions took over on Bougainville. At first, only occasional Japanese resistance was encountered. However, in late February and early March 1944 a sizable enemy offensive was defeated on the island. From November of that year through to the end of the war, the Allied presence on Bougainville was an Australian affair. The II Corps, commanded by Lieutenant General Sir Stanley Savige, conducted operations against a Japanese presence on the island that still numbered approximately 40,000 troops. Although by the time World War II in the Pacific ended Rabaul was an operational backwater, the Japanese on New Britain did not surrender until they received notification that the war was over.

Coda at Cape Gloucester

On December 26, 1943, a year after their long fight to wrest Guadalcanal from the Japanese ended with a major victory, the Marines of the 1st Division, now under Major General William H. Rupertus, were once again on the offensive.

After rest, recuperation, reequipping, and assimilating replacements, the 1st Division was hitting the two "Yellow" beaches at Cape Gloucester on the western end of the island of New Britain, 300 miles (483km) away from the major Japanese base at Rabaul. The Marine objective was control of the Japanese airfield complex at Tuluvu. General Douglas MacArthur, Commander-in-Chief, Southwest Pacific Area, wanted the complex for several reasons. Chief among them were the possibility of Allied airstrikes that could be launched against Rabaul in preparation for a direct assault on the enemy base, and the fact that Cape Gloucester dominated Dampier Strait through which Allied shipping would pass as MacArthur made later offensive moves toward the Philippines.

After Operation Cartwheel was altered to strangle Rabaul rather than to capture the base by direct assault, MacArthur still believed the capture of the two airfields at Tuluvu would allow aircraft to further tighten the noose. Some historians, however, have criticized the Cape Gloucester operation as unnecessary.

More than 10,000 Japanese troops defended the expanse of western New Britain. These were under the command of Major General Iwao Matsuda and consisted of elements of the 65th Infantry Brigade, the 51st Division, and the 1st and 8th Shipping Regiments. About 7500 troops were in the vicinity of Cape Gloucester.

After difficult landings on the narrow beaches due to rough surf that buffeted their LCVPs, two battalions of the 7th Marines moved inland.

They encountered more initial resistance from the inhospitable terrain than the defending Japanese. In a single day, 13,000 troops and more than 7500 tons (6804 tonnes) of supplies were brought ashore. Air Solomons provided fighter cover while bombers hit visible targets.

Supported by tanks and artillery, the 1st and 2nd Battalions, 5th Marines, took the airfields on December 30. Heavy rains impeded further operations, but by mid-January surrounding high ground was in Marine hands. The 3rd Battalion, 7th Marines, seized Hill 660 and held it against subsequent Japanese counterattacks.

The 1st Marine Division consolidated its hold in western New Britain during the coming days and succeeded in driving the Japanese from the area before withdrawing in two echelons during the first week of April and in early May.

For the Japanese defenders in western New Britain the cost was high with 3100 killed and wounded. Marine casualties were 248 killed and 772 wounded.

Below: Near Cape Gloucester, alert Marines man a defensive position on the island of New Britain during operations to isolate the sprawling Japanese base at Rabaul. The two Marines at center are manning a Browning .30-caliber water-cooled M1917 heavy machine gun, while the one in the foreground carries a Thompson submachine gun and the Marine in the background holds an M1 carbine.

CHAPTER 4

TAKING TARAWA

Nearly two years after the devastating attack on Pearl Harbor, American military strategists were set to take the first step in the Central Pacific on the long road to the Japanese Home Islands and victory.

The character of the Japanese plan of conquest in the Pacific and on the Asian mainland changed rapidly after their shattering defeat at the Battle of Midway. Japan's perspective on its far-flung empire necessarily became one of maintenance and defense rather than expansion. In Tokyo, the nation's senior war ministers and the inner circle of advisors that clustered around Emperor Hirohito knew that the Americans were coming.

Plotting a Course

The U.S. military's path lay across thousands of miles of trackless ocean and through a string of fortified islands, often just small spits of land among numerous coral shelves that peaked slightly above the water surrounding extinct volcanoes. Known as atolls, these might consist of only a few small islets or dozens of coral outcroppings. The first step in the Central Pacific was codenamed Operation Galvanic. In the summer of 1943, Admiral Chester W. Nimitz, Commander-in-Chief, United States Pacific Fleet, authorized the seizure of a pair of atolls in the Gilbert Islands, Tarawa and Makin. These specks of land were roughly halfway between Hawaii and Australia.

Opposite: A Marine of the 2nd Division takes aim at a Japanese pillbox, possibly to provide covering fire for other Marines who will assault the enemy position. This scenario was typical during the fighting on Betio at Tarawa Atoll as the Marines sought to take the fortified islet against fierce Japanese resistance.

As U.S. Marine, Navy, and Army forces battered their way across the Central Pacific, control of the Gilberts was essential to the expanding American zone of operations. The primary objectives were to eliminate the threat of air attack from the rear as the Americans pushed further across the Pacific to attack the Japanese base at Kwajalein Atoll in the Marshall Islands, 500 miles (805km) northwest of the Gilberts.

By far the largest amphibious operation ever attempted by the U.S. Marine Corps, Operation

Galvanic would also provide an opportunity to refine the skills needed for future amphibious assaults that would surely be necessary. As its combat role had evolved through more than a century-and-a-half of existence, the modern raison d'être of the Marine Corps, rapid landing and movement across a contested beach, would be validated—if not perfected—during the wresting of Tarawa from the Japanese.

Slated for November 20, 1943, the task of executing Operation Galvanic was given to the 2nd Marine Division and the 165th Regimental Combat Team of the U.S. Army's 27th Infantry Division. Vice Admiral Raymond A. Spruance, who had made the pivotal decisions that led to victory at Midway, commanded the Central Pacific Force, while three major generals named Smith assumed senior command roles in Operation Galvanic. Holland M. "Howlin' Mad" Smith commanded the V Amphibious Corps, Julian C. Smith the 2nd Marine Division, and Ralph C. Smith the 27th Infantry Division.

The combined strength of U.S. ground troops exceeded 35,000, and the naval task force that sailed from several locations in early November included an array of troop transports with a powerful escort of 17 aircraft carriers, 12 battleships, eight heavy cruisers, four light cruisers, and 66 destroyers. More than 200 ships of the U.S. Navy converged on a rendezvous point near the intersection of the International Date Line and the equator. From there, the armada split into three groups. The carrier group kept watch against Japanese air or naval attacks, particularly from the direction of Kwajalein, and the northern force headed for Makin, while the southern steamed toward Tarawa, about 100 miles (161km) distant.

Three days after the attack on Pearl Harbor, the Japanese had occupied Tarawa and Makin without opposition. For more than 18 months, they had worked to fortify the principal islets of the atolls, Betio and Butaritari respectively. In August 1942, the Marines' 2nd Raider Battalion under Colonel Evans F. Carlson conducted a raid against the small garrison at Makin, awakening the Japanese to the vulnerability of island outposts along their defensive perimeter.

By mid-1943, the Japanese had identified a "Zone of Absolute Defense" that encompassed territory from Burma in the west to the Dutch East Indies through New Guinea and the Marshalls and to the Kuriles in the north. Although the Gilberts were outside this zone, they were among several island groups to be defended to the last man, trading lives and resources for time to bolster the empire's inner defenses and to exact the heaviest possible toll on the Americans.

Rear Admiral Tomanari Saichiro brought 2600 troops of the 6th Yokosuka Special Naval Landing Force to bolster the garrison on

Right: A soldier from the 2nd Marine Division wears the two-piece herringbone-twill uniform that became the dominant dress code of Marines in the Pacific Theater. He is carrying a captured "Samurai" sword, a trophy of the battle on Tarawa.

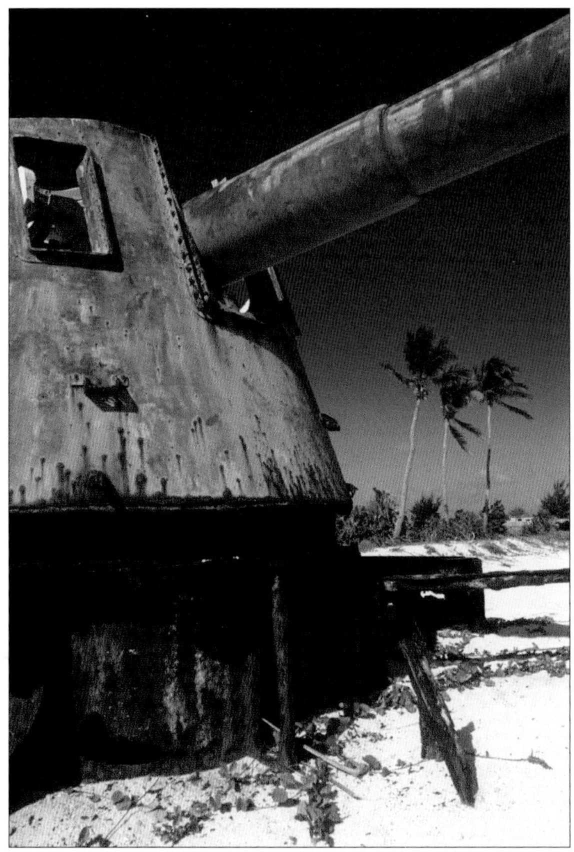

Left: This heavy gun, a rusted relic of the bitter struggle at Tarawa, rests where it was placed by the Japanese defenders on the islet of Betio nearly 75 years ago.

Betio. Along with 1200 Korean forced laborers and 1000 Japanese construction workers, they built concrete blockhouses with walls several feet thick, reinforced with steel and coconut logs and covered with tons of sand. Machine-gun nests and pillboxes were positioned with interlocking fields of fire, barbed wire entanglements were strung along the beaches, and sharp steel obstacles that could tear into the thin hulls of landing craft were submerged around Betio and in the lagoon that stretched 17 miles (27km) long and nine miles (14km) wide, fronting the beaches chosen by American planners for the coming assault. The Japanese even buried seven tanks in sand up to their turrets to fire into the lagoon.

More than 40 artillery emplacements studded Betio, and the islet bristled with the muzzles of 13mm heavy machine guns and field pieces of calibers up to 120mm. Four heavy 8in (20cm) guns of British manufacture that had been purchased by the Japanese at the height of the Russo-Japanese War in 1905 were positioned on Betio. Contrary to popular belief, these heavy weapons had not been captured at Singapore.

Roughly two miles (3.2km) from one end to the other and 2400ft (730m) across at its widest point, Betio is comprised of only 291 acres (118 hectares), approximately half the size of Central Park in New York City. Both Japanese and American commanders speculated that Betio, for its size, may well have been the most fortified territory on Earth. In August, Rear Admiral Keiji Shibasaki replaced Saichiro. Shibasaki was so impressed with the defenses at Betio that he boasted: "A million men cannot take Tarawa in a hundred years!"

General Holland Smith and Admiral Turner chose to accompany the Makin Force, designated Task Force 52, aboard the battleship *Pennsylvania*, while command of Task Force 53, the Tarawa force, was given to Rear Admiral Harry W. Hill aboard the battleship *Maryland*. The senior American commanders believed that the Makin operation would be completed rapidly. If a problem arose at Tarawa, Holland Smith and Turner could reach the scene quickly.

Lay of the Land

Shaped like a parrot, Betio is positioned with its lagoon on the north side and the main U.S. landing beaches, designated west to east as Red 1-3, running along the parrot's breast. Near the junction of Red 2 and 3, a long pier jutted more than 1500ft (457m) into the lagoon, and surely the Japanese had placed machine guns and snipers along its length. For the most part, the beaches were convex, which was expected to ease the

The battle-scarred landscape of Betio attests to the ferocity of the combat on Tarawa as the 2nd Marine Division assaulted its beaches in the face of heavy enemy fire from well-entrenched positions. About 4500 Japanese troops had occupied concrete pillboxes, blockhouses, and machine-gun nests with interlocking fields of fire to contest the Marine landings.

Above: Repaired and modernized after being heavily damaged at Pearl Harbor, the battleship USS *Maryland* fires its 16-inch main guns in support of the 2nd Marine Division landings at Tarawa on November 20, 1943.

landings to a degree. One notable exception was a small cove on the west side of Red Beach 1 that would allow the Japanese to simultaneously fire from three directions.

At a right angle to the west of Red Beach 1, Green Beach ran the length of the parrot's head from beak to crest. The primary landings, however, had been set for the Red Beaches because the waters of the lagoon would not be as rough as the open sea approaches to the ocean side of Betio at Green Beach, and Intelligence reports suggested that the defenses along the Red beaches were not yet completed.

The greatest concern to the planners of the Tarawa assault was the existence of a barrier reef that ringed the islet. The most common landing craft in use with American forces at the time was the LCVP (Landing Craft, Vehicle, Personnel), or Higgins Boat, and these flat-bottomed transports were capable of hauling a jeep and a squad of infantry, a 36-man platoon, or 8000lb (3628kg) of supplies. These were shallow draft boats, about 3ft (0.9m) aft fully loaded, but the depth of the water along the reef during tidal cycles might well be insufficient for the craft to enter the lagoon. If the LCVPs became hung up on the reef, infantrymen might be disgorged hundreds of yards from shore and required to wade some distance under enemy fire.

Tracked Amphibious Vehicles

Lieutenant Colonel David M. Shoup, Operations Officer of the 2nd Marine Division, led the planning effort for the Tarawa assault. Shoup chose the landing beaches for the right reasons but also recognized the potential for disaster if the LCVPs were unable to negotiate the barrier reef. Shoup was also aware of a possible solution to the problem. A limited number of tracked amphibious vehicles originally developed for use in the swampy Everglades of Florida were available. These vehicles, designated LVTs (Landing Vehicle Tracked) and commonly called amtracs or alligators, were capable of traversing the water and then engaging tracks to cross low barriers and put troops directly on the beaches.

Only 75 LVTs had been allotted to the Tarawa invasion, and Shoup requested an additional 100 that he knew were in storage on the U.S. West Coast. Holland Smith was a forceful advocate for Shoup, arguing vigorously against Turner, who asserted that time was of the essence. Transporting the LVTs to a combat zone meant the commitment of more ships and might even compromise the secrecy of Operation Galvanic.

Smith was adamant, and eventually the 100 LVTs were assigned to the deployed force. Half of these, however, would go to the Army's landing operation at Makin. A total of 125 LVTs would be available at Tarawa. LCVPs would carry the rest of the combat troops—hopefully all the way to the beaches.

Shoup's original invasion plan was evaluated during a senior level conference, and he was taken aback by the restrictions handed down from the highest echelon of Pacific command. A diversionary landing on an islet near Betio was canceled. Although heavy bombers from the Ellice Islands had hit Tarawa repeatedly for days, the duration of pre-invasion naval and air bombardment on November 20 were restricted to supposedly preserve the element of surprise as long as possible. One of the most shocking alterations to Shoup's plan was the decision that the 6th Marine Regiment would be held as V Corps reserve, lowering the Marine numerical superiority to only about two to one.

Shoup's revised plan called for the 2nd Marine Regiment and a landing team of the 2nd Battalion, 8th Marines, to hit the beaches, while the remainder of the 8th Marines served as 2nd Division reserve. On the eastern edge of the assault beaches at Red 3, the 2nd Battalion, 8th Marines (Landing Team 2/8), under Major

Below: This LVT-2 (Landing Vehicle, Tracked), capable of climbing across coral reefs and other obstructions, was a significant improvement over the flat-bottomed Higgins boat in carrying combat Marines to shore on hostile beaches.

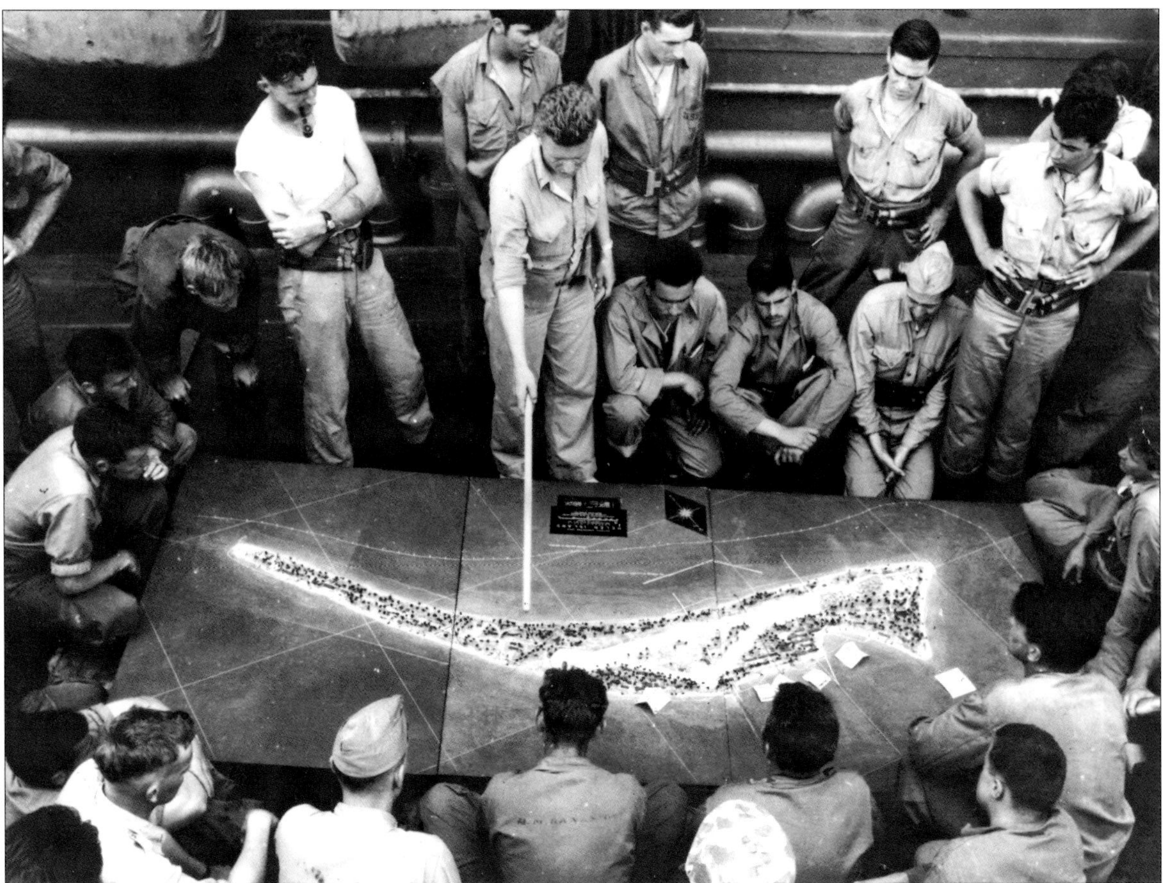

Above: The distinctive parrot shape of Betio is visible as Marines study the islet's terrain aboard a U.S. Navy transport vessel en route to the rendezvous point where the November 20, 1943, landing operation was launched.

Henry P. Crowe, would land simultaneously with the 2nd Battalion, 2nd Marines (Landing Team 2/2), under Lieutenant Colonel Herbert R. Amey, Jr. on Red 2, and the 3rd Battalion, 2nd Marines (Landing Team 3/2), under Major John F. Schoettel on Red 1. The 1st Battalion, 2nd Marines, under Major Wood B. Kyle was designated the regimental reserve. The first Marines to reach Tarawa would be the 34-man Scout Sniper Platoon, 2nd Marines, under the command of 1st Lieutenant William D. Hawkins, and their task was to seize the long lagoon pier.

Shoup shouldered the considerable burden of responsibility for planning the Tarawa landings; however, within days of the operation his load became much heavier. Colonel William Marshall, commander of the 2nd Marines, suffered a serious heart attack only days before the assault. Shoup was the logical choice to take field command and execute his own plan. Julian Smith promoted him to colonel and made it official.

Opposite: Colonel David M. Shoup planned the landings of Operation Galvanic at Betio and then was elevated to command the 2nd Marines during the actual landing, after the regiment's commanding officer, Colonel William Marshall, suffered a serious heart attack. Shoup served gallantly at Tarawa and received the Medal of Honor.

Shoup still agonized over the challenge presented by the barrier reef, and the new commander of the 2nd Marines told *Time-Life* correspondent Robert Sherrod that the earliest assault troops would head for the beaches in amtracs but following waves might have trouble during the run-in. "...We'll either have to wade in with machine guns maybe shooting at us, or the amtracs will have to run a shuttle service between the beach and the end of the shelf."

Before sunrise on November 20, steak, eggs, fried potatoes, and coffee were served up in the galleys of the transports carrying the Marines who would make the first major beach assault against prepared Japanese defenses during World War II. After eating what they could (some had trouble with food given the circumstances), the Marines emerged from the galleys, proceeded topside, and then clambered down cargo nets and into landing craft that bobbed below.

Below: As the landing operation at Tarawa gets underway, Marines clamber down cargo nets from a transport ship to Higgins Boats that bob in the choppy waters of the Pacific below them.

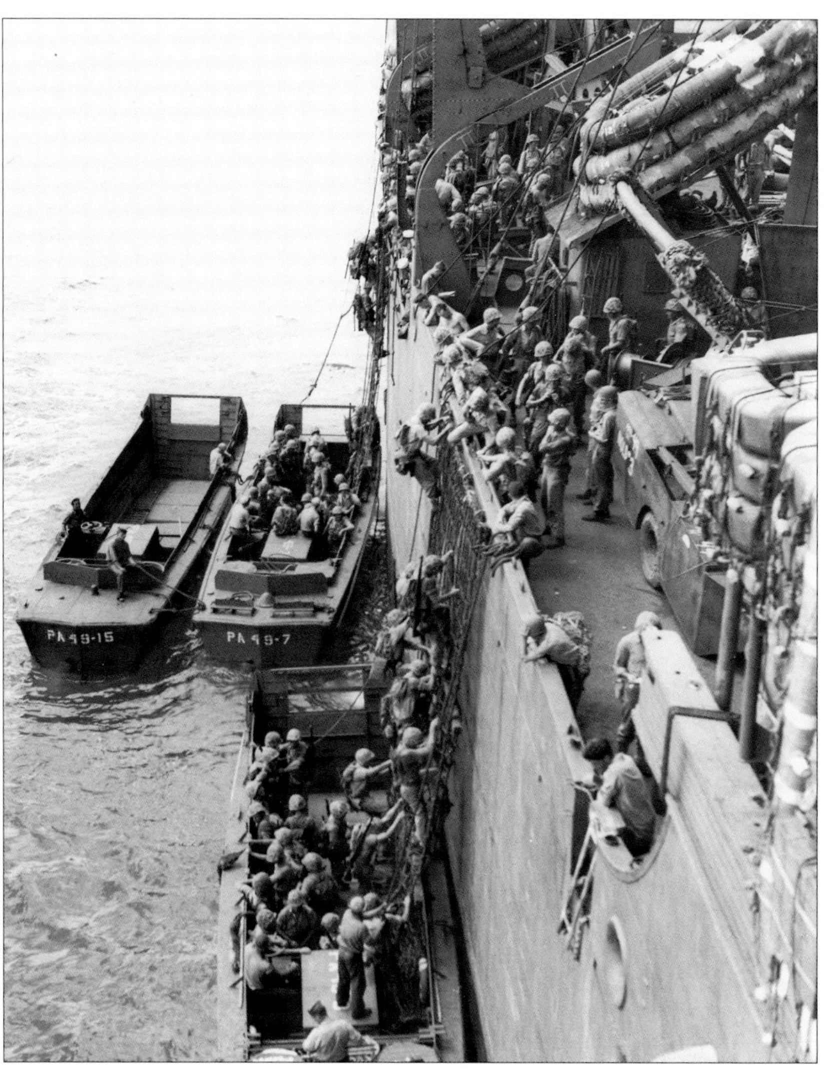

From the beginning, what had been conceived as a well-choreographed series of shelling, bombing, and strafing prior to the landings began to go awry. Rear Admiral Howard F. Kingman was so confident that the bombardment would do its job that he had remarked, "Gentlemen, we will not neutralize Betio. We will not destroy it. We will obliterate it!"

Admiral Hill, however, became aware that some of the transport ships were in the wrong place, obscuring the view of the gunners aboard the battleships and cruisers of the support force. He ordered the transports to relocate while some Marines were still scrambling down the nets, and confusion ensued as transports and landing craft became separated.

At 4.41 a.m., a red star shell streaked into

The Higgins Boat

Left: During exercises, Marines dash from the belly of a Higgins Boat, its ramp just lowered into the surf. The Higgins Boat was used by Allied forces in virtually every theater of World War II.

From the inception of amphibious warfare strategy and tactics, the Marine Corps sought the most efficient method of moving fighting men from ship to shore. Finding a proper landing craft that could reach the beach and discharge Marines swiftly sometimes seemed an insurmountable problem.

The solution lay with a hard-drinking Irishman from New Orleans, Louisiana, named Andrew Jackson Higgins. During the years before World War II, Higgins worked in the lumber business and then concentrated on the construction of small boats, which he marketed to hunters, trappers, and the oil industry. In the late 1930s, the U.S. Navy and Marine Corps tested one of Higgins' early designs, the Eureka Boat, and its performance was superior to a competing design that had originated with the Navy itself. Further tests took place during fleet landing exercises.

With the coming of World War II, Higgins was sure that the U.S. military would need small boats, and lots of them. He gambled with the purchase of the entire 1939 crop of mahogany from the Philippines and stored it for future use while insisting that the Navy "doesn't know one damn thing about small boats!"

The early Higgins design was modified to Navy specifications, including the addition of a frontal ramp, which lowered to allow the troops aboard to exit rapidly. The boats were constructed of both wood and steel and measured 36ft 3in (11m) in length with a beam of 10ft 10in (3.3m). They were armed with a pair of .30-caliber machine guns and carried up to 8000lb (3629kg) of cargo, either infantrymen or equipment.

Officially designated the Landing Craft, Vehicle, Personnel (LCVP) by the military, the boat weighed 18,000lb (8165kg) and was capable of a top speed of 12 knots. The most common powerplants were a 225-horsepower Gray Marine diesel engine and a 250-horsepower Hall-Scott gasoline engine.

Nearly 24,000 LCVPs, also popularly known as Higgins Boats, were produced by Higgins' own firm in New Orleans and other defense contractors. Although the coral reef at Tarawa laid bare the LCVP's glaring weaknesses—its inability to traverse obstacles in the water or operate on land—the little craft is remembered along with the Jeep, the C-47 aircraft, and the two-and-a-half ton truck as one of the transport systems that powered the Allied victory in World War II.

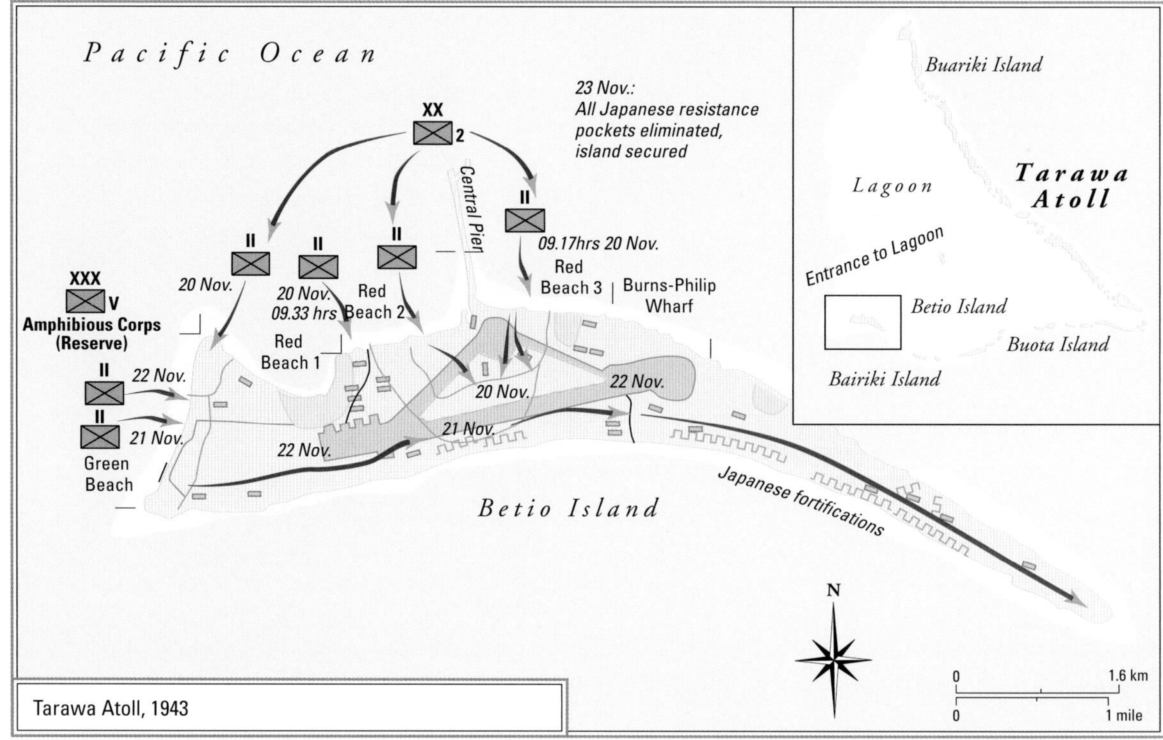

Above: The 2nd Marine Division were tasked with capturing the 0.59 square miles (1.54 sq km) of Betio Island on Tarawa Atoll. This tiny island was heavily defended by 4800 Japanese troops, and cost the Marines more than 3000 casualties.

the sky above Betio, and at 5.07 a.m. Japanese shore batteries fired the first shots of the day. Minutes later, the main batteries of the battleships *Maryland*, *Colorado*, and *Tennessee* opened fire.

The Hour of Attack

H-hour was set for 8.30 a.m., and fire support was to begin with air strikes by planes from the carriers *Bunker Hill*, *Essex*, and *Independence*. Naval gunfire was to follow for just over two hours, and then a second wave of aircraft would strafe and bomb until five minutes before the first Marines landed. When Admiral Hill ordered his ships to cease firing at 5.42 a.m., he expected carrier aircraft to arrive momentarily, but none came. For some unexplained reason, the strike was delayed by half an hour.

For more than 20 minutes, there was no activity against the Japanese on Betio. Finally, Hill ordered his bombardment force to commence firing again. Five minutes later, at 6.10 a.m, the carrier planes appeared overhead. The warships also took up their task once more.

The Marines in the landing craft were awed by the spectacular bombardment. A shell from *Maryland* detonated the ammunition bunker of one of the heavy Japanese guns, and a geyser of flame erupted skyward. It appeared that nothing could survive such a sustained rain of large caliber shells and bombs. However, it was soon painfully apparent that looks were deceiving. Many of the naval shells failed to penetrate the reinforced walls of the Japanese bunkers and blockhouses. The Marines would have to take care of these themselves.

Strong currents in the lagoon and the initial confusion forced a postponement of H-hour to

8.45 a.m. and then again to 9.00. Hill ordered his ships to continue their bombardment beyond the scheduled time, while aircraft kept up their support. Complicating matters, the concussion of the first salvo from *Maryland's* 16in (40cm) guns disrupted communications. Hill's order was not executed. Some observers reported that air support and naval fire ceased 18 minutes before the Marines landed. Others asserted that Hill ordered a ceasefire at 8.54 a.m., fearing possible friendly fire incidents. Carrier aircraft stayed in the vicinity and resumed their attacks moments later.

The first amtracs began crossing the line of departure, 18,000ft (5486m) from the beaches, at 8.24 a.m., and the destroyers *Ringgold* and *Dashiell* glided into the lagoon as close as their skippers dared without running aground, dueling with Japanese batteries and firing ahead of the Marines as long as they were able.

Amtracs churned toward the reef in three waves followed by two waves of LCVPs. When they saw the landing craft coming, the Japanese defenders along the lagoon summoned many of those on the ocean side to rush over as reinforcements. When the amtracs were within 9000ft (2743m), the Japanese guns began belching fire and spitting lead.

Lieutenant Hawkins and the intrepid Scout Sniper Platoon were five minutes ahead of the first line of amtracs. Unflinching in the face of heavy fire, Hawkins led the assault on the pier. His Marines followed, routing the Japanese with rifle, bayonet, grenade, and flamethrower. With his assignment completed, Hawkins stood erect in an amtrac as it crushed barbed wire and beach obstacles and climbed a 5ft (1.5m) seawall near the water's edge to engage Japanese strongpoints.

Below: Tracked LVTs churn toward the embattled beaches at Betio during the opening hours of Operation Galvanic on November 20, 1943. The 2nd Marine Division suffered grievous losses, but captured Betio during 76 hours of intense combat.

As the amtracs of the first wave reached the reef and ponderously climbed across, they were met with a hail of accurate Japanese fire. Private Newman M. Baird, a machine gunner aboard one of the craft, remembered the harrowing ordeal.

"We were 100 yards in now, and the enemy fire was awful damn intense and getting worse. They were knocking boats out right and left," Baird recalled. "A tractor'd get hit, stop, and burst into flames, with men jumping out like torches... Bullets ricocheted off the coral and up under the tractor. It must've been one of those bullets that got the driver. The lieutenant jumped in and pulled the driver out and drove himself 'til he got hit. Our boat was stopped, and they were laying lead to us from a pillbox like holy hell... I grabbed my carbine and an ammunition box and stepped over a couple of fellas laying there and put my hand on the side so's to roll over into the water. I didn't want to put my head up. The bullets were pouring at us like a sheet of rain. Only about a dozen of the 25 went over the side with me."

Major Henry Drewes, commander of the 2nd Amphibious Tractor Battalion, climbed up to an LVT machine gun when the crewman firing it was killed. Within seconds, Drewes was shot dead with a bullet to the head. A sergeant stood up in an LVT on Red Beach 1, and his men watched as machine gun bullets appeared to "rip his head off".

Schoettel's 3rd Battalion, 2nd Marines was being chewed up on Red Beach 1. Several of the unit's landing craft were hung up on the reef, forcing the Marines to wade ashore while enemy machine guns raked them. Schoettel was unable himself to get ashore for several hours and feared that his battalion had been wiped out.

Below: Rear Admiral Harry W. Hill, commander of Task Force 53 assigned to complete the capture of Tarawa, observes the fire of 16-inch guns aboard the battleship USS *Maryland* during the pre-invasion phase of Operation Galvanic off the islet of Betio.

Company L, commanded by Major Michael Ryan, had taken 35 percent casualties wading toward Red Beach 1 from the reef, but Ryan displayed tremendous initiative, gathering survivors from his company along with others he could pull together in a relatively quiet area that was actually on Green Beach.

At Red Beach 2, Corporal John Joseph Spillane was the crew chief of an LVT named "The Old Lady", which reached the seawall and came under heavy fire. Spillane was a professional baseball prospect, and scouts from the St. Louis Cardinals and the New York Yankees had visited his parents. When the Japanese began lobbing hand grenades into "The Old Lady", Spillane displayed incredible skill and bravery. Accounts vary as to how many hand grenades he fielded, spearing, trapping, and throwing them back like a shortstop. There were at least three and as many as six that hissed his way. "I didn't have time to think. I just kept

Below: Marines wade ashore on the lagoon side of Betio after the capture of the islet in November 1943. During the fight for Tarawa, many Marine landing craft were caught on the coral reef that ringed the lagoon side of Betio, forcing their Marine cargo to wade several hundred yards under enemy fire to reach the Red Beaches.

throwing them back," Spillane remembered. "Finally, one came over with a lot of blue smoke coming out of it. I picked it up anyway, and just as I pushed back my hand to throw it went off. I was stunned for a minute. There wasn't much left of my hand, but I felt no pain."

Spillane's baseball career was over. He held his bloody stump and yelled, "Let's get out of here!" He later received the Navy Cross and Purple Heart for his exploits.

On the west side of the pier at Red Beach 2, Lieutenant Colonel Amey tried to rally his beleaguered men. Amey raised his pistol and shouted, "Come on! These bastards can't stop us!" Instantly, he was riddled with machine-gun bullets and killed. Lieutenant Colonel Walter Jordan, an officer of the 4th Marine Division who had come along as an observer, took command of the 2nd Battalion, 2nd Marines. Moments later, he received the grim news that one company was pinned down while another had lost five of six officers.

The only battalion to land relatively intact on the bloody morning of November 20 was Major Crowe's 2nd Battalion, 8th Marines, at Red Beach 3, east of the pier where *Ringgold* and *Dashiell* had covered its approach. Once ashore, most of Crowe's command was held up by a complex of pillboxes and bunkers that included Shibasaki's command post. Two amtracs managed to push through to the edge of the 4000ft (1219m) airstrip that crisscrossed Betio.

While the initial landings were being punished, Colonel Shoup was frustrated in his attempts to get ashore. Sometime around 10.30 a.m. he transferred from an LCVP to an LVT and headed

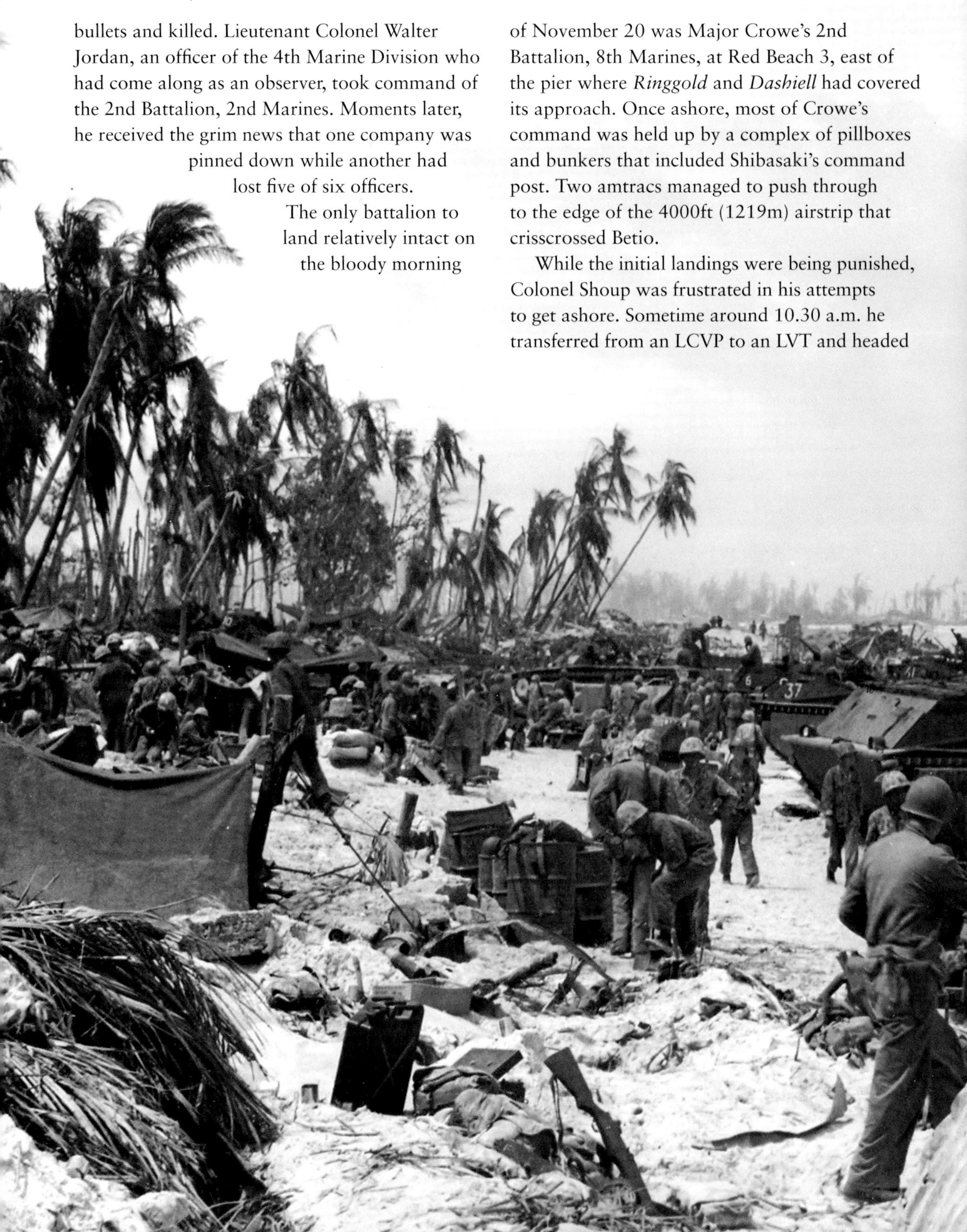

for Red Beach 2 near the pier. On its third attempt to land, the LVT was peppered with Japanese bullets, and Shoup was wounded in the leg by a shell fragment. He limped toward the shore and then stood in waist-deep water trying to assess the situation. Communications were difficult at best as most radios were lost or waterlogged. Around noon, Shoup moved inland about 150ft (46m) and set up a command post only 3ft (0.9m) from a log bunker still occupied by the Japanese. Neither could bring their guns to bear on the other.

Sketchy reports began to filter through, and Shoup realized that the situation was desperate. One said, "Have landed. Unusually heavy opposition. Casualties 70 per cent. Can't hold." Shoup committed the regimental reserve, Major Kyle's 1st Battalion, 2nd Marines, with orders to land on Red Beach 2 and fight westward to Red 1.

By this time, General Julian Smith had already released Major Robert H. Ruud's 3rd Battalion, 8th Marines, from the division reserve. He informed Holland Smith: "Successful landings on Beaches Red 2 and 3. Toehold on Red 1. Am committing one LT (Ruud) from Division Reserve. Still encountering strong resistance throughout."

Kyle's assault came apart rapidly as the Japanese shot up LVTs with accurate fire, several bursting into flames and sinking. Two companies were aboard these LVTs, and the weapons company was forced to wade in. A storm of Japanese shells pushed five boats away from Red 2. These fortuitously landed their Marines at Ryan's position on Green Beach. Kyle made it to the pier and flagged down an LVT for the run-in. A handful of his men extended the American position on Red Beach 2 a few yards inland.

Below: This photograph taken on Red Beach 2 at Betio after the battle for Tarawa ended gives some indication of the chaos that ensued as elements of the 2nd Marine Division landed there under fire on November 20, 1943. LVTs and an artillery piece sit temporarily unattended among the detritus of war.

Above: Wounded Marines are moved by raft following the capture of Tarawa.

Ruud's command was cut to pieces when no LVTs were available to shuttle his Marines from the reef to the beach. The 3rd Battalion suffered 70 per cent casualties wading through water that was chest deep. Two Higgins Boats were obliterated on the reef by direct hits, and the coxswain of another was so terrified by the sight that he lowered his ramp shouting, "This is as far as I go!" Marines carrying full combat gear sank like stones and drowned.

Sometime around mid-day, Julian Smith committed the last of the division reserve, the 1st Battalion, 8th Marines, under Major Hays, but only after Holland Smith confirmed that the 6th Marines had been released from Makin, where the capture of the islet proved a frustrating effort that would last four days was finally making sustained progress, and was heading toward Tarawa. A colossal communications failure resulted in Hays's command remaining aboard landing craft all night long rather than coming ashore near Red 3 and working westward as Julian Smith intended.

Although the Japanese had absorbed tremendous punishment, their fire slackened only slightly. Clearly, the Marines pinned down at the seawall, in the shadow of the pier, or dug in along a narrow strip of sand would have to silence the enemy guns the toughest way possible—with demolition charges, grenades, and flamethrowers.

Rising to the Challenge

Although the sight of their dead comrades bobbing in the lagoon, burned out LVTs littering the shoreline and drifting, and the scores of wounded were unnerving, those junior and noncommissioned officers that were left began rising to the occasion at the most critical time. Among the first to act was Staff Sergeant William Bordelon of San Antonio, Texas. A combat engineer with Lieutenant Colonel Amey's 2nd

Battalion, 2nd Marines, Bordelon reached Red Beach 2 after his LVT was ravaged, killing all but four of the men aboard. Bordelon destroyed two Japanese pillboxes with demolition charges. He was wounded by machine-gun fire as he tried to silence a third, but emptied an M1 rifle in support of Marines crossing the seawall.

Ignoring his own wounds, Bill Bordelon then pulled two wounded men from the water. He gathered himself and charged a fourth machine-gun position but was riddled by enemy fire and died instantly. Bordelon received a posthumous Medal of Honor, the first of four Marines so recognized for valor during the fight for Betio.

Heroic Navy and Marine personnel risked their own lives to treat and evacuate the wounded. Among these was a Naval Reserve lieutenant from Minneapolis, Minnesota, named Edward Albert Heimberger, who rescued 47 severely wounded Marines from the water and helped 30 others get back to ships offshore for treatment. He received the Bronze Star with Combat "V" for heroism. He went on to become a well-known actor with the stage name Eddie Albert.

The Marines had received little training with armor, but they knew that tanks could use their guns to good effect in reducing Japanese strongpoints on Betio. A company of 14 medium M4 Sherman tanks and a few light M2s of the 2nd Tank Battalion had been attached to the 2nd Marine Division for Operation Galvanic. The tanks headed for the invasion beaches at Betio aboard LCMs (Landing Craft, Mechanized) and ran into trouble just as the infantry units had.

Several LCMs were destroyed by Japanese guns, taking their tanks to the bottom of the lagoon. None of the light tanks aboard these LCMs reached the shore. Shermans fell into deep holes off the beaches and were lost. Several were thrown into the fight piecemeal with orders to simply engage any enemy position encountered. At least two were put out of action by American dive-bombers.

As the day wore on, only two Shermans remained in action. On Red Beach 3, Colorado, commanded by Lieutenant Louis Largey, supported Major Crowe's thrust toward the airstrip, shrugging off fire from Japanese antitank guns and undeterred when it detonated a mine. Still, Colorado came on, blasting bunkers and pillboxes with its 75mm gun. With Major Ryan at the extended position on Green Beach, a Sherman nicknamed "China Gal", commanded by Lieutenant Ed Bale, destroyed a Japanese tank after a hit from the enemy vehicle had turned the inside of the Sherman's turret lemon yellow, but failed to penetrate the armor.

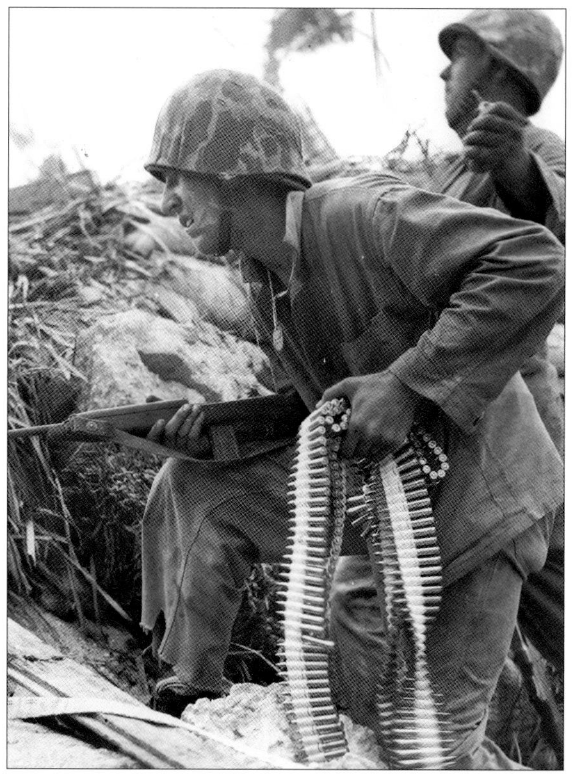

Right: A pair of Marines moves stealthily forward on Betio, expecting Japanese machine-gun fire to greet them if they are too exposed. The Marine in the background prepares to throw a hand grenade, while the other is armed with an M1 carbine and carries a belt of .30-caliber machine-gun ammunition.

Japanese light tanks were no match for the American Shermans, but a pair of them rumbled toward Crowe's embattled Marines. The crews of two 37mm antitank guns had wrestled their weapons ashore when the landing craft carrying them were sunk. When the seawall blocked any further movement forward, word was passed. The shout, "Lift 'em over!" was heard. Rapidly, the 900lb (408kg) guns were manhandled into position. A direct hit caused one of the Japanese tanks to lurch sideways billowing smoke and flame. The other turned and fled.

Although Ryan was out of position, the number of men under his ad hoc command had steadily grown. He sensed an opportunity. The Japanese defenses on Green Beach were sited to fire out to sea. They were vulnerable to flank attack. Marines moved from blockhouse to pillbox, from machine-gun nest to trench, and cleared a portion of Green Beach that could have been used to land reinforcements. However, the gains could not be exploited because there was no communication with Shoup.

Ryan had little in the way of substantial weapons, no flamethrowers, and many of his demolition charges were used in the fighting. Only the 75mm gun aboard the blackened hulk of "China Gal" provided anything heavier than standard infantry weapons. To avoid being cut off and overwhelmed by a Japanese counterattack, he wisely pulled back to a perimeter 600ft (183m) deep and about 300ft (91m) wide, an area he believed his makeshift command could hold. A 1800ft (549m) stretch of sand literally crawling with Japanese separated Ryan from Shoup, and runners attempted to establish communications but failed.

Left: Smoke darkens the sky as Marines clamber over a wall of coconut logs and advance toward the airstrip on the islet of Betio. The assault on Betio laid bare numerous shortcomings in American amphibious doctrine, and the lessons learned were applied to future such operations in the Pacific.

To the east at Red Beaches 2 and 3, the deepest penetration was 750ft (229m), about halfway across the airstrip. Elements of four Marine battalions stretched from left to right, Major Crowe's 2nd Battalion, 8th Regiment, Major Ruud's 3rd Battalion, 8th Regiment, Major Kyle's 1st Battalion, 2nd Regiment, and the 2nd Battalion, 2nd Regiment, under Lieutenant Colonel Jordan.

"This was the crisis in the battle ... Three-fourths of the island was in the enemy's hands, and even allowing for his losses he should have had as many troops left as we had ashore."

Night Maneuvers

When daylight faded, about 5000 Marines had come ashore on Betio on November 20, 1943, and 30 percent of them were dead or wounded. Pockets of Marines held positions that were often a significant distance away from the nearest supporting troops. The Marines were aware that the Japanese might mount a nighttime suicide charge, and they knew just how vulnerable they were. Sporadic gunfire pierced the darkness, but no attack came. Shibasaki's communications had been severed, and he had lost contact with his subordinate commanders. Attempts to organize an attack that might drive the Americans into the sea proved hopeless.

During the night the Marines braced for the Banzai charge that did not materialize. Some Japanese soldiers infiltrated to the lagoon and swam out to disabled LVTs and the hulk of a half-sunken freighter, *Saida Maru*, that was hit by American dive-bombers earlier and capsized in the shallow water. From these positions, they waited to rake any reinforcements that ventured toward the Red beaches as dawn streaked the sky.

Aboard *Maryland*, Julian Smith worried. "This was the crisis of the battle," he remembered. "Three-fourths of the island was in the enemy's hands, and even allowing for his losses he should have had as many troops left as we had ashore."

Smith radioed Spruance and Nimitz at Pearl Harbor with a succinct, unvarnished assessment. "Issue in doubt."

Hays and the 1st Battalion, 8th Marines, were still aboard their landing craft almost a full day after boarding. Waiting at the line of departure, Hays had never received orders to land. Julian Smith was shocked to learn later that the battalion had not come ashore. Through his assistant division commander, Brigadier General Leo Hermle, who had spent much of the day at the embattled pier, Smith learned that Shoup wanted Hays to land at Red Beach 2. Earlier orders for Hays to go in on Red 3 were changed. At 6.15 a.m. on November 21, the 1st Battalion, 8th Marines, finally began the agonizing slog of 1500ft (457m) or more from the reef to Red 2.

The horror of the first day on Betio was renewed with vigor on the second. The 800 men under Hays lost 350 of their number to murderous fire that poured from Japanese emplacements ashore and from the hulk of *Saida Maru*, even through repeated dive-bombing and strafing by American planes. Weakened by blood loss and numbed by 30 hours without sleep, Shoup realized that Hays needed help and ordered a general attack along the intermittent Marine line.

Two 75mm pack howitzers of Lieutenant Colonel Presley Rixey's 1st Battalion, 10th Artillery Regiment, had been brought ashore during the night and assembled on the beaches behind a sand berm constructed by a Seabee bulldozer. They bellowed in support, suppressing some of the Japanese fire.

At Red Beach 3, Crowe and Ruud started moving despite the interlocking fields of fire from three Japanese bunkers on their left. Once again, *Ringgold* and *Dashiell* went to work. A direct hit from one of their 5in (12.7cm) guns blew a bunker sky high. On Red 2, Jordan and Kyle directed their Marines in a push that reached the south shore of Betio, tenuously cutting the islet in two.

Although wounded on the first day, Lieutenant Hawkins, the quintessential Scout Sniper, was still full of fight. He had once pronounced that his platoon could whip any company-sized 200-man force in the field, and on the morning of November 21 few would have doubted it. Hawkins was ordered to silence a series of Japanese machine-gun nests and pillboxes that ringed a Japanese bunker pouring deadly fire into Hays's men near the small cove close to the junction of Red 1 and Red 2.

As his men laid down covering fire, Hawkins crawled toward a pillbox, fired through a gun slit, and tossed grenades inside. Screams were heard, and the Japanese weapons were silent—but not before Hawkins had been shot in the chest. He still refused to evacuate, declaring, "I came here to kill Japs, not to be evacuated!" Three more times, Hawkins led his men in successful attacks on Japanese positions until he was caught in the explosion of an enemy mortar shell. Within

Below: Marines crouch behind the temporary cover of the seawall on Red Beach 3. Although its presence was unexpected, the seawall offered some protection against intense Japanese fire.

Above: While one Marine takes a momentary break from combat, another rises to throw a hand grenade at an enemy pillbox. The Marines at Tarawa were obliged to clear heavily fortified Japanese strongpoints on the islet of Betio one at a time. They used explosive satchel charges and hand grenades, often rushing toward the enemy positions under heavy fire to clear the way.

minutes, he was dead. After Shoup learned of the young officer's heroism, he remarked: "It is not often that you can credit a first lieutenant with winning a battle, but Hawkins came as near to it as any man could."

The dashing Lieutenant William Deane Hawkins received a posthumous Medal of Honor for his bravery and remarkable leadership at Tarawa. He was 29 years old. Although his heroism had cost him his life, Hawkins had opened the way for Hays's 1st Battalion, 8th Marines to seize the initiative on the right (west) flank of Red Beach 2.

Ryan and company had been busy on Green Beach during the night gathering weapons, ammunition, and first aid kits from the dead and wounded. Another Sherman tank, "Cecilia", joined "China Gal" on the second day. Ryan's Marines had been able to get some rest since the Japanese had mounted little resistance overnight, and another stroke of luck appeared in the shape of Navy Lieutenant Thomas Greene, a gunfire spotter whose radio actually worked.

At 11.20 a.m., Ryan began to stretch his legs across Green Beach with a well-organized attack on the Japanese pillboxes and machine-gun nests there. Greene radioed map coordinates for destroyers in the lagoon, and the 5in (12.7cm) shells smashed into their targets with great accuracy. Within an hour, Green Beach was clear as Ryan's patchwork command retraced its steps from the previous day. The newly named Task Force Ryan then turned toward the southwest corner of Betio to eliminate Japanese resistance there, moving into position to attack further eastward toward the airfield.

Ryan finally got word to Julian Smith aboard *Maryland* that Green Beach was open. The 6th Marines were arriving from Makin, and Smith ordered the regimental commander, Colonel Maurice Holmes, to prepare for landings. Holmes sent Major Willie K. Jones and the 1st Battalion to Green Beach and Lieutenant Colonel Raymond L. Murray's 2nd Battalion to the neighboring islet of Bairiki, where some Japanese were holed up. When Jones's battalion reached Green Beach, its Marines were virtually unscathed. They came ashore with all their weapons and equipment.

As the sun rose higher, the situation continued to improve. The Marines were gaining ground yard by yard, pillbox by pillbox. Reports began filtering into Shoup's command post that some Japanese troops were turning their weapons on themselves. Shibasaki was desperate but resolute, with no intention of surrender, even though he exerted little control over his troops and no reinforcements or relief could be expected.

About 4.00 a.m., Shoup had gained enough confidence to send a situation report to Julian Smith. Its conclusion has become legendary—"Casualties: many. Percentage dead: unknown. Combat efficiency: we are winning."

After dark on November 21, Colonel Merritt A. "Red Mike" Edson, already famous for his defense of Bloody Ridge at Guadalcanal, came ashore to relieve Shoup, whose stellar performance would earn him the Medal of Honor. Exhausted and in need of medical attention, Shoup, who went on to attain the rank of four-star general and serve as Commandant of the Marine Corps, said to Robert Sherrod: "Well, I think we're winning, but the bastards have got a lot of bullets left. I think we'll clean up tomorrow."

Edson set to work with efficiency. Orders for the third day were straightforward. The gains on Green Beach were to be exploited with renewed attacks to the east spearheaded by the 1st Battalion, 6th Marines that would link up with the 1st and 2nd Battalions, 2nd Marines that had fought their way southward the previous day. Hays's 1st Battalion, 8th Marines was to thrust westward and eliminate the Japanese salient between Red Beaches 1 and 2. Crowe and Ruud, commanding the other two battalions of the 8th Marines, were to attack eastward.

"Casualties: many. Percentage dead: unknown. Combat efficiency: we are winning."

With the Shermans up front, Major Jones and the 1st Battalion, 6th Marines, killed 250 Japanese troops and made the junction with the 2nd Battalion Marines in about three hours. At Red Beach 2, Hays brought in halftracks mounting 75mm guns when the 37mm guns of light M2 tanks proved insufficient for the job of reducing some Japanese strongpoints. The 75s blasted away, but painfully slow progress against enemy positions around the cove required combat engineers with satchel charges and grenades to silence some of the persistent guns.

Crowe's Marines faced the triple threat of a coconut log bunker with multiple machine guns, a steel reinforced pillbox, and a large blockhouse that was reported to have been Shibasaki's headquarters. Their interlocking fields of fire had held the Marines at bay for two days. Finally, at 9.30 a.m. on the morning of November 22, a mortar round scored a direct hit on the ammunition storage compartment for the coconut log bunker, demolishing the strongpoint. The Sherman nicknamed "Colorado" cracked open the pillbox with a 75mm (2.95in) round. The blockhouse still spewed machine gun and rifle fire.

Above: After the bloody fight for Betio has ended, Brigadier General Thomas E. Bourke, commander of the 2nd Marine Division Artillery, Colonel Merritt A. Edson, 2nd Marine Division chief-of-staff, and Major General Julian C. Smith (left to right), commander of the 2nd Marine Division, assess the results of the heated combat.

Early on the morning of the third day, Shibasaki had sent a last communiqué to Tokyo: "Our weapons have been destroyed. From now on everyone is attempting a final charge. May Japan exist for 10,000 years." Shibasaki had no way of organizing for such a charge; however, the message was in keeping with the spirit of Bushido, the Japanese code of honor. Now, if he was actually inside the blockhouse, the Japanese commander did not have long to live.

The two-storey structure was the highest point on Betio, and it had to be taken by storm. First Lieutenant Alexander Bonnyman of Knoxville, Tennessee, led five engineers forward under covering fire. Bonnyman climbed the sandy slope, reached the roof of the blockhouse, and was confronted by dozens of Japanese troops who had emerged full of fight. Bonnyman made several of them human torches with his flamethrower and emptied his carbine into them. The Japanese pulled back in disorder, but the gallant engineer was killed.

As Bonnyman's body tumbled down the slope, the remaining engineers planted demolition charges while Japanese troops swarmed out of the blockhouse. These hapless men were remorselessly gunned down, and "Colorado" took out 20 of them with a single canister round. A Marine bulldozer shoved mounds of sand against stubborn firing slits. Gasoline was poured through ventilation shafts, followed by grenades. Explosives were detonated.

At long last, the Marines on Red Beach 3 had silenced their greatest tormenter. More than 200 blackened Japanese corpses were later found

The 75mm Pack Howitzer

Nicknamed "Little Dynamite", the 75mm pack howitzer proved its worth with the 1st Battalion, 10th Artillery in support of the Marines on Tarawa. Under the command of Lieutenant Colonel Presley Rixey, the Marine howitzers fired 2366 rounds at Japanese targets during the four-day fight for the islet of Betio.

Developed in the early 1920s by the U.S. Army and standardized in 1927 as the M1 pack howitzer, the weapon could be broken down into several components: rear trail and axle, front trail, top sleigh and cradle, bottom sleigh and recoil mechanism, breech and wheels, and tube. These could be carried by men or pack animals and assembled in the field. The gun was light at 1439lb (653kg) and capable of an impressive rate of fire of five rounds per minute, with a maximum range of about 5.4 miles (8.7km).

At Tarawa, the Marines of the 1st Battalion, 10th Artillery, brought their howitzers ashore under heavy enemy fire, traversing the waist-deep water of the lagoon and then crossing the exposed pier to reach firing positions. Shortly after assembling the weapons, the artillerymen went to work, blasting away at Japanese strongpoints. Early on the second day of fighting, they destroyed two enemy bunkers that had been raking elements of the 8th Marines as they struggled toward the shore. The howitzers were also instrumental in breaking up a Japanese Banzai charge against the 6th Marines on the third night of the battle.

While the fighting raged the Marines were under continuous enemy fire, but served their howitzers steadily. Rixey and 1st Lieutenant Norman Miller, a forward observer who directed highly accurate fire, received the Silver Star for their heroic actions at Betio. By the time the islet was secured, seven Marines of the 1st Battalion, 10th Artillery, had been killed and 18 wounded.

During the course of World War II, heavier weapons of 105mm and 155mm were introduced in Marine artillery units; however, the versatile "Little Dynamite" remained in service to the end of the conflict. When production ceased in 1944, more than 8000 had been produced.

Below: The 75mm pack howitzer was versatile. It could be disassembled, carried to locations as needed, reassembled, and then brought to bear against enemy targets with the firepower that was necessary to crack stubborn strongpoints.

inside the blockhouse. Shibasaki's body was never positively identified. The 33-year-old Bonnyman received a posthumous Medal of Honor for his act of bravery.

Julian Smith came ashore on Green Beach at about noon and quickly decided to move to the lagoon side of Betio near the pier where heavy fighting was still going on between Hays's men and the Japanese along the edge of the small cove. Smith's landing craft was shot up and its coxswain killed. An LVT was located for the general. Two hours later, Smith found Edson and Shoup. Smith took formal command on Betio at 7.30 p.m.

During the night at least four uncoordinated suicide charges rattled the nerves of Marines at some of Major Jones's positions, but they held on, slaughtering hundreds of Japanese troops. One Marine killed three Japanese soldiers with his bayonet and was stabbed with a Samurai sword by a Japanese officer whose skull was then fractured by another Marine's rifle butt.

The howitzers of the 1st Battalion, 10th Artillery, fired more than 1200 rounds, and gunfire from the destroyers *Sigsbee* and *Schroeder* broke the back of the Japanese attacks, but the 1st Battalion, 6th Marines, suffered 40 dead and 100 wounded. By the morning of November 23, the fresh 3rd Battalion, 6th Marines, under

Below: Lieutenant Alexander Bonnyman leads a Marine assault against a blockhouse on Tarawa that was reported to have been the headquarters of the Japanese commander on the atoll.

Lieutenant Colonel Kenneth McLeod, was rolling eastward along Green Beach against ebbing resistance. Japanese combat efficiency had blown itself out with the previous night's suicide charges. At 1.00 p.m., McLeod halted at the eastern end of Betio with nearly 500 dead or wounded Japanese in his battalion's wake.

The Japanese strongpoints near the cove and the junction of Red Beaches 1 and 2 were still tough nuts to crack. Majors Hays and Schoettel directed their 1st Battalion, 8th Marines, and 3rd Battalion, 2nd Marines, respectively in attacks from three directions, while halftracks provided suppressing fire from the reef, encircling the pillboxes and machine gun nests. Marine grit and Japanese suicides ended the fight.

Around 1.00 p.m., a Navy Grumman F6F Hellcat fighter plane landed at the airfield that would soon bear the name of the deceased

Above: Marines carrying machine gun ammunition boxes sprint forwards on Betio Island. Most of the Japanese fixed defenses were on the beaches. Once beaten on the beaches, the Japanese withdrew to bomb-proof ammunition and personnel shelters inshore, where they fought to the death.

Lieutenant Hawkins. Almost simultaneously resistance at the cove ended. Tarawa was declared secure after 76 hours of fighting, the likes of which few men had ever experienced. The veteran Lieutenant Colonel Carlson admitted: "It was the damndest fight I've seen in 30 years of this business."

Only 17 Japanese soldiers and 129 Korean laborers were alive to surrender. A total of 1027 Marines and 29 U.S. Navy personnel, most of them corpsmen attached to Marine units, died in the fighting on Betio, and 2292 Americans were wounded.

Above: When the fight for Tarawa was over, only 17 Japanese soldiers and 129 Korean laborers were left alive. The other defenders of Betio had been killed to a man. As the Marines fought their way across the Pacific during World War II, they encountered determined resistance from an enemy that preferred death to surrender.

Bitter Lessons

The lessons learned at Tarawa were bitter, but they actually saved lives during future amphibious operations. Among these lessons was the clear implication that overwhelming numerical superiority was essential and that the coordination of pre-invasion naval and air bombardment had to be improved. The big guns of battleships and cruisers would only be effective against reinforced strongpoints with armor-piercing shells and plunging fire.

Solid information on the tides and depth of surrounding waters was also needed for future operations. Amtracs would have to be available in quantity. Communications had to be improved, and the actual chain of command had to be clearly defined. On the ground, the Marines needed more automatic weapons and flamethrowers.

A public outcry followed Operation Galvanic. Newspaper headlines screamed of the high death toll, the cost of wresting a tiny, desolate mound of coral from its fanatical defenders. Admiral Nimitz and others were roundly criticized, but the Marines had been equal to the bloody task.

While the American public was profoundly shocked, the personnel of the U.S. Marine Corps knew to a man that the horror of Tarawa was only the beginning of the bloody work that had to be done to secure the ultimate defeat of Japan.

Opposite: Marines stare in disbelief at the carnage on the Red Beaches at Betio following the conquest of Tarawa in November 1943. The bodies of dead Marines lie at the water's edge and float in the lagoon, while a disabled M4 Sherman tank lies abandoned.

CHAPTER 5

MARIANAS MOMENTUM: SAIPAN, GUAM, AND TINIAN

The Marine Corps played a key role in the capture of strategically significant islands in the Marianas chain, bringing U.S. military might on air, land, and sea closer to the Home Islands of Japan.

The pamphlet was published by the command of the 2nd Marine Division, and its title was one word—*Saipan*. Its message was clear: "For the first time, this division is going to be operating in what has been the Japanese Empire for 25 years. Until now, we have been reconquering former Allied territory, and the zone of action has been in relatively unexploited, wild parts of the Pacific... Now, however, we are going to be fighting in what has almost been part of the Japanese homeland."

By the summer of 1944, World War II in the Pacific had turned in favor of the Allies for good. The Marine Corps, the amphibious fist of the U.S. military, had been forged in strenuous training and tempered in the fire of nearly two years of combat. It had grown from a relative few in number to a colossus of nearly half a million men. Now, the fight against Imperial Japan was indeed entering a new phase. Guadalcanal, Bougainville, and Tarawa were hard-won victories on the periphery of the enemy's defensive ring. As the Marines girded for yet another amphibious operation, the next target was the Marianas, specifically three islands in the archipelago, Saipan, Guam, and Tinian, deep in the heart of the Japanese inner security zone.

The two-pronged strategy of island hopping in the Central Pacific and northwest progress through the Solomons and northern New Guinea to the doorstep of the Philippines proceeded. In the south, the string of U.S. victories thus far had resulted in the isolation and de facto imprisonment of 100,000 Japanese troops at Rabaul on New Britain and the establishment of a massive U.S. forward base at Seeadler Harbor on Manus Island in the Admiralty group. From there, the warships of the U.S. Pacific Fleet could

Opposite: In preparation for the major assault on the Marianas, U.S. Marines and Army troops seized the islands of Roi-Namur in the Marshalls in the winter of 1943–44. In this photo taken on Namur on February 2, 1944, a dazed Japanese prisoner, stripped of his clothing, sits under the watchful eyes of two Marines.

operate and aircraft could fly in support of future operations in the Philippines and the Central Pacific.

Pacific Advancement

Progress in the Central Pacific included the capture of Tarawa in the Gilbert Islands after four days of heavy fighting and the occupation of the Marshall Islands, particularly the former Japanese base at Kwajalein Atoll, Eniwetok Atoll, and the island of Roi-Namur, captured by the Army's 7th Infantry Division, the 4th Marine Division, and 22nd Marine Regiment in the winter of 1943–44.

For the Central Pacific thrust, led by Admiral Chester W. Nimitz, Commander-in-Chief, Pacific Ocean Areas, the conquest of the Marianas, only 1200 miles (1931km) from the home islands, would bring Japan's great cities, its military-industrial complex, and its civilian population within range of the Boeing B-29 Superfortress heavy bomber, destined to rain unprecedented destruction on the enemy.

To accomplish the seizure of the key Marianas islands, Nimitz amassed a staggering array of firepower on land, sea, and air. While the Fifth Fleet under Admiral Raymond A. Spruance provided fire support and engaged any elements of the Imperial Japanese Navy that might sortie in response to the American thrust, both the III and V Amphibious Corps were slated to take part. Codenamed Operation Forager, the offensive eventually involved 130,000 troops and a fighting fleet, referred to as Task Force 58, that included 15 aircraft carriers, 10 battleships, and more than 500 smaller warships and transport and supply vessels.

Left: American progress through the Marshall Islands was marked by multiple amphibious assaults. During fighting at Eniwetok Atoll in February 1944, Marines crouch while a U.S. Navy fighter plane attacks Japanese positions. In the distance, smoke rises from earlier airstrikes against Japanese fortified pillboxes, bunkers, and machine-gun nests.

Above: On the embattled beach at Saipan in the Marianas, two Marines pass one another while under enemy fire as they move toward their assigned positions. In the background, an amphibious LVT(A)-4 landing craft is visible.

Saipan, second in landmass to Guam in the Marianas with a length of 12 miles (19km) and a width of nearly six miles (10km), was the biggest prize and the first island to be invaded. With the landings set for June 15, 1944, the job of taking Saipan fell to Marine Major General Holland M. "Howlin' Mad" Smith's V Amphibious Corps, consisting of the 2nd and 4th Marine Divisions with the Army's 27th Infantry Division, a former National Guard unit from New York, in reserve.

The assault plan involved landings on a stretch of beaches named Red, Green, Blue, and Yellow from Agingan Point in the south toward Garapan in the north along the southwestern tip of the island. The pre-invasion bombardment began before daylight, and Navy pilots flew countless missions to soften up the landing zones.

A few minutes before 9.00 a.m., the 6th Marines, under Colonel John P. Riseley, hit the Red beaches on the left flank, while the 8th Marines of Colonel Clarence R. Wallace stormed ashore on the Green beaches 450ft (137m) from Riseley's left. Around 2400ft (732m) to the right of these 2nd Division assault regiments the 23rd and 25th Marines of the 4th Division, commanded by Colonel Louis R. Jones and Colonel Merton J. Batchelder respectively, landed on Blue and Yellow beaches.

Landing Under Fire

Confusion reigned as some landing craft came ashore in the wrong sectors, Marines were jumbled up on the shore, and in some locations the fire was so intense that LVTs (Landing Vehicle, Tracked) backed away from the beaches before disgorging their cargoes of machine guns, mortars, and extra ammunition.

The Marines were facing well concealed guns and tough Japanese troops of the recently organized 31st Army under the command of Lieutenant General Hideyoshi Obata, who was actually caught while returning from an inspection trip when the invasion was launched and able to get no closer than Guam. Overall command devolved to Lieutenant General Yoshitsugu Saito, commander of the 43rd Division, while Admiral Chuichi Nagumo, who had commanded the Combined Fleet during the Pearl Harbor attack in 1941 and the debacle at Midway six months later, exercised nominal control over roughly 700 troops of the 1st Yokosuka Special Naval Landing Force. Total Japanese strength on Saipan approached 23,000, including the 47th Independent Mixed Brigade, various engineer and artillery regiments, and the 48 tanks of the 9th Tank Regiment.

Despite heavy losses, the 6th Marines pushed into the village of Charon Kanoa by noon on June 15, while the 8th Marines worked its way through heavy vegetation and knocked out Japanese machine-gun emplacements and bunkers at Afetna Point. The fight was close quarter at times, and some of the Marines were armed with shotguns that they employed to good effect.

To the south, the artillery of the 4th Marine Division supported the advance, but by the end of the day the assault had gained only about half of the expected territory, a lodgment about 5.6 miles (9.1km) long and 3000ft (914m) deep. The 6th Marines had sustained roughly 35 percent casualties. During the night, the Japanese mounted several counterattacks. Artillery fire and the big guns of the battleship USS *California* broke up one of these, and tank support rumbled in to help finish the job. The 6th Marines killed about 700 enemy soldiers of the 136th Regiment.

At 3.30 a.m. the 25th Marines halted a Japanese advance, but the enemy reemerged an hour later using civilians to screen their approach. The 1st Battalion perimeter was nearly breached, but well directed artillery fire from 105mm

Below: Marines use a captured Japanese mountain gun during the attack on Garapan, the administrative center of Saipan.

howitzers broke up this attack as well. One Japanese shell set a 75mm self-propelled gun on fire, forcing Marines to withdraw 600ft (183m) as the ammunition cooked off.

The Japanese did their best to mount a coordinated effort to defeat the Americans on land and the powerful Task Force 58 at sea, and Spruance knew that the Combined Fleet under Admiral Jisaburo Ozawa was approaching the Marianas. Spruance prepared for action while elements of the 27th Infantry Division came ashore, allowing the Navy's transports to move to safer waters. On June 19–20, Spruance engaged the Japanese Navy in the decisive Battle of the Philippine Sea. Three Japanese aircraft carriers were sunk, and so many land- and carrier-based planes were shot down that American carrier pilots referred to the one-sided aerial encounter as the "Great Marianas Turkey Shoot". The American victory broke the back of Japanese carrier aviation for the remainder of the war.

Meanwhile, on the night of June 16, General Saito massed the largest concentration of Japanese tanks during the Pacific War—44 medium and light armored vehicles of the 9th Tank Regiment, along with most of the 1st Yokosuka Special Naval Landing Force and the remnants of the 136th Division. He hurled them at Major General Harry Schmidt's 4th Marine Division positions.

Noise, Tracers, and Flashing Lights

The 1st Battalion, 6th Marines, was hit hard. At 3.30 a.m., a star shell illuminated the valley where the battalion was positioned, and the engines of

Below: During early 1944, US forces pushed beyond their recent victories in the Solomons and Marshall Islands to Saipan, Tinian, and Guam, providing a jumping-off point for invasions of the Philippines and, later, the Japanese Home Islands.

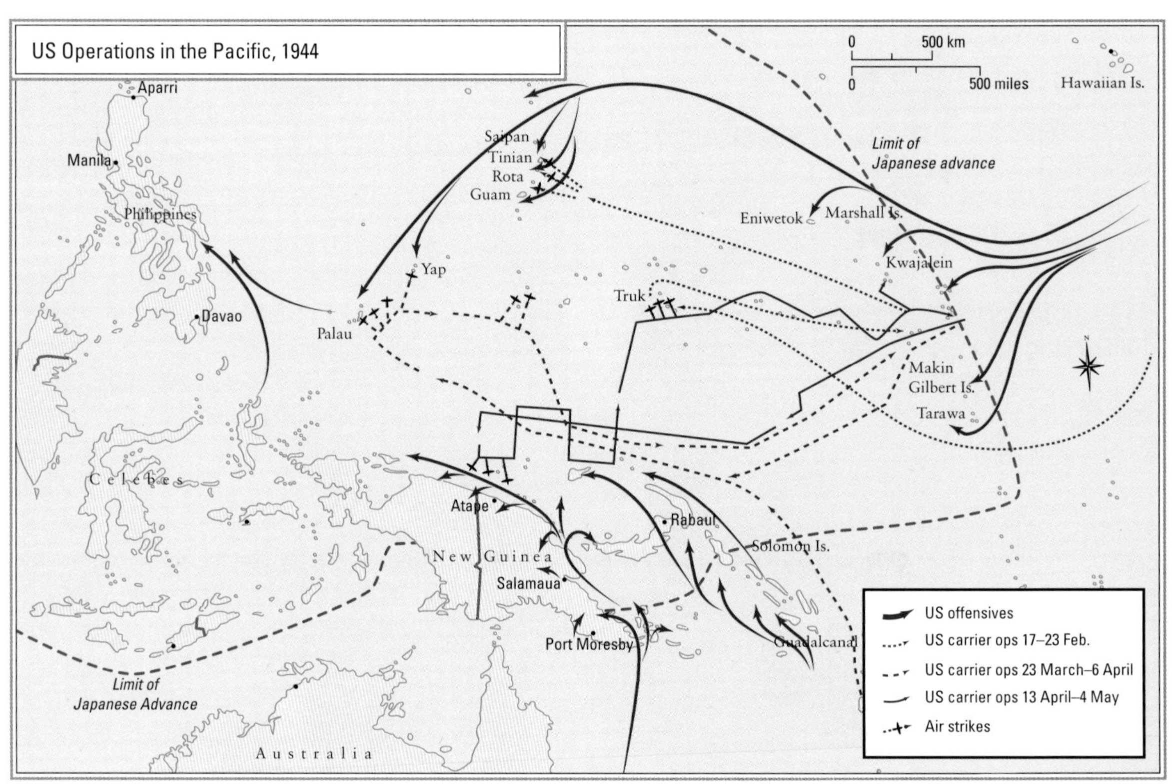

tanks became audible. A platoon of M4 Sherman medium tanks with 75mm guns, heavier than anything mounted by the Japanese tanks, rumbled forward while artillery and mortar fire greeted the enemy attack that began minutes later.

Major James A. Donovan, Jr., the executive officer of the 1st Battalion, remembered: "The battle evolved itself into a madhouse of noise, tracers, and flashing lights. As tanks were hit and set afire, they silhouetted other tanks coming out of the flickering shadows to the front or already on top of the squads."

Artillery, anti-tank weapons, and the superior Shermans blasted 24 of the Japanese tanks and decimated the infantry that accompanied them. When the battle was finished, Marine artillery had fired more than 1000 rounds. The Marines lost about 100 killed and wounded, but Japanese dead numbered more than 300 among approximately 500 infantrymen engaged.

The next day the 24th and 25th Marines moved eastward toward Aslito Airfield, where their patrols discovered that the Japanese had abandoned the facility. The 165th Infantry Regiment, 27th Division, moved in to occupy the key objective.

On June 18, elements of both Marine divisions continued toward their expected progress points. The 8th Marines ran into opposition at Hill 240 and with the help of the 10th Marines artillery destroyed Japanese positions in a coconut grove. The 23rd Marines brought up halftracks that fired 75mm guns into caves where the enemy had holed up. From June 19–22, the Marines reached the east coast of Saipan and then pivoted on the 2nd Marines, holding positions on the island's west coast. The move reoriented the American focus northward in the direction of General Saito's main line of defense anchored along high ground and the slopes of Mount Tapochau. The rugged terrain of the island's interior made the Marines and the soldiers of the 27th Division pay dearly for every yard gained.

The 105th Infantry Regiment struggled against Japanese positions at Nafutan Point, while the 106th and 165th Regiments were ordered toward the center of the American line of advance. Difficulties with the terrain, coordination between Marine and Army commands, and perhaps Holland Smith's less-than-stellar impression of the performance of 27th Division commander, Major General Ralph Smith—a belief held over from the assault on Makin Atoll the previous November—contributed to rising dissatisfaction with the overall progress of the northward advance.

"The battle evolved itself into a madhouse of noise, tracers, and flashing lights. As tanks were hit and set afire, they silhouetted other tanks coming out of the flickering shadows …."

Eventually, Holland Smith became fed up with Ralph Smith and the slow movement of the 27th Division. After stern warnings, Holland Smith obtained permission to relieve Ralph Smith of command and replaced him with Major General Sanderford Jarman, who had been designated to lead the occupation forces once Saipan was secured. Holland Smith's action touched off a firestorm of interservice controversy, prompting several inquiries and a debate that continues to this day.

While the dark clouds of Army versus Marine Corps accusations boiled up, there was still a potent Japanese enemy to deal with on Saipan. In fairness to Holland Smith, the Marines on the 27th Division flanks were absorbing heavy casualties from enfilading fire due to the lack of progress in the center. However, from Ralph Smith's perspective the dirty job of rooting the Japanese from defensive positions in rugged terrain was a substantial undertaking for any fighting unit. The Army troops took heavy casualties as well, trying to clear the enemy from positions they nicknamed Hell's Pocket, Purple Heart Ridge, and Death Valley.

As the Japanese grudgingly gave ground against the relentless Marine attacks and the newly revived 27th Division effort, the 24th Marines and other elements of the 4th Division secured the Kagman Peninsula on June 25. Flamethrowers, engineers flinging satchel charges, and Marines with hand grenades cleared the stubborn enemy from concealed positions in caves near the shoreline.

In the early morning hours, the 1st Battalion, 6th Marines, fought off a Japanese counterattack, and Pfc. Harold Epperson gave his life, pouncing on a live hand grenade that had been tossed into his machine-gun emplacement and saving those around him. He received a posthumous Medal of Honor.

On the same day to the west, the 8th Marines fought directly up the slope of Mount Topachau while a battalion of the attached 29th Marines moved around the right flank, up the mountain in single file, and reached the summit miraculously without losing a man. By June 28, the 105th Infantry had cleared Nafutan Point, and the 106th eliminated the concentrated resistance at Hell's Pocket. Major General George W. Griner arrived that day to take command of the 27th Infantry Division on a permanent basis.

Below: Marines blast a Japanese strongpoint on the island of Saipan with a demolition charge. Riflemen stand poised to engage any enemy soldiers who might emerge from the position.

Left: Two Marines take cover in a shell hole on the island of Saipan during operations in the Marianas in June 1944.

Bait and Trap

As the 2nd Marine Division took on stiff resistance while advancing toward the population center of Garapan, the Japanese stubbornly defended high ground nicknamed Flame Tree Hill. The Marines baited the enemy into the open, firing a heavy artillery, mortar, and small arms barrage at the mouths of caves and bunkers. This was followed by a layer of smoke, convincing the enemy that the Marines were moving forward on foot. The Japanese were decimated when they rushed into the open to meet the expected assault, only to be greeted by a sheet of flame from Marine mortars, rifles, and machine guns.

In the 4th Division sector, the Marine left flank was cocked back toward the 27th Infantry Division line. However, after the 105th Infantry finally cleared Nafutan Point on the 27th, the Army troops renewed their offensive effort, closing up with the 8th Marines and—at long last—overcoming the ferocious Japanese defense of Purple Heart Ridge and Death Valley. The 27th Infantry Division had taken on both the enemy and some of the most inhospitable terrain encountered during the Pacific War. Even Holland Smith grudgingly acknowledged that the 27th Division had finished a tough task.

Completion of these operations gave the Americans control of central Saipan. Saito knew that the end was coming but vowed to fight on. To execute Holland Smith's plan for the final conquest of the island, the 4th Marine Division moved two miles (3.2km) to the north, past the village of Tanapag on the west coast, against light opposition. With the 27th Division moving north, the 2nd Marine Division would be pulled back to reserve as the front narrowed. The 4th and the 27th would then administer the coup de grâce to the Japanese on Saipan.

Still, the fighting was bitter. When three American tanks took a wrong turn and were swarmed by Japanese soldiers, a call for help went out. The 1st Battalion, 25th Marines, was close by, and its commander, Lieutenant Colonel Hollis U. Mustain, rallied his men to the rescue. "Get some people there and get those tanks out!" he ordered. Major Fenton Mee, the battalion executive officer, recalled admiringly, "They got there and the Japs pulled out. This let the tanks get out and they were saved. It was one of the bravest things I ever saw people do."

Fighting to the death, many Japanese soldiers "played possum", smearing their uniforms with blood and lying in wait for unsuspecting Americans to venture near—then pulling the pins on grenades and taking Marines with them. At times, the Japanese continued to use civilians as human shields, and for the Americans clearing the enemy it meant rising concerns for casualties among noncombatant men, women, and children.

The increasing desperation of the Japanese resistance made American commanders keenly aware that the likelihood of a massed suicide or banzai charge was growing daily. Holland Smith warned his frontline units to be wary, especially after dark. Saito and his lieutenants were holed up in a cave north of Tanapag, and on the morning of July 6, he did issue orders for a final bloody banzai assault. "Whether we attack or whether we stay where we are, there is only death," Saito said. As an aide shot him in the head, Saito plunged a dagger into his own abdomen, committing ritual suicide, or seppuku. Admiral Nagumo committed suicide as well.

Fight to the Death

Before dawn on July 7, the largest banzai charge of the Pacific War spilled across the battle-scarred Saipan landscape. Hundreds of Japanese soldiers, some of them walking wounded and even on crutches, along with a number of civilians surged toward a gap between two regiments of the 27th Infantry Division. Some of the Japanese troops were fortified with sake, Japanese rice wine, and some were armed with nothing more than primitive spears.

The human tidal wave crashed into the 1500ft (457m) gap, intending to overwhelm the front line of defense and surge along the coast all the way to Charan Kanoa. The charge swept across the line and fell upon the artillerymen of the 10th Marines. The Marines and beleaguered men of the 105th Infantry Regiment fought back; the guns of 105mm howitzers were depressed to fire point-blank at the onrushing Japanese.

The fighting raged late into the afternoon. The 165th Infantry Regiment came up to help stem the charge, and finally the attack was stalled just 2400ft (732m) from the command post of the 105th south of Tanapag. When the shattered remnants of the Japanese attack faded, the enemy had suffered 650 killed and 250 wounded.

Opposite: An M3A1 light tank with an E5R2-M3 flame-gun attacks a Japanese position on Saipan while a single Marine crouches in a foxhole and provides some security for the armored vehicle against Japanese attackers.

Marine casualties totaled 127 dead and wounded. Among them was Pfc. Harold Agerholm of the 4th Battalion, 10th Marines. Agerholm personally evacuated 45 wounded men before a sniper's bullet killed him. He was awarded a posthumous Medal of Honor. Two soldiers of the 27th Infantry Division, Lieutenant Colonel William O'Brien and Sergeant Thomas Baker, also received the nation's highest award for valor during the action on July 7. Japanese losses were horrendous, with more than 4300 dead.

On July 8, Holland Smith called the 2nd Marine Division forward to join with the 105th Infantry Regiment and the 4th Marine Division for the final push to secure Saipan. Organized resistance was sporadic, but Marines were still dying. Sitting in the open turret of his tank, Sergeant Grant Timmermann covered the blast of a hand grenade that would otherwise have gone down the hatch and exploded inside the armored vehicle. He received the Medal of Honor posthumously.

Mass Suicide

As they approached Marpi Point at the extreme northern end of Saipan, the Americans were confronted with a new kind of horror. Japanese soldiers and civilians were committing suicide in droves. Some civilians were observed in clusters, herded together by soldiers who then detonated hand grenades in their midst.

The Japanese military had convinced many of the civilians that the Americans would torture them and commit terrible atrocities against them if they were captured. They chose suicide, jumping from the jagged cliffs to drown in the sea. Mothers clutched their children to their breasts and simply walked into the ocean.

Marines scurry for cover amid the ruins of the village of Garapan, the principal town on the island of Saipan. Clearing the Japanese from Garapan remained a deadly business even after Marine artillery had destroyed numerous enemy positions and set buildings afire.

The Americans were aghast at the spectacle and did what they could to convince some civilians to surrender. They distributed food and water and provided medical care to the suffering people, many of whom were on the verge of starvation.

At 4.15 p.m. on July 9, the island of Saipan was declared secure. Pockets of Japanese troops remained to be mopped up, but fighters and bombers of the Army Air Forces were already operating from the airfield along with two Marine observation squadrons that helped spot enemy troop concentrations and artillery targets.

The cost had been high. American casualties totaled 3225 killed and 13,061 wounded. More than 300 were missing. The Japanese lost nearly 24,000 troops. The terrible task in the Marianas, however, was only partially complete.

Below: Coming off the line, exhausted Marines on Guam walk toward a rest area following hard fighting.

Guam

Twelve days after Saipan was declared secure, Marines of the III Amphibious Corps stormed ashore on the beaches of the Orote Peninsula on the west side of Guam, the southernmost and largest of the Marianas Islands with an area of 209 square miles (541 square km).

The III Amphibious Corps commander, Major General Roy S. Geiger, told his troops via loudspeaker: "You have been honored. The eyes of the nation watch you as you go into battle to liberate this former American bastion from the enemy. The honor which has been bestowed on

you is a signal one. May the glorious traditions of the Marine Corps' esprit de corps spur you to victory. You have been honored."

The young Marines crouching in landing craft stiffened when they saw a flare arch skyward and the order went out at 7.30 a.m. to "Land the landing force!" Whether they felt honored or not was up to each Marine. They were certain, however, that the Japanese were waiting.

The III Amphibious Corps included the 3rd Marine Division under Major General Allen H. "Hal" Turnage, the 1st Provisional Marine Brigade commanded by Brigadier General Lemuel C. Shepherd, Jr., and the Army's 77th Infantry Division under Major General Andrew D. Bruce. The 3rd Division included three rifle regiments, the 3rd, 9th, and 21st Marines, the engineers of the 19th Marines, and the artillery of the 12th Marines. Many of these men were veterans of Bougainville, who had rested and absorbed replacements on Guadalcanal late in 1943.

The 1st Provisional Marine Brigade included veteran troops, and in one of its regiments—the 4th Marines—were men of the former Marine Raider battalions that had recently been disbanded. The brigade's other rifle regiment, the 22nd Marines, had seen action during the capture of Eniwetok in the Marshalls.

The 77th Infantry Division, originally an outfit raised during World War I and populated with draftees from New York City and its environs, wore the distinctive Statue of Liberty shoulder patch. The division was activated on March 25, 1942, with the 305th, 306th, and 307th infantry regiments and the 304th, 305th, 306th, and 902nd Field Artillery Regiments and supporting elements. The combined strength of the assembled Army and Marine units slated for the recapture of Guam totaled well over 50,000 troops.

Opposing the Americans, and keenly aware of the fate of their comrades on Saipan, were 18,500 Japanese troops, including soldiers of the 29th Infantry Division, the 48th Independent Mixed

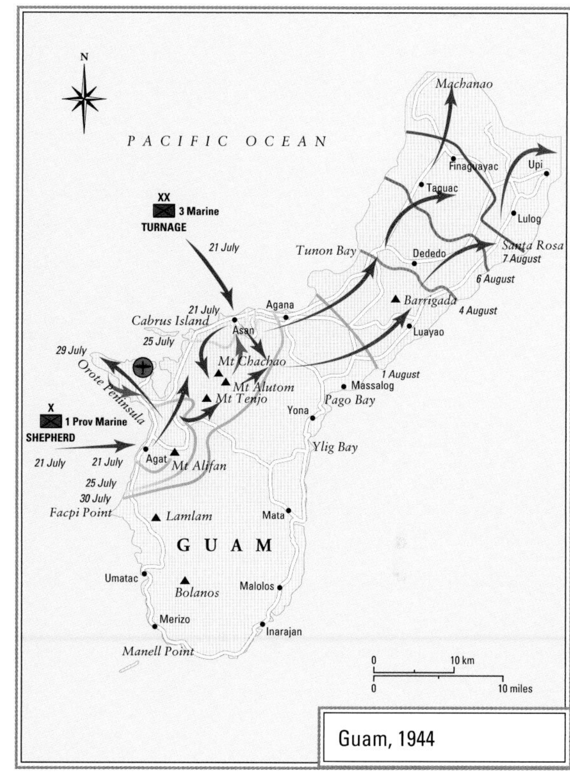

Above: It required three weeks of intense fighting for Geiger's 3rd Marine Division to capture Guam from the 18,500 Japanese troops defending the island.

Brigade, the 10th Independent Mixed Regiment, naval troops of the 54th Guard Force, and about 2000 airmen and ground crewmen at Orote Field, one of the primary Marine objectives on Guam. As the invasion of Guam drew near, General Obata allowed Lieutenant General Takeshi Takashina of the 29th Division to exert tactical command.

On the morning of July 21, the 3rd, 9th, and 21st Marines rushed ashore at the Red, Blue, and Green beaches north of the Orote Peninsula between Adelup and Asan Points, while the 4th and 22nd Marines landed south of the peninsula between Apaca Point and Bangi Point on the White and Yellow beaches. Takashina had established his command post in a cave above the Adelup-Asan beaches, and the Marines landed

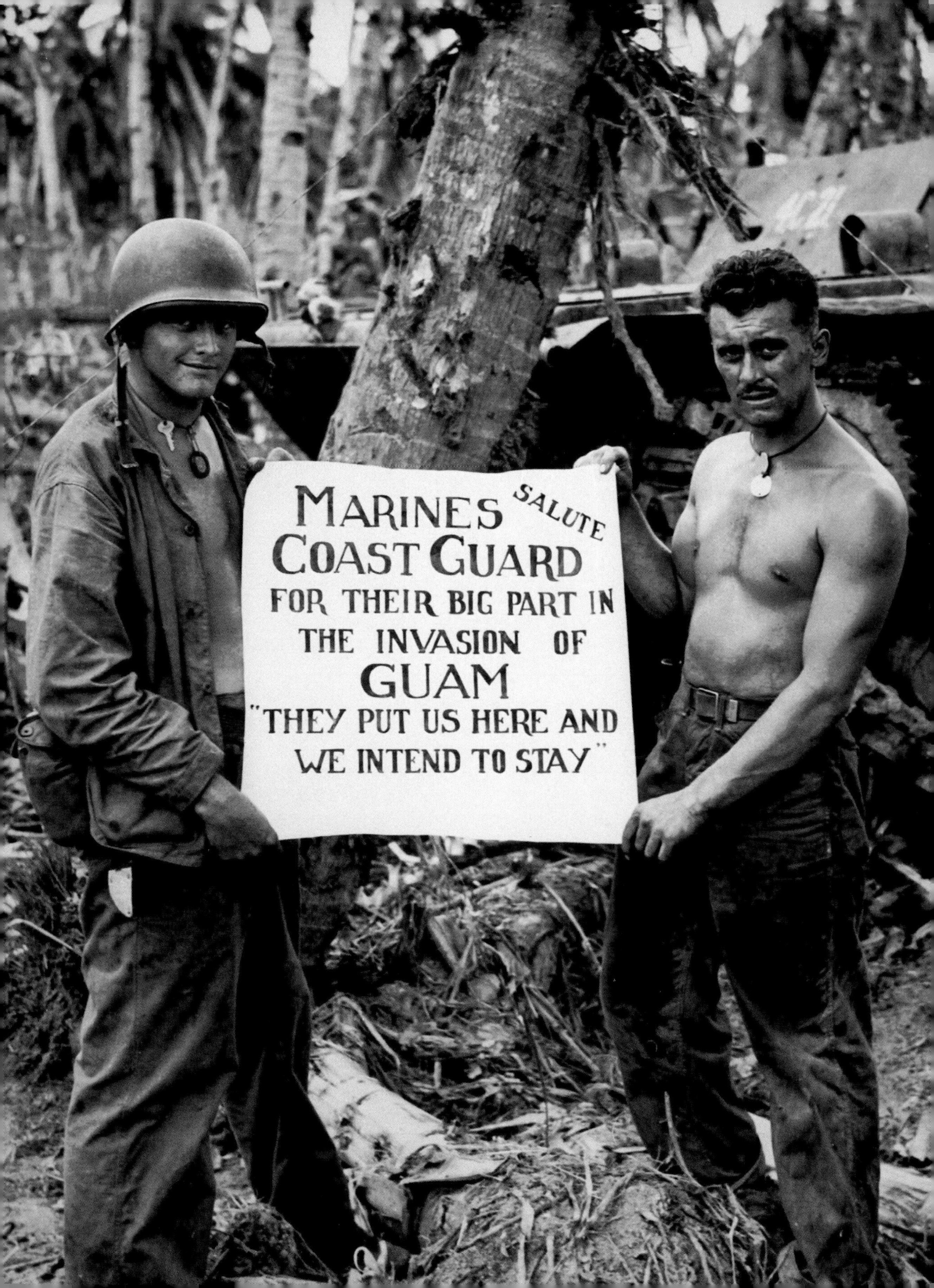
MARINES SALUTE
COAST GUARD
FOR THEIR BIG PART IN
THE INVASION OF
GUAM
"THEY PUT US HERE AND
WE INTEND TO STAY"

literally in front of him. As darkness fell on the first day, the Americans had advanced more than 6000ft (1829m) in some sectors, but the fighting was bitter in several locations.

Early resistance at Asan Point was stiff, but the Marines brought up tanks and moved forward steadily. The three brigades stretched toward a line of hills, and once the defenders at Asan Point were outflanked movement was brisk. The 3rd Marines took mortar, artillery, and small arms fire across the beach and during the move inland. The Japanese 320th Independent Infantry Battalion, ensconced on a small promontory, held fast against a heavy 81mm mortar barrage followed by a charge from the 1st and 2nd Battalions, 3rd Marines.

The Japanese held tenaciously to the position that came to be known as Bundschu Ridge, named for Captain Geary Bundschu who was killed in the early fighting, until their withdrawal on the night of the July 22–23. The 3rd and 21st Marines finally established contact with one another on July 24. The 3rd Marines suffered 615 killed and wounded around Bundschu Ridge, and two men earned the Medal of Honor. Private First Class Luther Skaggs led a mortar section in support of the repeated Marine assaults and defended his ground against several counterattacks before he was seriously wounded. Private First Class Leonard F. Mason, firing a Browning Automatic Rifle (BAR), wiped out an enemy machine-gun nest, but was seriously wounded in the fighting and later died.

On the southern beaches, the Japanese put up a serious fight against the 1st Provisional Brigade landings. At Gaan Point in the center, a pair of 75mm guns and a 37mm weapon fired rapidly from a reinforced concrete blockhouse that had been well camouflaged and unscathed by pre-invasion bombardment. Before the Gaan Point position was enveloped from the rear and silenced, as many as 24 landing craft of the 22nd Marines were destroyed.

Opposite: Two battle-hardened Marines of the III Amphibious Corps hold a sign saluting the U.S. Coast Guard and its role in delivering the fighting men to the shores of Guam in the Marianas, August 1944.

Above: His face camouflaged, a Marine armed with an M1 carbine awaits the signal to advance against Japanese positions on Guam. The M1 carbine was ideal for use in the jungle since it was lighter and easier to handle in heavy vegetation than the M1 Garand rifle.

On the right of the southern landings, the 1st Battalion, 4th Marines, ran into a buzzsaw at Hill 40, which directly overlooked the beach at Bangi Point. Marine armor and reinforcements from the 3rd Battalion reduced the enemy position, and by the end of the day the 4th Marines held a line 4800ft (1463m) deep and within sight of adjacent Marine units.

During the first night of battle, the Japanese mounted counterattacks against both the northern and southern beachheads and attempted to infiltrate the Marine lines. The 4th Ammunition Company, made up of African-

American Marines, guarded the ordnance of the 1st Provisional Brigade and shot dead 14 enemy soldiers laden with explosives and intent on blowing up the ammunition dump.

Fierce Resistance at Hill 40

At Hill 40, the 3rd Battalion, 4th Marines, fought off approximately 750 Japanese troops that hit their line about 9.30 p.m. Major Anthony N. "Cold Steel" Walker, the operations officer of the 3rd Battalion, remembered the grim battle to hold the high ground. "Finding a gap in our lines and overrunning the machine gun which covered the gap the enemy broke through and advanced toward the beaches. Some elements turned to their left and struck Hill 40 from the rear. K Company with about 200 men fought them all night long from Hill 40 and a small hill to the rear and northeast of Hill 40."

Walker continued: "When daylight came the Marines counterattacked with two squads from L Company... and two tanks... and closed the gap. A number of men from Company K died that night, but all 750 Japanese soldiers were killed. The hill... represents in miniature ... the whole hard-fought American victory on Guam."

A dirt path named Harmon Road ran near the 4th Marines' perimeter, and four Japanese tanks rolled toward Pfc. Bruno Oribiletti, who knocked out two of them with a bazooka before he was killed. A platoon of Shermans from the 4th Tank Company accounted for the other two, and Oribiletti received a posthumous Navy Cross.

By July 28, the 3rd Marines had expanded its perimeter beyond the old U.S. naval installation at Piti, and the heights of Fonte Ridge were cleared of Japanese. During the battle for Fonte, Captain Louis H. Wilson, a future Commandant of the Marine Corps, earned the Medal of Honor in 10 hours of hand-to-hand fighting. He was wounded three times, but led his 17-man patrol to the summit of the ridge and refused to budge.

As General Takashina directed the survivors of the battle around Fonte Ridge to new positions, a burst of machine-gun fire from a Marine tank killed him. General Obata assumed tactical command as the defenders' situation deteriorated. He ordered a fighting withdrawal toward the northwest corner of the island and a final defensive line around Mount Santa Rosa.

"A number of men from Company K died that night but all 750 Japanese soldiers were killed."

Throughout the Marine advance, Japanese counterattacks were steady and their casualties horrendous. A heavy attack along the length of the 3rd Marines' line was repelled on the night of July 25–26. About 50 fanatical enemy troops reached the 3rd Division hospital well behind the perimeter before they were cut down. Two companies of the 3rd Pioneer Battalion killed 33 Japanese soldiers in a three-hour firefight.

On July 25, the Marines working from both north and south had sealed the Orote Peninsula with the 22nd Regiment driving up the coast from Agat and the 4th Marines in possession of Mount Alifan. Elements of the 77th Infantry Division came up in support on the southern flank. On the night of July 26, a vicious Japanese counterattack was beaten back under a hail of artillery fire that killed more than 400 enemy soldiers just yards from Marine foxholes.

Japanese Retreat

At daylight on the 26th, a Marine counterattack went forward through mangrove swamps and a large coconut grove. As they emerged from these natural obstacles the Japanese opened fire from strong defensive positions, but soon enough they broke off the engagement and fled. The Americans advanced to within 900ft (274m) of

Orote Field and the old Marine barracks that had been under Japanese control since three days after the Pearl Harbor attack.

On the morning of the 29th, tanks of both the Army and the Marines led the final assault that recaptured the Orote Peninsula. The defenders committed suicide, singly and in groups. The Marines found a bronze plaque that had been affixed to the wall at the old barracks entrance. It was later reinstalled, and a formal ceremony was held to mark the symbolic victory.

General Geiger wasted no time in organizing the final push northward with the 3rd Marine Division on the left and the 77th Infantry Division on the right. The advance began early on July 31, and by midday the 3rd Battalion, 3rd Marines, had liberated the capital city of Agana. The seizure of the Agana–Pago road that bisected the island helped speed the advance, particularly in the 77th Division sector. Within five days, the 305th and 307th Infantry Regiments had taken the town of Barrigada and nearby 674ft (205m) Mount Barrigada.

The Japanese attempted to slow the 3rd Marines at the village of Finegayan on August 3. They fought from prepared positions that were

Below: Captain Phillip P. Santon, intelligence officer for a Marine battalion, points out a landmark on the island of Guam during a pre-invasion briefing aboard an LST (Landing Ship, Tank). Santon's audience includes the members of a Marine pack howitzer battalion designated to provide fire support.

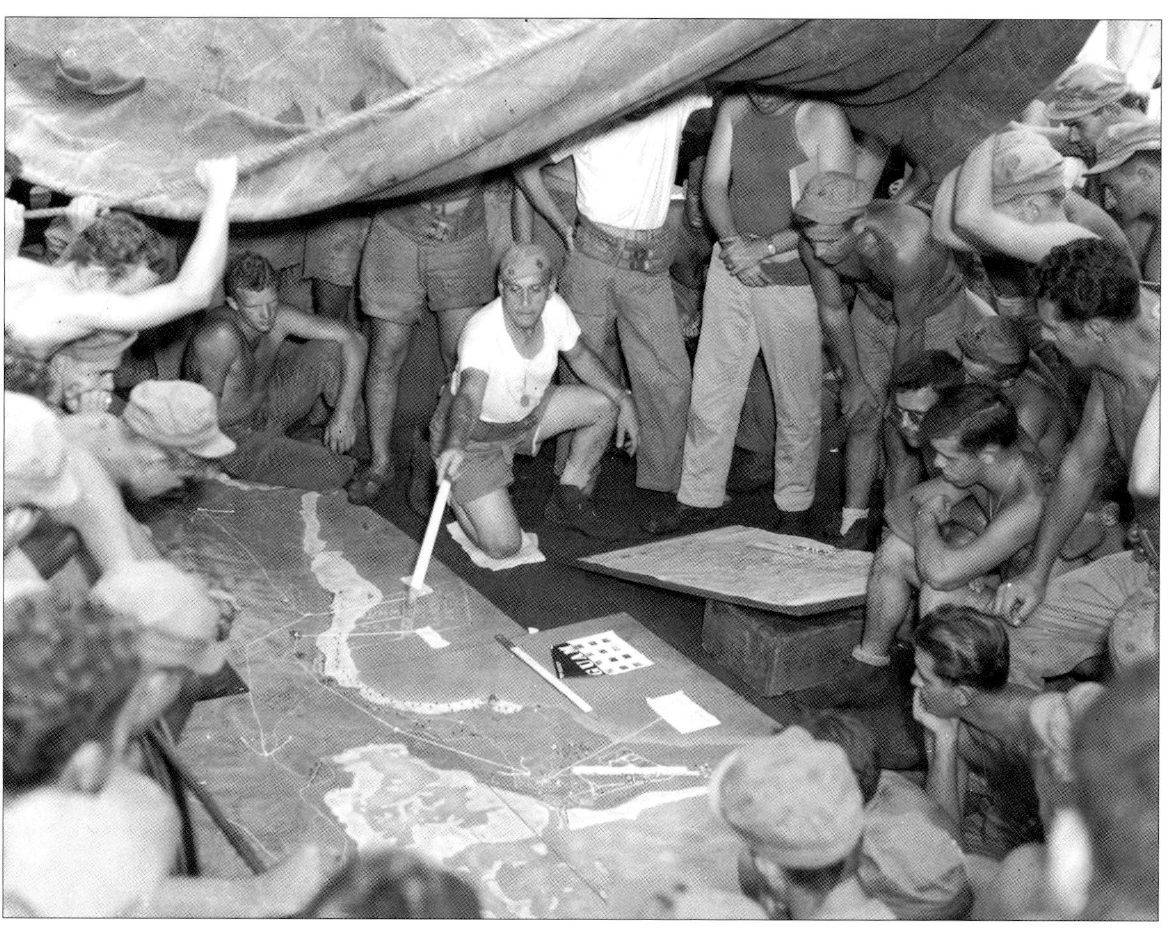

softened up by Marine and Army artillery, but proved to be among the toughest encountered in the battle for Guam. The Japanese threw the last of their tanks at the Marines along the Finegayan–Mount Santa Rosa road, but these were driven back. Private First Class Frank P. Witek of the 1st Battalion, 9th Marines, rushed ahead of his own advancing tanks and killed eight enemy soldiers occupying a defensive position before he was shot dead. Witek was awarded the Medal of Honor for his heroism.

By August 4, the imminent fall of Guam was a foregone conclusion. The 3rd and 21st Marines moved smartly forward, while the 9th negotiated dense jungle. The primary responsibility for capturing Mount Santa Rosa was given to the 77th Division. At nightfall on August 6, the Marines had advanced 2.8 miles (4.6km) to the vicinity of Ritidian Point and had made visual contact with the Army troops.

The 77th Division began its assault on Mount Santa Rosa at noon on August 7. Just over 24 hours later, the heights were in the Army's hands. However, several thousand Japanese were still at large on Guam, sniping and harassing the Americans wherever they could. By August 10, most organized resistance was over. The battle had cost the Japanese nearly 11,000 dead. During the next year, 8500 more were killed or taken prisoner. Nearly 1600 Marines had been killed and over 5000 wounded in the struggle to liberate

Below: An M4 Sherman tank advances down a dirt road on Guam at the height of the battle for control of the island in July 1944. Riflemen of the 3rd Marine Division have halted in the scant cover at the edge of the roadway to allow the tank to clear the way.

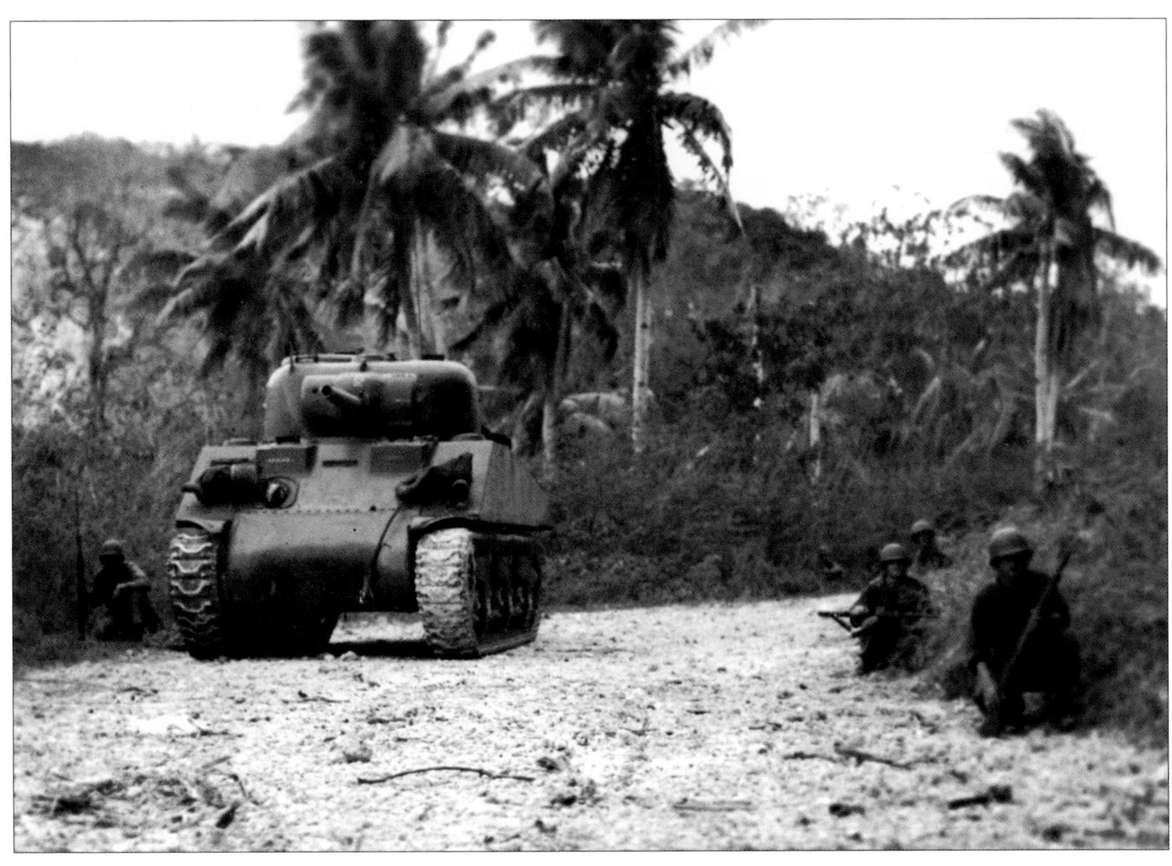

Guam, while the 77th Division had 177 dead and 662 wounded.

In contrast to the interservice angst experienced at Saipan, the 3rd Marine Division and the 77th Infantry Division had cooperated almost seamlessly on Guam. So well, in fact, that some Marines referred to their Army comrades as the "77th Marine Division".

The Battle for Tinian

The third amphibious operation during the reconquest of the Marianas took place at Tinian, three miles (4.8km) off the southwest coast of Saipan, where Marines of the 2nd and 4th Divisions went ashore on July 24. Although preliminary plans for the capture of the island that encompassed 39 square miles (101 square km) and where the Japanese had constructed several airfields had been drawn, the original assaults that placed the Marines landings on heavily defended beaches were shelved. Instead, the 4th Marine Division would land on two narrow strips of sand designated as the White beaches on the northwest side of the island, while the 2nd Division executed an amphibious feint at the population center of Tinian Town to the southwest.

Facing the Marines were 9000 Japanese defenders under the command of Army General Keishi Ogata of the 50th Regiment, detailed

Below: This aerial photograph shows Marine landing craft churning white wakes as they shuttle back and forth to deliver troops to the beach at Tinian. On July 24, 1944, Marines of the 4th Division came ashore at Tinian, while the 2nd Marine Division conducted a feint to draw Japanese attention elsewhere.

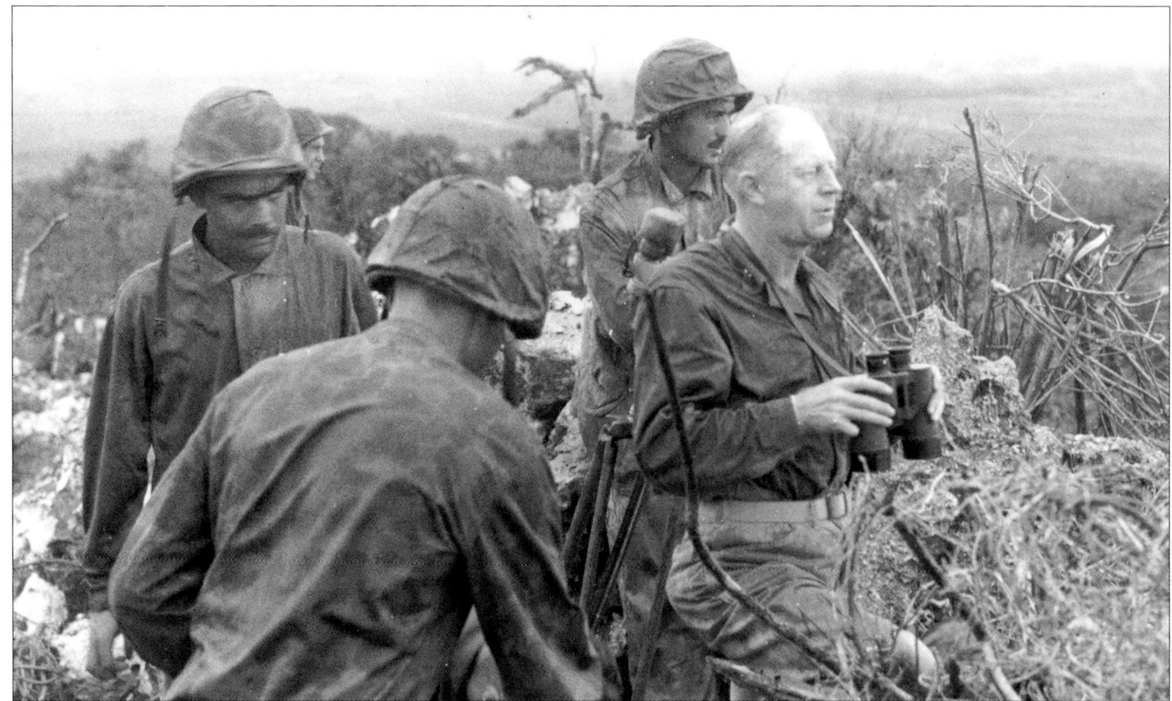

Above: Brigadier General Merritt A. "Red Mike" Edson, assistant commander of the 2nd Marine Division, holds a pair of binoculars as he surveys the battlefield from a command post on Mount Lasso on the island of Tinian.

from the 29th Division that was being chewed up on Saipan. The remainder of the Japanese contingent included the 1st Battalion, 135th Infantry Regiment, and elements of the Imperial Navy's 56th Guard Force. At least 1000 displaced airmen and ground crewmen who were no longer performing their primary functions contributed to the defense as well.

The Japanese on Tinian were armed to the teeth with artillery, hundreds of machine guns, and a dozen light tanks. They had also liberally sown mines and booby traps across all the potential landing beaches.

Early on the morning of July 24, the 4th Marine Division, departed Tanapag harbor on Saipan. Elements of the 1st and 2nd Battalions, 24th Marines, under Colonel Franklin A. Hart, landed on White Beach 1, while the 2nd and 3rd Battalions of Colonel Batchelder's 25th Marines struck White Beach 2. Both the 1st and 2nd Battalions, 24th Marines, were ashore at White Beach 1 within an hour. By 4.00 p.m., the 24th had advanced more than 4200ft (1280m) and reached the edge of one of the airfields.

The 25th Marines encountered so many mines that it took six hours to clear the explosives from White Beach 2, and a spirited Japanese defense, particularly from a pair of 47mm guns, was overcome after some effort. Several enemy strongpoints were bypassed and cleaned out by follow-on waves of Marines. Late in the afternoon, the 3rd Battalion, 25th Marines, had penetrated 4500ft (1372m), achieved its primary objective for the day, and established contact with the adjacent 24th Marines.

Despite delays and communication problems, the 23rd Marines began landing at 2.00 p.m. on July 24. The 1st Battalion, 8th Marines of the 2nd Division was ordered to land in support of the 24th Marines, but experienced delays as well before securing its positions ashore at 8.00 p.m.

Nighttime Counterattack

As night fell, the Marines were firmly ensconced on Tinian and waiting for the inevitable Japanese strike. "Destroy the enemy on the beaches with one blow, especially where time prevents quick movement of forces within the island", read Colonel Ogata's order. However, communications had been disrupted to the extent that no coordination could be achieved. Nevertheless, the Japanese attacks managed some penetrations, knifing between the junction of the 24th and 25th Marines all the way to the beach.

Lieutenant Colonel Justice M. "Jumping Joe" Chambers, commander of the 3rd Battalion, 25th Marines, remembered the fury of the Japanese attack. "Over in K company's area... was where the attack really developed. That's where [Lieutenant] Mickey McGuire... had his 37mm guns on the left flank and was firing canister. Two of my men were manning a machine gun... These two lads laid out in front of their machine gun a cone of Jap bodies. There was a dead Jap officer in with them. Both of the boys were dead."

Corporal Alfred J. Daigle and Pfc. Orville H. Showers received a posthumous Navy Cross and Silver Star, respectively, for their gallantry. A Marine correspondent recorded that the two Marines "held their fire until the Japanese were 100 yards away, then opened up. The Japanese charged, screaming, 'Banzai', firing light machine guns and throwing hand grenades. It seemed impossible that the two Marines—far ahead of their own lines—could hold on... The next morning they were found slumped over their weapons, dead. No less than 251 Japanese bodies were piled in front of them."

Numerous acts of heroism solidified the Marine beachhead, and American casualties totaled fewer than 100 dead and wounded. The Japanese, however, lost 1241 killed. In a single night, the defenders of Tinian had effectively shot their bolt. The remaining battalions of the 2nd Marine Division, the 2nd and 6th, came ashore on July 26. Pockets of resistance in the north of the island were systematically cleared, and a line of infantry and tanks was cobbled together for the drive southward to secure Tinian.

Below: One of the challenges faced by Marines executing amphibious landings on hostile beaches was the ability to bring increased firepower to bear against prepared Japanese defenses. One solution was the development of the LVT(A)-4, a tracked and armored landing craft that had a turret-mounted 75mm howitzer.

The endgame took shape on July 27. Resistance was fragmentary as the 6th Marines wiped out a 20-man Japanese patrol that tried to infiltrate its lines. The 25th Marines kept its collective heads down as snipers' bullets whizzed above the men. Two days later, more than half of Tinian belonged to the Americans.

Hart's 24th Marines entered Tinian Town on July 30 after half a day of fighting. Enemy soldiers mounted machine guns in the mouths of caves and fired steadily at the Marines of the 1st Battalion until flamethrowing Sherman tanks were brought up to immolate the defenders. When the Marines reached the center of Tinian Town at about 2.30 p.m., they found it deserted.

The Japanese made their last stand on the island atop a plateau outside Tinian Town. More than 2000 enemy troops occupied the expansive flatland, which stretched 2.8 miles (4.5km) long and 1.1 miles (1.8km) wide. Accurate Marine artillery on Tinian and the Army's XXIV Corps Artillery firing from Saipan hit the Japanese hard, and at daylight the battleships USS *Tennessee* and USS *California* joined in the bombardment along with cruisers and destroyers.

Below: His M1 carbine slung over his shoulder, a weary Marine pauses to give a child a piece of candy. The civilians on Tinian were temporarily relocated to internment camps as American forces took control of the island.

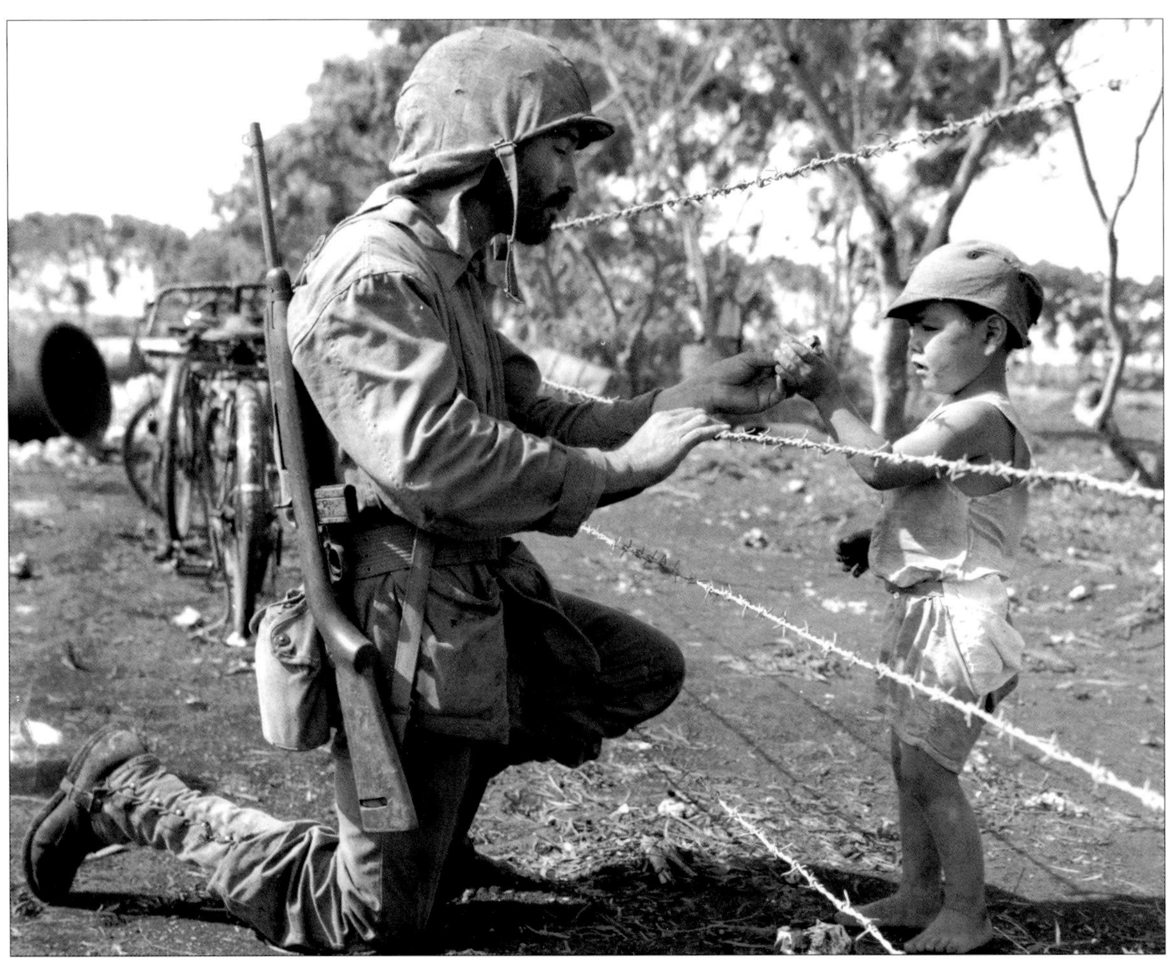

Women in the Marine Corps

On August 3, 1918, at the height of U.S. involvement in World War I, the first woman was sworn into the Marine Corps Reserve. Opha Mae Johnson led 305 women into the reserve, allowing more male Marines to serve in combat areas. A quarter century later, the Marine Corps Women's Reserve was authorized on February 13, 1943, under the direction of Major Ruth Cheney Streeter, its first director. During the course of World War II, 23,145 women, officers, and enlisted personnel served in more than 200 roles, from office clerks to parachute riggers and welders. Early officer candidates trained at Mount Holyoke College in Massachusetts, and the first enlisted recruits were trained at Hunter College in New York. In July 1943, a permanent recruit training center at New River, North Carolina, became active, turning out nearly 20,000 female reservists by 1945.

Difficult terrain hampered some operations, but late on the afternoon of July 31, the 1st Battalion, 23rd Marines, along with an attached company of the 2nd Battalion, had reached the top of the plateau and established a toehold. Soon the 3rd Battalion came up, expanding the lodgment.

Then the 1st Battalion, 8th Marines, reached the top with two companies of the 2nd Battalion trailing. The 3rd Battalion, 8th Marines made it to the base of the escarpment where the plateau reached the tangled ground below.

Victory on Tinian

The Japanese began probing the tentative Marine positions on the plateau after dark and then mounted a heavy banzai attack right at the muzzles of a 37mm gun position with the Marines firing canister into their faces. The Japanese lost two-thirds of the 150 men that assaulted the 1st Battalion, 28th Marines. Early on August 2, the 3rd Battalion, 6th Marines, killed 119 of 200 enemy troops executing a futile attack. By then, the Japanese on Tinian were finished as a cohesive fighting force.

The brief struggle for Tinian ended with 1100 casualties in the 4th Marine Division, 212 of them killed. Among them was Private Joseph W. Ozbourn, who smothered a live hand grenade to save other men of the 1st Battalion, 23rd Marines on July 30. The 2nd Marine Division suffered 105 killed and 655 wounded. One of them was Pfc. Robert L. Wilson of the 2nd Battalion, 6th Marines, who threw himself on a grenade while his unit was mopping up on August 4, sacrificing his own life to save his comrades. Both received the Medal of Honor.

Over 5500 Japanese were killed on Tinian, and many more were wounded or missing. Only 252 were taken prisoner.

With the seizure of the Marianas complete, the Marines were poised to continue their drive across the Pacific toward the home islands of Japan. Within hours of their capture, numerous airfields on Saipan, Guam, and Tinian were operational. Others were completed swiftly. Tinian was soon serving as the base for two wings of the 20th Air Force, whose B-29s became the scourge of Japan's cities.

On August 6, 1945, a B-29 rose into the sky from North Field on Tinian. The *Enola Gay* carried the atomic bomb that devastated Hiroshima, ushering in the Nuclear Age of modern warfare.

CHAPTER 6

PELELIU: PAINFUL PARADOX

"Rough but fast... we'll be through in three days. It might only take two." Such was the prediction of Major General William H. Rupertus, commander of the 1st Marine Division, as he contemplated the assault on the island of Peleliu in the Palau archipelago.

Nicknamed the "Old Breed", the 1st Marine Division had earned its reputation as a formidable fighting unit at Guadalcanal and Cape Gloucester. Pulled back to tiny Pavuvu in the Russell Islands, the division then received replacements and new equipment, although there were some shortages.

By the late summer of 1944, the combat veterans of the 1st Marine Division had been deployed to the Pacific for nearly two years. The drive toward the Japanese Home Islands had been costly but successful thus far. As Admiral Chester Nimitz's island hopping across the Central Pacific and General Douglas MacArthur's advance toward the Philippines converged, a difference of strategic opinion arose. Nimitz advocated the capture of Formosa and then a move against Okinawa. MacArthur, however, for both strategic and sentimental reasons wanted to return to the Philippines and then strike at Okinawa. In each case, staging areas for the invasion of Japan would then be available.

Opposite: Marines clamber down cargo nets from a transport ship to waiting Higgins Boats during the invasion of Peleliu.

The final strategic decision for the prosecution of the Pacific War went all the way to the White House. President Franklin D. Roosevelt flew to Hawaii in July 1944 and conferred with both senior commanders. The President chose MacArthur's proposal, and Nimitz pledged to protect his right flank during the coming offensive. The high-level decision thrust the little island of Peleliu, approximately five square miles (13 square km) in area and shaped somewhat like a lobster claw, into the spotlight.

A speck of land in the Palaus group about 600 miles (966km) east of the Philippines, Peleliu is near the western end of the Caroline Archipelago that stretches 1000 miles (1609km) across the Central Pacific. MacArthur worried that an airstrip there and another on a nearby spit of land called Ngesebus posed a threat of aerial attacks against his troop transport and supply lines to the Philippines. Nimitz concurred, and plans began taking shape for Operation Stalemate II, the capture of Peleliu, Ngesebus, and the island of Angaur about six miles (10km) to the southwest.

Flawed Intelligence

Rather than the swift victory predicted by General Rupertus, the 1st Marine Division and the U.S. Army's 81st Infantry Division, commanded by Major General Paul Mueller, were to experience some of the most bitter fighting of the Pacific War. Several significant factors influenced the nature of combat at Peleliu. Among these was the failure of American reconnaissance and photoanalysis to accurately assess the terrain, which consisted of deep draws, canyons, and rugged mountains dotted with scores of fortified caves, their entrances concealed by jungle.

Another factor, and likely the most significant, was a profound change in Japanese strategic and tactical defensive philosophy. Previous Marine and Army amphibious landings in the Pacific had been met with fierce opposition at the water's edge. Spirited banzai attacks were followed with the persistent expectation that the Americans would be driven into the sea. When previous outcomes failed to materialize as the Japanese expected, a change to defense in depth was adopted. The beaches would be contested; however, the object would then be to exact the highest toll possible in American blood—to make the conquest of further Japanese-occupied territory so costly that the enemy would tire of war and sue for peace. The battle for Peleliu

Below: Smoke shrouds the beaches of Peleliu as landing craft crowded with Marines prepare for the last run to the shoreline. The Japanese resistance to the initial landings at Peleliu was ferocious, and volunteers from non-combat Marine units were eventually called upon to augment the ranks of riflemen.

Above: On September 15, 1944, Marines of the III Amphibious Corps hit the beaches at Peleliu in the Palaus island group. During the opening hours of the invasion, Marines scurry across the beach toward the island's airfield, one of their initial objectives.

would mark the debut of the new Japanese defensive plan.

Delays in the capture of the Marianas extended the timetable for the Peleliu operation and exacerbated a debate as to whether the invasion of the island was necessary at all. Some contemporary observers, among them Admiral William F. "Bull" Halsey, commander of the U.S. Third Fleet, believed it was unnecessary. Modern historians have also continued to debate the judgment of McArthur and Nimitz; however, it may also be concluded that the two senior commanders acted properly in light of the information available to them at the time.

On the eve of the Peleliu invasion, Halsey approached Nimitz with a recommendation to cancel the operation altogether and accelerate the invasion of the Philippines, hitting the beaches on the central island of Leyte in October, two months earlier than the planned invasion of the southern island of Mindanao. The latter portion of Halsey's recommendation was adopted, but the Peleliu landing would proceed as planned.

As with previous amphibious operations, the Peleliu assault would be preceded by an intense naval and air bombardment. The five old battleships *Pennsylvania*, *Tennessee*, *Maryland*, *Idaho*, and *Mississippi* led a contingent of cruisers and destroyers that were originally slated to pound Peleliu for three days, up to the brink of the landings. Aircraft from three fleet carriers and eight light and escort carriers were to attack targets ashore.

When the task of executing Operation Stalemate II was handed to Marine Major General Roy S. Geiger's III Amphibious Corps (consisting of the 1st Marine Division and the 81st Infantry Division), the executive officer of the 1st Marine Division, Brigadier General Oliver P. Smith, led the planning effort while Rupertus was in Washington for an extended period. Early on the morning of September 15, 1944, three Marine regiments—the 1st under Colonel Lewis B. "Chesty" Puller, the 5th commanded by Colonel Harry D. "Bucky" Harris, and the 7th led by Colonel Herman H. Hanneken—were to assault a 6600ft (2012m) stretch of sand in the southwest of Peleliu, from which the Marines could drive due east toward one of their primary objectives, the island's airfield. The artillery of the 11th Marines and the III Amphibious Corps artillery were to begin landing within an hour of the assault.

Landing Party

From north to south, the invasion beaches were designated White 1 and 2, where the 1st Marines would hit the beach; Orange 1 and 2, the responsibility of the 5th Marines; and Orange 3, where the 7th Marines were to come ashore. Once clear of the beaches, Puller was to advance eastward and then pivot northward to assault the southwestern end of the formidable Umurbrogol Mountains and move steadily northward along the coast while the 1st Battalion, 5th Marines, provided flank protection and the 2nd Battalion, 5th Marines, crossed the island to the east and took the airfield in the process. The 7th Marines were to drive east and then south, isolating and annihilating resistance in that sector.

Meanwhile, the 81st Division's 322nd Regimental Combat Team was to capture Angaur with the support of the 321st and then revert to III Amphibious Corps reserve. Altogether, more than 40,000 Marines and soldiers were made available for Operation Stalemate II, apparently maintaining a substantial superiority in manpower. However, as Colonel Puller pointed out, only 9000 true riflemen populated the ranks of the 1st Marine Division. The rest were support personnel and other specialists.

Formidable Defenses

The Japanese defenses on Peleliu were challenging indeed. Colonel Kunio Nakagawa commanded the 2nd Infantry Regiment and two battalions of the 15th Infantry Regiment from the veteran 14th Division. Many of these soldiers had gained combat experience with the Kwantung Army in China, and their number substantially exceeded 10,000. For months, the Japanese had also been preparing defensive positions. A honeycomb of caves and subterranean complexes had been blasted from the rock of the Umurbrogol. Some of these were protected with sliding steel doors that made them virtually impossible to detect from the air. Heavy guns, mortars, and machine-gun nests with interlocking fields of fire were placed in concealed positions. Aerial bombs were rigged with tripwires and set as mines on the likely invasion beaches. By the time the Americans landed on Peleliu, more than 500 caves had been fortified, some of them extending several levels below ground.

At 8:32 a.m. on September 15, the 3rd Battalion, 1st Marines, commanded by Lieutenant Colonel Stephen V. Sabol, was first to land on Peleliu, on the far left flank of White Beach 1. Enemy fire was accurate and intense, particularly against Sabol's command, and spread rapidly along the Marine beachhead. Within an hour, scores of landing craft and other vehicles had been knocked out, including numerous LVTAs,

Below: The jumble of Marines and equipment on Orange Beach 3 at Peleliu is evident as smoke billows from stricken landing craft, and riflemen of the 1st Marine Division struggle to maintain unit cohesion and move inland.

Above: A Marine of the 1st Division uses a flamethrower to spray a lethal stream of fire into a Japanese pillbox on Peleliu, where an enemy sniper has holed up. The fighting on Peleliu gave the Marines their first taste of defense in depth, a costly tactic of attrition the Japanese used to exact high casualties.

amphibious tractors equipped with 75mm guns to deal directly with enemy strongpoints. During the first 10 minutes of close combat 26 LVTs were destroyed. Puller's LVT took a direct hit, and he barely escaped with his life.

While the 2nd Battalion, 1st Marines penetrated 1050ft (320m) inland and made contact with the 5th Marines on its right, Sabol's 3rd Battalion struggled from the outset. Just 300ft (91m) off the beach, it ran into a coral ridge rising 30ft (9m) and capped with strong defenses, including a 47mm gun that pounded the Marines continually. Nicknamed "The Point", this troublesome high ground had to be taken and the task fell to Company K, 3rd Battalion, capably led by Captain George P. Hunt.

After the war, Hunt became a managing editor with *Life* magazine, but on this day he was occupied with staying alive and keeping his Marines focused on their arduous mission. "The Point" had not been identified on any maps of the island, and its existence proved to be merely the first of many nasty surprises the Marines were forced to deal with on Peleliu.

Captain Hunt's well-trained men moved forward, attempting to flank the gun embrasures that spewed fire incessantly and then silence them with demolition charges and rifle grenades. The 47mm (1.85in) weapon and several other guns positioned in a large blockhouse were demolished when a Marine corporal named Anderson fired a rifle grenade that ricocheted off the muzzle of a Japanese gun and set off tremendous explosions inside the structure. Enemy soldiers ran from the blockhouse exit, their uniforms aflame and rounds of ammunition cooking off in their belts. The vengeful Marines shot them down.

As the afternoon shadows lengthened, Company K held "The Point", but its manpower had been reduced to only platoon strength. Nevertheless, Hunt's Marines beat back numerous counterattacks during the next 30 hours. When finally relieved, the colonel counted only 18 men able to shoulder a rifle. Company K had been shredded. Of its original 235 riflemen, only 78 Marines survived the ordeal.

The 5th Marines advanced steadily through coconut groves and jungle, reaching its first objective within an hour of the initial landings and the airfield by the afternoon of the first day. The 7th Marines took ferocious enemy fire at Orange Beach 3, and some landing craft were diverted to Orange Beach 2. The 3rd Battalion, 7th Marines, advanced 1500ft (457m) before running into a line of pillboxes and concrete blockhouses near an old Japanese barracks compound. Tank support was inadvertently misdirected and created a gap between adjoining elements that required a halt to offensive operations to shore up coordination. It took nearly six hours for Lieutenant Colonel John Gormley's 1st Battalion, 7th Marines to reach its objective.

Enemy Tanks

Rupertus watched the progress of the 1st Division and became concerned that its momentum was waning. He committed the last of his reserve, the 2nd Battalion, 7th Marines, in the afternoon. As the 5th Marines consolidated its hold on the airfield, at 4:50 p.m. Nakagawa launched a counterattack spearheaded by deploying about 15 Type 95 light tanks supported by infantry.

Moving north to south, the Japanese encountered a prepared defensive line and soon came under fire from both the 1st and 5th Marines. One Marine destroyed a pair of enemy tanks with a bazooka, while the M4A1 Sherman tanks of the 1st Tank Battalion flanked the Japanese and raked the inferior enemy armor with 75mm fire. Within minutes, most of the Japanese tanks were flaming wrecks. They had outdistanced the bulk of their infantry and left the foot soldiers exposed to withering American small arms and artillery fire as the attack foundered and melted away.

Although the Marine assault had achieved a secure lodgment, the Americans had not reached all of their objectives for the first day. The Japanese mounted numerous counterattacks after dark, and one of these against the 7th Marines was repulsed with the help of a Black Marine support unit that volunteered to take up rifles and moved inland from the beach.

One Marine destroyed a pair of enemy tanks with a bazooka.

Puller's 1st Marines had suffered heavy casualties, and their hold on "The Point" was tenuous. The colonel's report to Rupertus was overly optimistic, due in part to his limited knowledge of the tactical situation in the confused battle. During the first day of combat, the 1st Marine Division suffered 1111 casualties, 209 of these killed in action. Worse was yet to come. During the following week, temperatures soared above 100 degrees Fahrenheit while the 5th and 7th Marines continued their advances. Steadily destroying pillboxes, blockhouses, and machine-gun nests, the 7th Marines completed its initial assignment, securing southern Peleliu on September 18.

The 5th Marines secured the area around the airfield on September 16 and encountered heavy enemy fire across a patch of open ground to the north. The 2nd Battalion became locked in a vicious fight with numerous Japanese strongpoints in a swampy area to the east. As they moved north to support the 1st Marines the following day, elements of the 2nd Battalion came under flanking fire from enemy strongpoints directly in front of the 1st Marines' positions. Heavy jungle impeded progress, but the 5th Marines pushed forward, reaching the eastern

Desegregation of the Marine Corps

Although President Harry S. Truman did not sign the legislation that officially desegregated the U.S. armed forces until July 26, 1948, African-American Marines had trained and served in a segregated Marine Corps since early in World War II. In June 1942, the Marine Corps authorized African-Americans to enlist in all-Black units, and separate training facilities were then established for them.

African-American Marines received basic training at Montford Point, North Carolina, and the first group of 13 recruits arrived there on August 26, 1942. These men formed the nucleus of the 51st Composite Defense Battalion, a coastal artillery formation. Opportunities for African-American Marines were quite limited—rather than allowing them to train fully as combat infantrymen, the Corps restricted their assignments to those of cooks, stewards, supply, and other non-combat roles.

Nevertheless, when manpower was short and the Japanese threatened to counterattack on the island of Peleliu, the African-American 11th Marine Depot Company and 7th Marine Ammunition Company responded to the call for replacement combat riflemen. "My company, when we went in, we went in with our rifles blazing", remembered Marine Lee Douglas, Jr. After the battle, Major General William H. Rupertus, commander of the 1st Marine Division, sent letters of commendation to the commanding officers of both companies. Following a similar performance on the island of Saipan in the Marianas, General Alexander A. Vandegrift asserted, "The Negro Marines are no longer on trial. They are Marines, period."

During World War II, approximately 8000 of the more than 19,000 African-American Marines in uniform served during combat operations. Although their total manpower accounted for less than five per cent of total Marine strength, their contribution to the U.S. victory over Japan is significant not only in the triumph itself, but also in the advancement of equal rights at home.

Below: African-American Marines stand at parade during an inspection at Montford Point, North Carolina.

Above: The devastated landscape of Peleliu provides a backdrop for a column of Marines moving toward the front lines. The Japanese took full advantage of the rugged terrain of Peleliu, fortifying caves, cliffs, mountains, and valleys and constructing concrete blockhouses, pillboxes, and machine-gun emplacements.

shore on September 20. Three days later, effective resistance in southern Peleliu had ended.

Meanwhile, on the left flank the ordeal of Puller's 1st Marines was coming sharply into focus. On the second day, Puller was obliged to come to the aid of Hunt's Company K, 3rd Battalion at "The Point" and then take on the Japanese in a desperate fight northward through the dense jungle toward the ridges, valleys, and rocky crags of the Umurbrogol. It was readily apparent to those on the ground that the thick canopy of jungle foliage had obscured the true nature of the Umurbrogol from aerial reconnaissance, and Puller's command would pay a bloody butcher's bill as a consequence.

Bloody Nose Ridge

On September 17, the 1st Marines encountered the rough terrain of the Umurbrogol for the first time. As their ferocious advance commenced, they soon found that the capture of one promontory meant subjecting themselves to direct fire from the next high ground to the north. Attacking on a front approximately 3000ft (914m) wide, the Marines were obliged to engage in a frustrating, bloody, and time-consuming endeavor to blast the enemy defenders from every cave, defile, and rocky peak of the Umurbrogol, which they nicknamed Bloody Nose Ridge.

During five days of intense fighting from the beaches into the labyrinth of Bloody Nose Ridge, the 1st Marines suffered 1749 casualties,

Above: Marines stay low on Bloody Nose Ridge at Peleliu. The 1st Marines took heavy casualties during five continuous days of fighting at Bloody Nose Ridge, clearing the Japanese from every cave entrance and defile in the Umurbrogol.

just six fewer than the entire 1st Marine Division had absorbed during the extended battle for Guadalcanal the previous year. All the while, Rupertus continued to urge Puller forward, insisting that the drive maintain critical momentum. Rupertus refused to accept the idea that reinforcements from the 81st Division were needed and ordered the Army division to proceed with the planned invasion of Angaur on September 17.

The 1st Battalion, 1st Marines, moved forward steadily until confronted by a concrete blockhouse that the Navy had reported destroyed during the pre-invasion bombardment. Obviously this was not the case, even after the Navy reported it had run out of targets on Peleliu and ceased its bombardment ahead of schedule. The blockhouse was taken only after heavy fire from the 14-inch guns of the battleship *Mississippi* was directed against its 4ft- (1.2m-) thick walls.

On September 19, Company B, 1st Battalion, 1st Marines, attacked Hill 100 near Horseshoe Canyon at the eastern edge of the Umurbrogol. Captain Everett Pope had brought 242 fighting Marines ashore and by this time commanded only 90 effective riflemen. Pope stepped off with tank support but quickly lost it as two Shermans slipped from a narrow causeway as the elevation increased. The Marines pressed on under heavy Japanese small arms and mortar fire.

When they reached the summit of Hill 100, which the Japanese called East Mountain, Pope's men found themselves under fire from high ground beyond and from the caves that laced a parallel ridge on the western flank that had been dubbed the Five Brothers. When night fell, the Japanese began a series of counterattacks to dislodge the Marines, whose ammunition, food, water, and medical supplies were running dangerously low. The fighting was hand-to-hand—knives flashed and rifle butts rose and fell as the Marines held on by their fingernails.

Lieutenant Francis Burke and Sergeant James McAlarnis survived a harrowing fight with two Japanese soldiers, one of whom thrust a bayonet into Burke's leg. The lieutenant killed the enemy soldier with his bare hands, repeatedly pounding him with his fists. McAlarnis crushed the other's skull with his rifle butt. The bodies of the Japanese attackers were then unceremoniously tossed down the slope.

U.S. Casualties

As the sun rose, what was left of Company B still held Hill 100, but Pope was down to only eight men in fighting condition. He was ordered to withdraw and got his wounded out, but had to leave the bodies of his dead Marines behind. These were not recovered until two weeks later when Hill 100 was taken for the last time. Pope received the Medal of Honor for his gallantry.

Aware that the 1st Marines had lost 1500 killed and wounded by September 19, Major General Geiger visited the regiment's command post on the 21st and discussed the situation with Rupertus and members of his staff. Despite the grievous losses, Rupertus was adamant that the Marines did not require Army assistance to complete the capture of Peleliu. Geiger, however,

Below: A Marine bends to offer a drink of water from his canteen to a wounded comrade on the island of Peleliu.

had seen enough. He overruled Rupertus and directed the 321st Regimental Combat Team to redeploy from Angaur to Peleliu.

As this was accomplished, Rupertus was instructed to withdraw the 1st Marines. The gallant regiment had virtually ceased to exist as a fighting force, and one veteran of the hellish Peleliu combat remarked, "I resigned from the human race. We were no longer human beings. I fired at anything in front of me, friend or foe. I had no friends. I just wanted to kill."

Life Magazine war artist Tom Lea accompanied the Marines on Peleliu and produced haunting images that reflected his experience there. One of these depicts a Marine staring blankly from hollow eyes, a victim of the stress of days on the line in horrific combat.

"As we passed the sick bay, still in the shell hole, it was crowded with wounded, and somehow hushed in the evening light," Lea captioned the painting. "I noticed a tattered Marine standing quietly by a corpsman, staring

Below: Their faces showing the signs of fatigue after days of combat, Marines trudge along a dirt road toward the northern end of the island of Peleliu.

stiffly at nothing. His mind had crumbled in battle, his jaw hung, and his eyes were like two black empty holes in his head."

At this point, the advance of the 1st Marine Division had reached the main Japanese line of defense, eliminating several observation posts that the enemy had used to direct artillery fire on the Marines from the high ground. With the airfield operational, supporting fighter-bombers were conducting regular missions. Supplies were flowing onto the island, but the elimination of Japanese resistance in the Umurbrogol remained an ugly business.

Enemy Reinforcements

By September 23, the necessity of capturing northern Peleliu was recognized more fully as the Japanese managed to land a battalion of reinforcements from the nearby island of Babelthuap. The arrival of the 321st Regimental Combat Team from Angaur the following day facilitated operations to isolate the Umurbrogol and secure northern Peleliu. The plan involved a northward thrust past the Umurbrogol by the Army troops, with the 5th Marines advancing through them into northern Peleliu as the 7th Marines took over the positions formerly held by the 1st Marines.

Only a single road was available for the movement of tanks or other vehicles, and this was subjected to Japanese fire from the surrounding hills. Therefore, the advancing troops were often on their own with only their light weapons available. As Marine Air Group 11 began arriving at the airfield in force, its fighter-bombers assumed the primary responsibility for tactical air support. Major Robert F. "Cowboy" Stout and the pilots of Marine Fighter Squadron 114 (VMF-114) were conspicuous in pressing home their attacks against ground targets.

On September 25, the offensive movement had been accomplished sufficiently for the 5th Marines to advance to the shattered village of Garekoru in the north and secure neighboring high ground. The following day, the 321st initiated a three-pronged attack on the northern edge of the Umurbrogol, confining the Japanese to a defensive pocket.

The 5th Marines assaulted the successive promontories of Hills 1, 2, 3, and Radar Hill, known to the Americans as "Hill Row". Approximately 1500 Japanese troops occupied these knobs and the Amiangal Ridge, which extended northward. The 3rd Battalion, 5th Marines, captured Hill 80 and reached the eastern shore of Peleliu. On the 27th, the northern portion of the island was effectively secured,

Rupertus and the Marine Rifleman's Creed

Major General William Rupertus was a tough old school Marine. He grudgingly refused to relinquish the preeminence of his 1st Marine Division on Peleliu to the Army's 81st Infantry Division. Commissioned into the Marine Corps in 1913, Rupertus had served as commander of a ship's Marine troop detachment during World War I, and later in Haiti and China.

By the time of Operation Stalemate II, Rupertus had been with the 1st Marine Division since early 1942, serving as its assistant commander during the Guadalcanal Campaign. He took command of the division prior to the landings at Cape Gloucester, and after it was withdrawn from Peleliu he was placed in command of the Marine Corps School at Quantico, Virginia. Just four months later he suffered a massive heart attack and died on March 25, 1945.

In addition to his command of the 1st Marine Division, Maj. Gen. Rupertus is best known as the author of the famed Marine Rifleman's Creed. It reads:

"This is my rifle. There are many like it, but this one is mine.

My rifle is my best friend. It is my life. I must master it as I must master my life.

My rifle, without me, is useless. Without my rifle, I am useless. I must fire my rifle true. I must shoot straighter than my enemy who is trying to kill me. I must shoot him before he shoots me. I will...

My rifle and I know that what counts in war is not the rounds we fire, the noise of our burst, nor the smoke we make. We know that it is the hits that count. We will hit...

My rifle is human, even as I, because it is my life. Thus, I will learn it as a brother. I will learn its weaknesses, its strength, its parts, its accessories, its sights and its barrel. I will keep my rifle clean and ready, even as I am clean and ready. We will become part of each other. We will...

Before God, I swear this creed. My rifle and I are the defenders of my country. We are the masters of our enemy. We are the saviors of my life.

So be it, until victory is America's and there is no enemy, but peace!"

Right: Major General William Rupertus commanded the 1st Marine Division on Peleliu and stubbornly refused to allow Army troops to enter the fight. Rupertus is perhaps best known as the author of the *Marine Rifleman's Creed.*

Above: A Marine Vought F4U Corsair fighter bomber drops its load of ordnance on a Japanese position in the rugged Umurbrogol Mountains of Peleliu. Marine and Navy tactical air support provided much-needed firepower against enemy targets.

although sporadic resistance continued for some time. After four days of combat, the Marines claimed the tops of the "Hill Row" promontories.

When the 2nd Battalion, 5th Marines, took on Amiangal Ridge it requested artillery support, which came in the form of a single barrel of the 8th 155mm Gun Battalion. Japanese observers saw the weapon in place on the morning of September 28 and peppered the artillerymen with their machine guns and rifles. The harassing fire was quickly suppressed, and all morning long the 155mm gun plastered the visible caves and enemy positions along the ridge. Only one troublesome strongpoint escaped the rain of shells, the mouth of a large tunnel at the northwestern base of the ridge that was too close to Marine positions for the big gun to fire on.

Buried Alive

Bulldozers filled in an anti-tank ditch that blocked the approach to the tunnel, and a combined tank-infantry assault rushed forward to toss demolition charges and fire point-blank into the tunnel mouth. Bulldozers then rolled up and sealed the entrance with mounds of earth and rubble. Subsequently, the Marines seized the crest of Amiangal Ridge. However, they remained heavily engaged for some time with the Japanese burrowed inside the warren of tunnels and caves beneath them.

The 3rd Battalion, 5th Marines, landed on the small island of Ngesebus just 1800ft (549m) north of Peleliu on September 28 to stifle further Japanese efforts to run more reinforcements down from Babelthuap and capture the airfield.

The close air-support of VMF(AW)-114, the first such all-Marine operation of the war, paved the way in the 36-hour fight that subdued 500 Japanese troops.

The Umurbrogol Pocket remained defiant, and the Japanese on Peleliu made their last stand there. Stretching about 3000ft (914m) by 1500ft (457m), the pocket was thick with Japanese defenders in their well-concealed bunkers, pillboxes, and labyrinthian cave complexes. From the hills nicknamed the Five Sisters in the south to Baldy Hill in the north, the enemy had already exacted a terrible toll. The 1st Marines had begun the dirty job and neutralized the early threat of artillery fire against the invasion beaches and the initial Marine movement inland.

Now, the 2nd and 3rd Battalions of the 321st Regimental Combat Team pushed from the north, while the 7th Marines stepped in for the 5th Marines and pressed ahead from the south. The 2nd Battalion, 321st, captured Hill B at the northern edge of the pocket on September 26, setting the stage for penetration into the Umurbrogol from that direction. On the 29th, the 2nd and 3rd Battalions, 7th Marines, relieved the Army troops. To accomplish the transition, ad hoc Marine units were pieced together to maintain the static line previously occupied by the two battalions of the 7th Marines.

With their maneuverability restored, the 2nd and 3rd Battalions, 7th Marines, forged ahead, capturing high ground at Boyd Ridge. Recalled from Ngesebus, the 3rd Battalion, 5th Marines came up in support of the 7th Marines on October 3. Although days of combat had reduced them closer to company strength, the Marines then executed a coordinated assault with four battalions against the eastern and southern sectors of the Umurbrogol Pocket, including Baldy Hill and Hill 300. Simultaneous diversionary attacks were mounted against the cluster of hills known as the Five Sisters and Horseshoe Canyon.

The attacks achieved their objectives with the exception of the 3rd Battalion, 5th Marines, assault on the Five Sisters. Marine riflemen reached the tops of four of these hills west of Horseshoe Canyon, but were forced to withdraw when the fifth was too heavily defended. On the

Right: With the slogan "The Bloody Trail" scrawled on its flank, an armored amtrak landing craft provides some cover for Marines on Peleliu. After landing the riflemen, the landing vehicle has remained to offer fire support with machine guns and a turret-mounted 75mm gun.

same day, the highest-ranking Marine to lose his life on Peleliu, Colonel Joseph F. Hankins, was killed by a sniper. Hankins had moved down the West Road to sort out a traffic snarl when he was shot.

The Battle for Hill 120

A renewed effort against the Five Sisters on October 4 was momentarily successful, but the heights had to be abandoned once again. The 3rd Battalion, 7th Marines, rushed to the top of Hill 120, and for a time it was believed that this advantageous position could provide a springboard for the seizure of the next ridgeline. However, characteristically for the Peleliu operation, the 3rd Battalion soon found itself under heavy fire and taking substantial casualties. The Marines were withdrawn.

During the attack on Hill 120, Captain James Shanley, commanding Company L, 3rd Battalion, was killed in action. Shanley dashed from cover to rescue two wounded Marines, dragging them

to safety behind a tank, and then went back to save a third. As he stepped forward, an exploding mortar round wounded him fatally. While Shanley lay dying, his executive officer, Lieutenant Harold J. Collins, attempted to reach the captain and was killed by an anti-tank shell. Shanley received a posthumous gold star for the Navy Cross he had earned at Cape Gloucester.

Two weeks of heavy combat in the Umurbrogol had taken their toll on the 7th Marines, and the attacks of October 4 were its last of the campaign. The 7th Marines had suffered 1486 casualties, roughly 46 percent of its strength, killed or wounded. General Rupertus still wanted the reduction of the pocket to be a Marine affair as much as possible, but acknowledged that the 7th Marines should be withdrawn. He replaced it with the 5th Marines.

Colonel Harris, the 5th Marines' commander, had conducted an aerial reconnaissance of the rugged terrain of Peleliu's interior during the first week of Operation Stalemate II, prompting him to declare that he intended to be "lavish with ammunition and stingy with... men's lives". When Rupertus handed him this latest assignment, Harris viewed the tactical situation as something of a siege. He determined that the

Below: A Marine LVT (Landing Vehicle, Tracked) equipped with a flamethrower emits a jet of fire at a Japanese strongpoint on the island of Peleliu during the bitter battle that occurred there in the autumn of 1944.

Marines held the greatest advantage in the north. The offensive would continue there while those Marines in the east and south would generally remain static and in reserve.

A disassembled 75mm pack howitzer was placed in a sandbag revetment, reassembled, and began firing at the mouth of a large cave.

Moving into its new positions on October 5, the 5th Marines sent patrols out to probe the Japanese defenses and called up bulldozers to carve roads into the box canyons and jungles to its front. Tanks and LVTs equipped with flamethrowers would then be able to provide support to the riflemen.

For nearly a week, the 2nd Battalion, 5th Marines fought to take Hill 140, knocking out numerous Japanese positions with satchel charges and hand grenades, while the 3rd Battalion to the north launched a tank-infantry assault into Horseshoe Canyon. The 3rd Battalion objective was to clear the stubborn Japanese from the Five Sisters and the lower western slope of Hill 100. The 2nd Battalion's capture of Hill 140 signaled the completion of the comprehensive effort.

With Hill 140 in Marine hands, a disassembled 75mm pack howitzer was placed in a sandbag revetment on the West Road, reassembled, and began firing at the mouth of a large cave at the base of the next ridgeline. Repeating this technique with the versatile pack howitzer brought successive Japanese positions under fire, greatly assisting in the capture of several hilltops and the clearing of two box canyons that had previously been deathtraps. Although the 5th Marines were taking Japanese positions on the western flanks of Boyd Ridge and Walt Ridge under fire, enemy troops were still under the cover of guns along the Five Brothers, which ran parallel.

In mid-October, the 3rd Battalion, 5th Marines, was sent to relieve the spent 2nd Battalion, and the slow but steady collapsing of the Umurbrogol Pocket, which had thus far reduced the enemy perimeter 1500ft (457m) to the south, continued. The Japanese enclave was now only 2400ft (732m) wide by 1500ft (457m) long. For all practical purposes, enemy resistance was contained to that area and Peleliu was secured.

Rupertus, however, remained fixated on the Marines completing the conquest of the Umurbrogol. That is until a pair of significant events compelled him to relent, including Major General Geiger, who urged that the 5th and 7th Marines should be withdrawn from the fighting altogether and that Major General Mueller's 81st Infantry Division should complete the assignment. First, the 81st Division's 323rd Regimental Combat Team returned from the capture of the island of Ulithi, bringing the division back to full strength. Second, a communiqué from Admiral Nimitz at far-off Pearl Harbor proclaimed that Peleliu was secure and further instructed Geiger to turn over tactical command to Mueller.

On October 15–16, the relief of the remnants of the 1st Marine Division was accomplished. Four days later, Mueller established his command post on southeast Peleliu.

Flushing Out the Enemy

For six more weeks, the troops of the 81st Infantry Division methodically destroyed countless Japanese strongpoints, particularly in the vicinity of the Five Brothers, Five Sisters, and a formidable rise called the China Wall. Army engineers used satchel charges and flamethrowers to root the enemy soldiers out, entomb them, or burn them alive.

Nakagawa sent his last message to superior officers on the island of Koror on November 24, advising, "Our sword is broken. We have run out of spears". He further related that he had burned the colors of the 2nd Infantry Regiment and that the handful of troops who remained at his disposal were being grouped into infiltration teams "to attack the enemy everywhere". After dark, 25 Japanese soldiers were killed attempting to slip through the American lines. When daylight came, a prisoner informed his Army captors that Nakagawa had committed suicide.

On the 74th day of Operation Stalemate II, American troops converged from north and south and linked up near the site of Nakagawa's former headquarters. Isolated pockets of Japanese resistance took many more days to clear, but the horrific battle for Peleliu was effectively over.

Along with Captain Pope, seven more Marines received the Medal of Honor for valor on Peleliu. Corporal Louis Bausell, PFCs. Richard Kraus, Charles Roan, and John D. New, and Private Wesley Phelps smothered hand grenades to save their comrades, while 1st Lieutenant Carlton Rouh was seriously wounded when he placed himself between his men and the blast of another grenade. Private First Class Arthur Jackson was credited with destroying 12 fortified Japanese positions and killing 50 enemy soldiers singlehandedly on September 18. Rouh, Pope, and Jackson survived the battle to receive their medals.

The fight for Peleliu had shattered the 1st Marine Division, which absorbed 1300 dead and 5450 wounded, while 36 Marines were missing. The 81st Division suffered more than 3000 casualties on Peleliu and Angaur, with 468 of them killed in action. The Japanese garrison on Peleliu and the nearby islands was annihilated. Only 241 prisoners were taken, and of the 202 captured on Peleliu just 19 were Japanese. The remainder were Korean and Okinawan laborers.

Right: Two Marines take a moment to rest and smoke a cigarette on Peleliu. Private First Class Douglas Lightheart (right) cradles his .30-caliber M1919 Browning machine gun, while Pfc. Gerald Thursby, Sr., relaxes beside him. This photo was taken during mopping-up operations on the island.

USMC

Counting the Cost

Was possession of Peleliu worth the cost? The debate continues to this day. Because of assurances that the campaign would conclude swiftly, only six reporters accompanied the Marines to the island, and the brutal battle received scant coverage. MacArthur's looming return to the Philippines also relegated the operation to the back pages of American newspapers. In the years after World War II, Nimitz never fully explained his decision, although it can be concluded with certainty that he did not allow the invasion to proceed for personal glory or pride.

The real payoff for the bloodshed at Peleliu lay in its future use as a base for American bombers to strike the Philippines, the sealing of the final cork in the bottle that isolated 250,000 Japanese troops on other islands in the Carolines, and the invaluable lessons learned in tank-infantry coordination and the subduing of fixed, in-depth fortifications. These lessons would be applied at Okinawa, but sadly there was no time to impart the hard-won wisdom to the Marines of the V Amphibious Corps, who were ordered to take the island of Iwo Jima to the north a few weeks after major combat operations on Peleliu ended.

Eclipsing any other conclusions, the battle for Peleliu validated the combat prowess, dedication, and pure heroism of the United States Marines and confirmed the honor and prestige of the 1st Marine Division for all time. Yet, for many the American victory at Peleliu remains Pyrrhic.

Below: Combat-weary Marines, one of them blaring a bugle, pose for a photographer with a war trophy. These Marines have battled for days to capture this enemy flag, and only 19 Japanese prisoners were taken during the weeks-long battle for Peleliu.

Marine Tactical Air Support in the Philippines

During the spring and summer of 1944, the buildup for the long-awaited return of General Douglas MacArthur and the U.S. Army to the Philippines was proceeding at a rapid pace. Amid the preparations, Major General Ralph J. Mitchell, commander of the 1st Marine Aircraft Wing, flew to Australia twice to offer the services of his battle-hardened pilots to MacArthur.

Each time, Mitchell received the administrative stiff-arm. The Army's senior commanders wanted the liberation of the Philippines to be an exclusive undertaking. Mitchell, however, reasoned that Japanese air assets had effectively been swept from the skies of the northern Solomons and that nearly two years of continuing air operations made his pilots veterans with invaluable combat experience.

General MacArthur waded ashore on the Philippine island of Leyte on October 20, 1944, and rather than Marine aircraft it was the artillery of the V Amphibious Corps that arrived to provide initial support to the Army offensive. The Marines' big guns were on loan to the Army since its own XXIV Corps artillery had been sent to aid the Marines then fighting in the Marianas.

The first Marine fighter aircraft arrived in the Philippines from Peleliu at MacArthur's request. The mission of VMF(N)-541, a night fighter squadron equipped with specialized Grumman F6F Hellcats, was to neutralize the threat of Japanese Nakajima Ki-43 Oscar night fighters. MacArthur traded an Army night fighter squadron whose Northrop P-61 Black Widow fighters were too slow to catch the Oscars. At the same time, growing concern over Japanese kamikaze suicide attacks against U.S. Navy ships off the Philippine coast prompted Third Fleet commander Admiral William F. Halsey to suggest that land-based Marine aircraft were well suited to provide air support for the Army troops ashore.

Thus, the night-fighting Hellcats of VMF(N)-541 arrived on December 3, 1944, hours ahead of 66 Marine Vought F4U Corsair fighters that completed an arduous 1957 mile (3149km) flight to the Philippine airstrip at Tacloban from Emirau in the Bismarck Islands. Soon, Marine fighter strength grew to 85 Corsairs as planes of VMF-115, VMF-211, VMF-218, and VMF-313, constituting Marine Air Group 12 (MAG 12), roared in to land on the muddy strip.

Serving under the command of the 308th Bombardment Wing, Fifth Army Air Force, the Marine pilots coordinated operations with the Lockheed P-38 Lightning and Curtiss P-40 Tomahawk squadrons of the Army Air Forces. Both the Hellcats and Corsairs proved more than a dogfighting match for the Japanese Mitsubishi A6M Zero fighters in the Philippines. The Marine pilots also interdicted enemy resupply and reinforcement efforts at sea, devastating Japanese vessels with .50-caliber machine-gun fire.

During the Leyte operations, MAG 12 pilots were credited with destroying 40 Japanese aircraft, sinking seven destroyers, nine freighters, and three troop transports, and damaging 11 more ships. In less than a month, the Marines had flown 264 missions. The Japanese ruefully nicknamed the Corsair the "Whistling Death".

By September 1944, Marine Corps' air strength reached its peak, with 145 squadrons, and in the coming months the commitment of Marine air power to the Philippines Campaign steadily grew. The dive-bombers of MAG 24 and MAG 32 supported Army ground troops during the fighting on the island of Luzon, completing 8842 missions and dropping 19,167 bombs.

CHAPTER 7

UNCOMMON VALOR AT IWO JIMA

On the afternoon of March 4, 1945, the Boeing B-29 Superfortress bomber nicknamed *Dinah Might* struggled to stay in the air. Shot up during a perilous bombing mission over Tokyo and critically low on fuel, its pilot, Lieutenant Fred Malo, fought to maintain control of the heavy aircraft.

Returning to base on the island of Tinian in the distant Marianas was a long shot. However, providence smiled on Malo and his 10 crewmen that day. There was an alternative. He headed for Iwo Jima, a speck of land in the Volcano Islands 650 nautical miles (748 miles/1204km) south of his target for the day's mission, and requested an emergency landing on the principal of three airfields located on the porkchop-shaped, otherwise inhospitable landmass that was only eight square miles (21 square km) in total area.

When Iwo Jima came within sight, Malo dropped from the thick cloud cover and slapped down on the strip. A wing snapped a telephone pole as the big silver bomber came to a shuddering stop just 50ft (15m) from the end of the runway. Within a half hour, temporary repairs had been made, the fuel tanks were topped off, and the plane was airborne, headed once again for Tinian.

Dinah Might was the first of many crippled aircraft engaged in the strategic bombing campaign against Japan that found a temporary haven on Iwo Jima, and its crewmen were among an estimated 25,000 American airmen whose lives were probably saved when they avoided ditching in the vast expanse of the Pacific Ocean.

On the day of *Dinah Might*'s salvation, U.S. Marines were still fighting to secure Iwo Jima. For two long weeks they had battled the determined Japanese enemy, seldom seen, usually burrowed deep in a fortified labyrinth of caves and tunnels, and virtually to a man preferring death in combat to surrender. Many of those weary Marines who saw the big bomber descend from the overcast sky and land safely stopped the business of killing for a moment to celebrate life. They cheered loudly and then took up their ugly task anew.

Opposite: A lone Marine sentinel stands watch on the summit of Mount Suribachi as the Stars and Stripes ripples in the breeze at Iwo Jima. The flag has been lashed to a pole and secured with ropes atop the 550ft (167m) extinct volcano.

Casualties of War

Although the Marines had been told why they were fighting for the desolate, sulfuric island, the event validated their purpose. Before Iwo Jima was secured, three more weeks of bitter fighting lay ahead. When the battle ended, the Marines had suffered mightily with 6821 killed and a staggering 17,000 wounded. The defending Japanese force of 25,000 men was nearly annihilated. Only 216 prisoners were captured.

The epic struggle for Iwo Jima was the largest and bloodiest battle in the history of the U.S. Marine Corps. It was a bitter fight with no quarter given and none expected—and it had to be won. Iwo Jima would certainly provide an important staging area for the planned invasion of Okinawa scheduled later in the spring of 1945, but there was another immediate reason for its capture.

The seizure of the Marianas in the summer of 1944 provided bases on the islands of Guam, Saipan, and Tinian, from which the big bombers of the U.S. Army Air Forces could lay waste to major Japanese cities as well as military and industrial targets. Although the Marianas brought the home islands of Honshu, Kyushu, Shikoku, and Hokkaido within range of the B-29s, the flight was still long and perilous.

One of the most direct air routes to Japan drew the bombers dangerously close to Iwo Jima, close enough for Japanese radar to alert anti-aircraft units and fighter squadrons that a raid was coming a full two hours before the American planes arrived above their targets. Three airstrips, two finished and the other under construction, allowed Japanese fighters to intercept American bombers en route to their targets and on the return flights, when crippled planes made easy kills. Occasionally, Japanese planes even ventured from Iwo Jima to bomb and strafe the American bases in the Marianas.

By November 1944, the stepped-up strategic bombing campaign against Japan was in full swing; however, senior American commanders knew well before that time that Iwo Jima had to be taken. In October 1944, the Joint Chiefs of Staff in Washington, D.C., directed by Admiral Chester Nimitz, the U.S. Navy's Commander-in-Chief Pacific, to formulate a plan to seize the island.

Nimitz handed the senior command role for Operation Detachment to Admiral Raymond A. Spruance. In turn, the V Amphibious Corps, commanded by Major General Harry Schmidt, three divisions and 70,000 strong, would assault Iwo Jima. The irascible Major General Holland M. "Howlin' Mad" Smith would join in with a titular role as commander of expeditionary troops. At this stage of World War II in the Pacific, Spruance's cadre of senior commanders was comprised of veterans of planning and amphibious warfare. They included Admiral Marc Mitscher commanding the fast aircraft carriers of Task Force 58, Admiral Richmond Kelly Turner leading the Joint Expeditionary Force, and others.

Operation Detachment

In late December, Schmidt completed the blueprint for Operation Detachment. The beaches on the southeastern coast of Iwo Jima appeared to offer the greatest advantage. From left to right they were designated Green, Red 1 and 2, Yellow 1 and 2, and Blue 1 and 2. The 5th Marine Division, commanded by Major General Keller E. Rockey, was to land its 28th Marine Regiment at Green Beach, while the 27th Marines landed on the Red Beaches. The 4th Marine Division, led by Major General Clifton B. Cates, was to land the 23rd Marines on the Yellow Beaches and the 25th Marines on the Blue beaches. The 3rd Marine Division, under Major General Graves B. Erskine, was designated as corps reserve.

The assault force was charged with three initial objectives. The 28th Marines was ordered to advance across a narrow peninsula to the northwest coast of Iwo Jima and then turn south, isolating and capturing the most prominent terrain feature on the island, 550ft (168m) Mount Suribachi, the cone of an extinct volcano that rose ominously at its extreme southwestern tip. The 25th Marines was to negotiate the steep, terraced landing beach with its loose, volcanic sand, and assault a jumble of scrub brush with sharp cliffs and crevices called the Rock Quarry before acting as the pivot point for a general reorientation to the north. The 23rd and 27th Marines were to capture the southernmost airfield, Motoyama No.1, before turning northward.

It was obvious that the heights of Mount Suribachi and the cauldron of the Rock Quarry would provide a stern test for the Marines, who would be subjected to heavy fire from both. D-day was set for February 19, 1945, and although some of the senior Navy and Marine commanders believed that Iwo Jima would fall within a week to 10 days, others were grim realists. Among them was Holland Smith, who opined: "This is going to be a rough one ... we could suffer as many as 15,000 casualties here."

Schmidt requested a 10-day preparatory naval bombardment to soften up the Japanese defenses. However, Admiral William H.P. "Spike" Blandy,

Below: A Marine lieutenant speaks into a microphone during one of many briefings that were held prior to the invasion of Iwo Jima. A map of the island, shaped like a pork chop, has been posted to the officer's right, and two of the island's airfields are clearly visible on it.

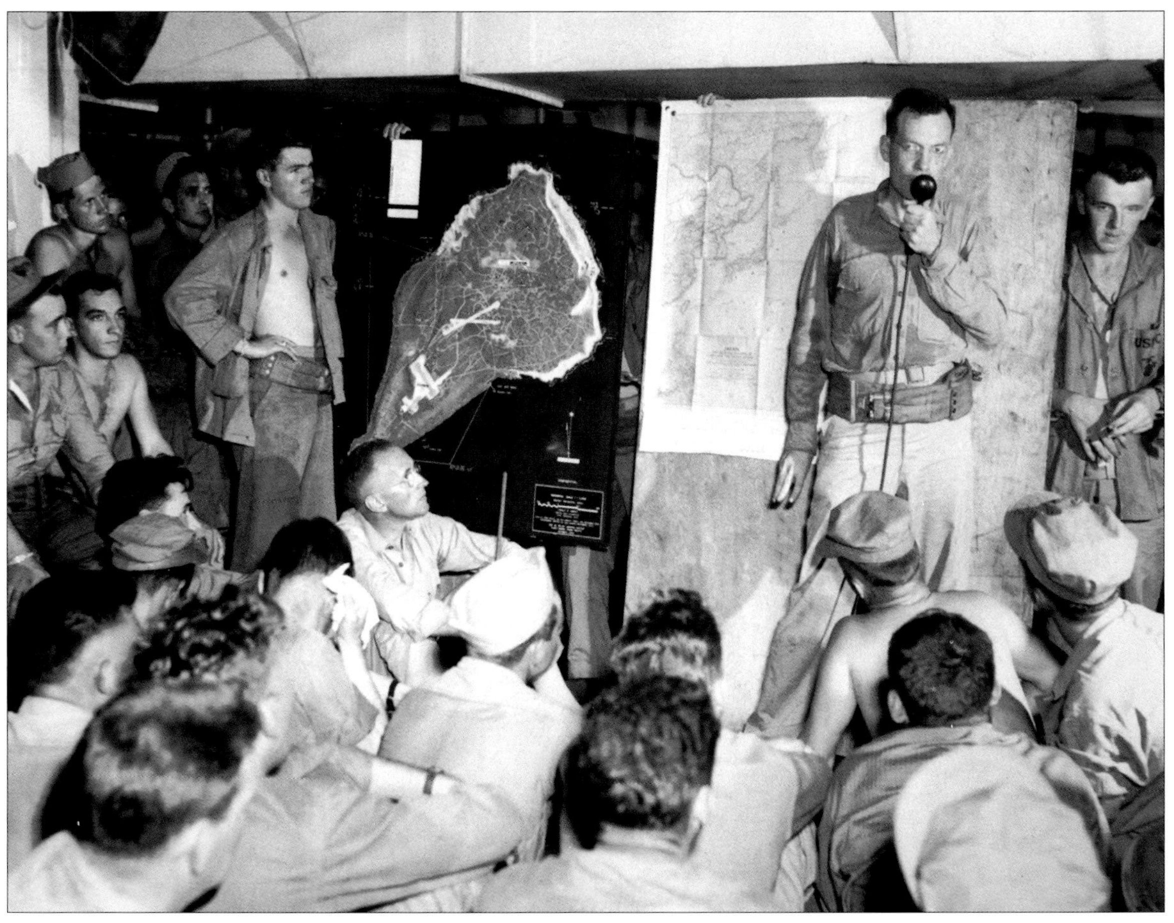

who commanded the amphibious support force and was responsible for the bombardment, demurred. Blandy argued that his ships could not replenish their stocks of heavy caliber ammunition with such a prolonged firing period. Schmidt countered with a request for a nine-day bombardment. Again, Blandy declined. To Schmidt's dismay, Blandy offered a three-day bombardment, and the V Amphibious Corps commander took what he could get. When Japanese guns began to pound the Marine riflemen on the beaches of Iwo Jima, several Marine officers blamed Blandy—at least partially—for the high casualties that resulted.

D-Day Assault

Before and during the landings, Marine and Navy aircraft roared above the disputed island to provide much-needed fire support. Accurate bombing and strafing forced the defenders to keep their heads low and to hunker in their caves and bunkers. On D-day, two Marine fighter

squadrons, VMF-124 and VMF-213, flying from the deck of the aircraft carrier USS *Essex*, put on a tremendous show for the men below.

Under the command of Lieutenant Colonel William A. Millington, the gull-winged Vought F4U Corsairs hit visible Japanese positions hard. The expeditionary force's air officer, Colonel Vernon E. Megee, had told Millington that the sight of his Marine fighters would hearten the riflemen on the ground. "Drag your bellies on the beach", he said. The Marine pilots gave a stellar effort, and Megee later noted that it was "... the first time a lot of them [riflemen] had ever seen a Marine fighter plane."

At 6.45 a.m. on February 19, Admiral Turner barked the order, "Land the landing force!" The naval guns thundered, followed by the air attacks. In half an hour, the LVTs carrying the Marines of the first wave were crunching onto the shoreline. If anything, they were punctual, arriving within two minutes of H-hour, the exact time prescribed.

One Japanese observer noted that the Marines hit the beaches like a tidal wave, swarming ashore. However, most of the enemy gunners did not open fire. They had been instructed to wait until the beaches were literally choked with men and materiel. That order had come from Lieutenant General Tadamichi Kuribayashi, the commander of all Japanese forces on Iwo Jima.

With the loss of the Marianas, the Japanese high command correctly deduced that Iwo Jima would be the next island the Americans would assault. Although only 1500 troops garrisoned the island early in 1944, the defending force was rapidly augmented while a near-frantic and ambitious construction initiative was undertaken. Iwo Jima was honeycombed with tunnels. Cave entrances were fortified. Machine-gun nests and artillery emplacements were positioned with interlocking fields of fire. Spider holes, large enough for only a single soldier, were dug into the volcanic terrain. The Japanese constructed pillboxes and bunkers that were reinforced with steel, concrete, and heaps of sand to absorb the shockwaves of plunging naval fire.

Kuribayashi embraced the concept of defense in depth as employed at Peleliu. He planned to

Left: Marines of the 4th Division were among the first to hit the beach at Iwo Jima. This image captures landing craft carrying some of the division's riflemen toward the shore. In the distance, warships of the U.S. Navy's bombardment force may be seen as they acquire targets for thousands of heavy caliber shells that pounded the island prior to the landings.

fortify and defend the interior of the island and Mount Suribachi, exacting a heavy toll in casualties and possibly discouraging the Americans from continuing the fight for Iwo Jima, let alone mounting an invasion of the Home Islands. He exhorted his troops to stand fast and to take 10 American lives for every Japanese soldier killed in the desperate fight to come.

While the Japanese waited, the greatest initial opposition to the Marine landings came from the crashing surf and the loose volcanic sand. Landing craft were pushed about like tub toys, and their instability caused delays in debarking riflemen and equipment. Both wheeled and tracked vehicles became mired up to their wheel wells and bogeys in the dark grit of the beaches. Individual riflemen struggled to maintain their footing.

Nevertheless, more than 5000 Marines were ashore in a few minutes and moving inland. In an hour-and-a-half, the 28th Marines had covered the 2100ft (640m) to the far shore, taking increasing casualties along the way. The 27th Marines moved steadily to the fringe of Airfield No.1 by noon. Coming off the Yellow Beaches, the 23rd Marines was held up by a pair of pillboxes during its advance toward the

eastern edge of the airfield. No armored support was forthcoming due to the traffic jam at the shoreline, but the 23rd Marines slugged away.

Led by Lieutenant Colonel Justice M. Chambers, the 3rd Battalion, 25th Marines, was hit hard by enemy fire as it attempted to move up the sloping Blue beaches toward the Rock Quarry. "The fire from automatic weapons was coming from all over", he recalled. "You could've held up a cigarette and lit it on the stuff going by. I knew immediately we were in for one hell of a time."

Nearby, the 1st Battalion, 25th Marines had its own trouble with the terrain and increasing Japanese small-arms fire, managing about 900ft (274m) in 30 minutes of heavy fighting.

From his command post near the center of the island, Kuribayashi watched the drama unfold. Just before 10.00 a.m. he passed the order to unleash a shattering barrage of artillery, mortar, and machine-gun fire on the invasion beaches clogged with Marines and their machines. The

Below: Combat veterans of the 4th Marine Division negotiate the black volcanic sand of Iwo Jima as they exit landing craft. The loose sand proved a formidable obstacle for individual Marines who lost their footing, and for armored and wheeled vehicles that were unable to gain traction.

Japanese troops that survived the pre-invasion bombardment and the aerial assault that followed had drilled continually in the efficient operation of their weapons. Every corner of the invasion beaches was pre-registered, zeroed in for this moment. The defenders unmasked barrels, loaded, and fired.

Veteran Marines remember the ensuing rain of shells as the most intense they ever experienced. Shells burst along the length of the 1.7 mile (2.7km) beachhead. One Marine officer said, "It was one of the worst bloodlettings of the war. They rolled those artillery barrages up and down the beach. I just didn't see how anybody could live through such heavy fire barrages."

For an hour, the Marines on the beaches were pummeled. However, as they were pinpointed a number of the Japanese positions were silenced by naval gunfire and planes that strafed and dropped bombs and napalm canisters. Despite the severe battering, the Marines were resolute.

"Greatest Possible Violence"

Correspondent Robert Sherrod, who covered the Pacific War for *Time* and *Life* magazines, had witnessed the carnage at Tarawa 15 months earlier. When he came ashore at Iwo Jima on the afternoon of D-day, he observed, "Whether the dead were Japs or Americans, they had one thing in common. They had died with the greatest possible violence. Nowhere in the Pacific War had I seen such badly mangled bodies. Many were cut squarely in half. Legs and arms lay 50 feet from the nearest cluster of dead."

The difficult first day on Iwo Jima left 2400 Marines killed or wounded—35 more murderous days were to follow before the island was declared secure. Among those killed early in the action was Gunnery Sergeant John Basilone, a recipient of the Medal of Honor for his heroism on Guadalcanal. While leading a machine-gun platoon of the 1st Battalion, 27th Marines, in an attack on the edge of Motoyama Airfield No.1, Basilone was fatally wounded by an exploding mortar round. Although he had been given ample opportunity to avoid further combat after Guadalcanal, Basilone had declined, saying: "I'm staying with my boys!"

Both Generals Cates and Rockey had fully committed their division reserves, the 24th and 26th Marines respectively, by evening on the 19th, and the cliffs surrounding the Rock Quarry were in the hands of the 3rd Battalion, 25th Marines, which lost 22 officers and 500 riflemen in the day-long fight. After dark, Kuribayashi dispatched teams of infiltrators to harass the Marines, many of whom expected a banzai charge that never came. Intermittent fire from Mount Suribachi was unsettling, and a direct hit on a foxhole killed Lieutenant Colonel Ralph Haas of the 1st Battalion, 23rd Marines.

Rain began to fall on February 20, and bad weather disrupted attempts to land artillery, armor, and additional troops. Schmidt's plan to bring the 21st Marines from the 3rd Marine Division ashore was thwarted, but early that morning those Marines that were ashore took up the arduous task of battle again. The waterlogged 21st Marines came in on February 21 to relieve the 23rd Marines, who had paid a high price to secure Motoyama Airfield No.1. The 26th and 27th Marines had occupied the west side of the airfield, while the 23rd finished the job by covering 2400ft (732m) from the east under murderous fire.

Fighting raged around the rim of the Rock Quarry. On the 22nd, Lieutenant Colonel Chambers took a Japanese bullet in the chest while urging his 3rd Battalion, 25th Marines, forward. When Chambers was shot, all three battalion commanders of the 25th Marines had been wounded before the Rock Quarry was taken. He survived to receive the Medal of Honor.

Assault on Mount Suribachi

The 28th Marines, commanded by Colonel Harry B. Liversedge, prepared to renew its

mission to take Mount Suribachi and dislodge the 2000 enemy soldiers who inhabited a maze of interconnected tunnels, caves, and strongpoints along the high ground. Nicknamed "Harry the Horse", Liversedge was well aware that his Marines had lost 400 casualties on the first day of fighting; however, the 1st and 2nd Battalions had reached the base of the mountain. While the 3rd Battalion successfully battered its way to the foot of Suribachi on the 20th, the 1st and 2nd Battalions slipped around the flanks in an attempt to surround it and then dig in.

Just to reach the positions they occupied, the 28th Marines were obliged to neutralize as many as 70 concrete blockhouses and pillboxes that dotted the base of Suribachi. At least another 50 strongpoints were positioned to open fire at them during the first 100ft (30m) of their ascent.

Above: Riflemen of the 5th Marine Division negotiate a slope just off Red Beach 1 at Iwo Jima in preparation for their movement toward Mount Suribachi, the extinct volcano at the southwestern end of the island that commanded the invasion beaches.

Nevertheless, on the third day of the battle Harry Liversedge's Marines were ready to directly assault Mount Suribachi.

The 28th Marines moved out. Naval gunfire and 105mm artillery assisted the 1st Battalion in its ascent along the west face, but the fighting was savage. Marines placed covering fire on the mouths of caves while intrepid comrades rushed forward and threw satchel charges inside or flipped grenades into gun ports. The Japanese were blasted from concealed positions or sealed inside.

Acclaimed author Richard Wheeler, a corporal in the 1st Squad, 3rd Platoon, 2nd Battalion, was

Above: Marines man an M1917 Browning machine gun somewhere near the foot of Mount Surabachi, providing fire support for the Marines' assault of the mountain.

wounded during the fighting around the base of Suribachi and remembered what it was like to scale the heights in the face of fanatical resistance. "It was terrible, the worst I can remember us taking", he recalled. "The Japanese mortarmen seemed to be playing checkers and using us as squares."

Wheeler wrote two books on his experience at Iwo Jima, *Iwo* and *The Bloody Battle for Suribachi*. He recalled seeing one Marine engaged in a fight to the death on the mountainside. "Hand-to-hand fighting sometimes resulted when enemy soldiers would suddenly dart from cover to attack or make a break for the safety of more remote defenses. There were a number of bayonetings and knife killings. One Marine, attacked by a saber-swinging Japanese officer, caught the blade with his bare hands, wrested it from the man and hacked him to death with it. I saw this Marine later when he was brought aboard the hospital ship I occupied a mile or two offshore. He stopped by my bunk and told me his story. Both his hands were badly gashed and were swathed in bandages—but he still had the Japanese sword."

The battle for Suribachi continued throughout the next day as the 28th Marines crawled upward yard by yard. At the end of the day, patrols from the 1st and 2nd Battalions reached the extreme southwestern tip of Iwo Jima at Tobiishi Point.

At 8.00 a.m. on the morning of February 23 (D+4), the 25 riflemen of the 3rd Platoon, Company E, 2nd Battalion, 28th Marines—along with a few replacements from other Company E outfits that raised their number to 40—moved out with orders to reach the summit of Suribachi.

Under the command of 1st Lieutenant Harold G. Schrier, the company executive officer, the Marines picked their way forward. Japanese snipers took shots at them, and individual enemy soldiers jumped up from spider holes. The Marines tossed grenades, fired into the mouths of caves, and cut down those enemy soldiers that lunged toward them.

Rifleman Harold Keller took the point and encountered the first enemy soldier. He remembered: "The Jap started to climb out of a deep hole, his back toward me. I fired three times from the hip, and he dropped out of sight."

Raising the Flag

Schrier's patrol, visible across the island and some distance out to sea as it snaked its way to the top of the mountain, had specific orders to raise the U.S. flag, in this case a small 54in by 28in (137cm by 71cm) example of Old Glory, from the summit. Marine photographer Louis R. Lowery recorded their progress, asking them to stop once and display the flag as he snapped the shutter of his camera. Once they fought their way to the crater, the Marines looked around for a suitable flagpole and found a length of pipe. It would do nicely. Schrier and three other Marines lashed the flag to the pipe. At approximately 10.30 a.m., the makeshift pole was planted and the small flag snapped in the breeze. The Marines below began to cheer, and whistles blew aboard ships.

General Holland Smith was escorting Secretary of the Navy James V. Forrestal, who had come to observe the operations. When the secretary saw the banner from a distance, he exclaimed: "The raising of that flag means a Marine Corps for another 500 years!"

Strangely, the Japanese clustered in caves and holes near the scene had remained quiet. One Marine even urinated into the crater to rouse their ire. Then, it broke. Bursts of rifle fire and a

Below: Riflemen of the 3rd Battalion, 28th Marines execute a direct frontal assault against a fortified Japanese position near Mount Suribachi. On February 23, 1945, a patrol from Company E, 2nd Battalion, 28th Marines reached the top of the mountain.

few grenades were heaved from hidden positions. A Japanese officer burst into the open wielding a sword that he had broken in half to limit its value to American souvenir hunters. One Marine stepped forward with a .45-caliber pistol and aimed at the crazed enemy officer. He pulled the trigger, and the weapon only clicked. He dove out of the way, and the Japanese officer was riddled by bullets from a dozen Marine rifles.

The dead officer had come from the entrance to a large cave, and the Marines went to work, first with grenades, then flamethrowers, and finally demolition charges to seal the multiple entrances to the substantial cave-tunnel complex shut. When the cave was reopened days later, the bodies of more than 150 enemy troops were discovered.

Below: Crouched low on the ground, two Marines unleash a sheet of flame against a Japanese bunker near the foot of Mount Suribachi.

About three hours after Schrier's patrol successfully completed its mission, Lieutenant Colonel Chandler Johnson, commander of the 2nd Battalion, 28th Marines, decided that the original flag was too small. A runner was sent to the beach to find a larger flag. He returned from the *LST-779* with a replacement that measured 8ft by 4ft 8in (2.4m by 1.4m). A second patrol set out to deliver the flag to the summit of Suribachi, and Associated Press photographer Joe Rosenthal decided to follow along.

When Rosenthal reached the crater, the raising of the second flag was already in progress. He tried not to obstruct the view of Marine William Genaust, filming away with a movie camera. "Hey Bill! There it goes!" he yelled.

"Out of the corner of my eye, I had seen the men start the flag up," Rosenthal remembered. "I swung my camera around and shot the scene. That is how the picture was taken, and when you

Iconic Photograph

While the names of the Marines who raised the first flag on Suribachi were relegated to the status of a historical footnote, those of the six men who raised the second flag became household words. Sergeant Michael Strank, Pharmacist's Mate 2nd Class John H. Bradley, Corporal Harlon H. Block, and Pfcs. Ira H. Hayes, Franklin R. Sousley, and Rene A. Gagnon will forever be remembered. Block, Sousley, and Strank did not survive the battle for Iwo Jima. Bradley, Gagnon, and Hayes became celebrities.

Since the enduring photograph captured the second flag raising, some observers declared that it had been staged. They were wrong. Rosenthal's film was flown to Guam and developed. Associated Press editor John Bodkin knew it was something special and blurted, "Here's one for all time!" He flashed the photo to the AP office in New York, and within 18 hours of the event it was in distribution.

Sculptor Felix de Weldon used Rosenthal's photograph as the model for the sculpture at the U.S. Marine War Memorial in Arlington National Cemetery, which was dedicated in 1954. The image has been reproduced on everything from postage stamps to coffee mugs and T-shirts. In 1999, a New York University survey named it number 68 on the list of the 100 best examples of journalism in the 20th century. It has become the symbol of the Marine Corps for all time.

Above: This historic image of the second flag raising on Mount Suribachi was taken by Associated Press photographer Joe Rosenthal, who later said that he snapped the defining moment somewhat by accident.

Joe Rosenthal, who died in 2006 at the age of 94, remembered the Marines and their great sacrifice as being much more significant than his photograph. He once said, "What I see behind the photo is what it took to get up those heights, the kind of devotion to their country that those young men had, and the sacrifices they made. I take some gratification in being a little part of what the U.S. stands for."

take a picture like that, you don't come away saying you got a great shot. You don't know."

Rosenthal captured on film a moment that defined the courage and fortitude of the U.S. Marine Corps and the will of a nation to see the war through to final victory. The image of five Marines and a Navy corpsman raising the flag is the most iconic symbol of the American fighting man in World War II. For the sake of history and for their valor, here are the names of the first group of flag raisers: 1st Lieutenant Schrier, Platoon Sergeant Ernest T. Thomas, Jr., Sergeant Henry O. Hansen, Corporal Charles W. Lindberg, and Pfcs. Louis C. Charlo and James Michels.

Although the moment of the flag raising had electrified the Marines on Iwo Jima and those within sight of it at sea, the Japanese were far from finished. The island would not be secured for another month.

Japanese Defensive Command

The fall of Suribachi was a serious blow to Kuribayashi's scheme of defense in depth. Still, he took cold comfort in the performance of his command, particularly the skillful handling of his artillery by Colonel Chosaku Kaido, whose prominent blockhouse on the flat Motoyama Plateau, an area the Marines nicknamed the Turkey Knob, seemed impregnable to American fire. Marines came to grudgingly respect the fighting prowess of the Japanese soldier on Iwo Jima, and most agreed that Kuribayashi, who they were unaware was even on the island until intelligence confirmed his presence on February 27, was the best defensive commander they faced in the Pacific.

General Schmidt's plan for the conquest of northern Iwo Jima was straightforward. Three Marine regiments—the 26th on the left, 21st in the center, and 24th on the right flank—were to advance with the combined support of the armored formations that had been assigned to all three Marine divisions. Colonel William R. "Rip" Collins commanded the largest concentration of tanks in the Pacific War. About 150 medium M4A2 and M4A3 Shermans were armed with 75mm guns, and some were modified to carry the Mark I flamethrower and assigned to the 4th and 5th Tank Battalions. Earlier versions, equipped with the E4-5 mechanized flamethrower mounted in the bow in the former position of the .30-caliber hull machine gun, were assigned to the 3rd Tank Battalion.

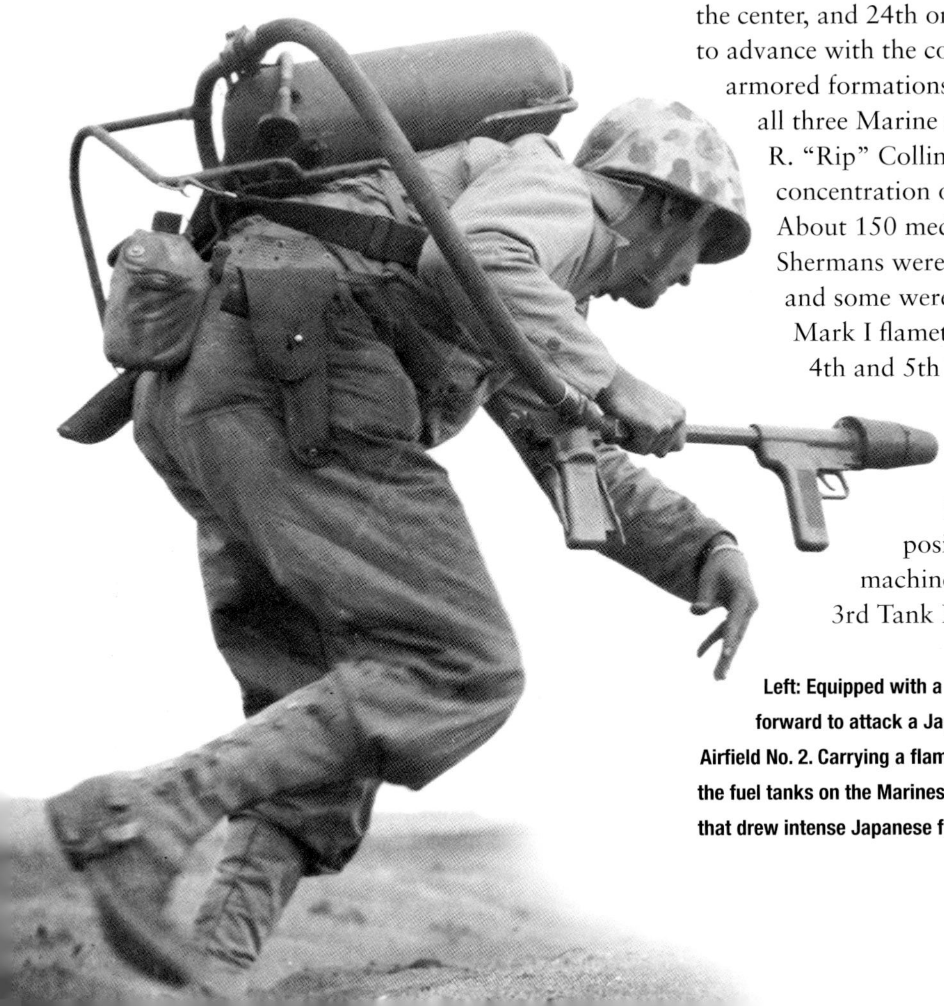

Left: Equipped with a flamethrower, a Marine rushes forward to attack a Japanese pillbox near Motoyama Airfield No. 2. Carrying a flamethrower was hazardous duty, as the fuel tanks on the Marines' backs were conspicuous targets that drew intense Japanese fire.

Above: A Marine observer in a forward position on Iwo Jima pinpoints the location of a Japanese machine-gun nest. Within minutes, the map coordinates were relayed to artillery positions to the rear, and shells began to plummet onto the enemy strongpoint.

Nicknamed Zippos or Ronsons after popular cigarette lighters of the day, the flamethrower Shermans were often the best weapons available to combat Japanese strongpoints. They were capable of spewing a napalm jet of flame up to 450ft (137m) for more than a minute. Japanese soldiers were either burned to death or suffocated as the flame consumed the available oxygen in the confined space.

Schmidt's northward thrust began on February 24, and the enemy's main defensive line awaited. Motoyama Airfield No.2, an early objective, proved a killing ground. Open areas around the runways allowed the Japanese machine-gunners excellent fields of fire. The superb enemy 47mm anti-tank guns were well concealed and took their toll on the Marine tanks. Everywhere the coordinated Marine offensive broke down into individual and squad size actions. Lieutenant Colonel Alexander A. Vandegrift, Jr., the son of General Vandegrift who had won the victory at Guadalcanal and then been elevated to Commandant of the Marine Corps, was wounded and relinquished command of the 3rd Battalion, 24th Marines, to Major Doyle Stout.

On the same day, General Schmidt moved his headquarters to Iwo Jima from a command ship offshore, and General Erskine, commander of the 3rd Marine Division, came ashore along with the 9th Marines, under the command of Colonel Howard N. Kenyon. During the next several days, the 3rd Division's 12th Artillery continued to land, joining the 13th and 14th Artillery Regiments of the 5th and 4th Marine Divisions on the island. The last major infantry reserve was the 3rd Marines, under the command of Holland Smith at the expeditionary force level, and Schmidt made the first of several requests for the unit's release, but these troops were never committed despite the need for reinforcements. Eventually, in a controversial move, Holland Smith ordered the 3rd Marines to retire to Guam.

For more than a week, the Marines struggled to take control of Motoyama Airfield No.2 and the series of hills and ridges to the north. Fire support was problematic as the Marine artillery was often too light to deal with the well-entrenched Japanese, their concrete fortifications with walls so thick that they were impervious to shellfire. At times the locations of Japanese strongpoints prevented the fire of cruisers and destroyers offshore from being truly productive. Positioned in ravines and on the reverse slopes of hills and ridges, they were shielded from the plunging fire. Complaints emerged concerning the availability and quantity of naval air support, but the situation was temporary. Soon, the Marine commanders were satisfied with its volume and accuracy.

When elements of the 3rd, 4th, and 5th Marine Divisions turned north to assault Motoyama Airfield No.2, they were also well aware that their next objectives would include the high ground that lay beyond. During 10 days of heavy fighting, the Marines advanced about 2.27 miles (3.66km) and absorbed a staggering 7000 killed and wounded.

Elements of the 26th, 27th, and 28th Marines fought for several days to occupy Nishi Ridge and then secure Hill 362-A, where the 28th took 200 casualties before the job was finished. On February 27, the 1st Battalion, 27th Marines, advanced on the high ground and ran into a complex of Japanese pillboxes spewing machine-gun fire. A halftrack mounting a 75mm gun was called up to blast several of the pillboxes in succession.

Individual Marines with flamethrowers and satchel charges were obliged to take care of the rest, and one of these was 1st Lieutenant Clair Voss, whose 1st Platoon, Company A, pushed ahead to a small knoll and was raked by Japanese fire from several directions. Voss gathered hand grenades and demolition charges and managed to work his way to one of the pillboxes. He tossed a grenade into a firing slit, and the machine guns stopped. Then, knowing that Japanese soldiers were still inside, he climbed atop the concrete fortification and placed a charge that wrecked the structure with the ensuing explosion.

Voss was wounded but survived, and received the Navy Cross for his effort. Eight Marines of Company A were killed and 50 wounded on the hill. By March 3, the 5th Marine Division had been in combat for 12 days and taken horrific casualties—1000 dead, 349 wounded, and 49 missing.

Left: This Marine is typical of the fighting men who battled the Japanese on Iwo Jima for more than a month. His M1 rifle is slung around his shoulder, while his canteen and ammunition belt are clearly visible.

On the same date, the 26th Marines captured Hill 362-B on the left flank as Company F of its 2nd Battalion took the brunt of the casualties with 47 killed or wounded, including the last of the platoon commanders who had landed with the 2nd Battalion on February 19. Some units advanced as far as 1800ft (549m) to take the hill, and during the night more than 100 Japanese infiltrators were killed as they approached the new Marine positions. The 26th Marines suffered 500 casualties in the fight from dawn to dusk at Hill 362-B, and five Medals of Honor were earned in a single day on the embattled island.

The Meat Grinder

Across Iwo Jima, the deadly Japanese concentrations of troops and firepower received colorful nicknames. While the 3rd Battalion, 25th Marines, fought at the Rock Quarry, the 28th Marines pushed through a contested area at the base of Mount Suribachi that they dubbed the Jungle of Stone. Now, in front of three Marine divisions that were already depleted, rose several prominent terrain features that would live as infamous reminders of the blood and death at Iwo Jima. The defenses in the north of the island were formidable, including Hill 382, the Amphitheater, Turkey Knob, and the small village of Minami, which had been ravaged by naval and aerial bombardment. Collectively, these mutually supporting Japanese strongpoints were referred to as the Meat Grinder.

During the first week of March, the Marines had breached Kuribayashi's main line of defense. However, the price had been high. Among the dead was Lieutenant Colonel Chandler Johnson, whose 28th Marines had secured Mount Suribachi a few days earlier. On March 5, the 1st Battalion, 27th Marines, lost its commander when Lieutenant Colonel John Butler's jeep took a direct hit from a Japanese 47mm anti-tank shell.

Despite grievous losses, the Marines were making painful gains on Iwo Jima. Kuribayashi acknowledged the situation by relocating his command post from the compromised center of Iwo Jima to the north, where his troops would continue to resist to the last man.

The 26th Marines suffered 500 casualties in the fight to capture Hill 362-B, and five Medals of Honor were earned in a single day.

From February 26–28, the 23rd Marines fought to capture Hill 382, a steep warren of machine-gun nests, bunkers, and pillboxes, along with a bombed-out Japanese radar station on its crest that had been repurposed as a strongpoint with artillery and small arms in abundance. Japanese tanks were pulled into crevices that obscured them from vision and played their 47mm guns along the avenues of approach. As they had done elsewhere on Iwo Jima, the Japanese had burrowed a maze of interconnecting tunnels and gun emplacements into the hill.

On March 1, the 2nd Battalion, 24th Marines, relieved the 1st Battalion, 23rd Marines, in the battle for Hill 382, and by the afternoon of the following day the Americans had finally claimed the summit and prepared to turn toward the northwest to renew the advance against the enemy beyond the high ground. However, the 2nd Battalion was in need of rest and replacements as Company E had lost four company commanders in a brief but deadly timeframe. Still, the 4th Marine Division pressed forward against the elevation of Turkey Knob.

The high ground of Turkey Knob rose 1800ft (549m) south of Hill 382, and the Japanese had fortified it with an observation post and communications center ringed by machine-gun and mortar positions. Down the slope of Turkey Knob, the ground formed a natural bowl—hence the nickname of the Amphitheater. The Japanese recognized the potential for defense in the area and built three concentric defensive rings on the southern slope of Turkey Knob, including reinforced bunkers and anti-tank and machine-gun emplacements. Their lethal weapons easily swept the open ground before them.

While fighting raged around Hill 382, the 4th Marine Division continued to batter away at the Amphitheater. By the end of February, the 23rd and 25th Marines had reached the hills north and south of the Amphitheater and were in position to outflank the deadly bowl and Turkey Knob as well. In a single day flamethrower tanks spewed 1000 gallons (3785l) of fuel against enemy strongpoints, and on March 2, the Marine pincers reached to within 195ft (59m) of each other in an attempt to close the ring before a torrent of Japanese artillery shells forced the riflemen to withdraw.

Four days of heavy fighting did significantly weaken the defenses of the Amphitheater and Turkey Knob, where machine guns continued to rattle from the massive communications bunker despite heavy bombardment and direct assaults that were stymied. Nearly two weeks of heavy fighting were ultimately required before the 4th Marine Division subdued the salient formed by the double envelopment around the two centers of resistance. At the same time, the division made progress on both flanks.

Banzai Charge

To the Japanese, it was clear that with every day their grip on the Amphitheater and Turkey Knob were slipping, and on the evening of March 8 the local commanders abandoned the concept of defense in depth. Pulling out of their prepared defenses, the Japanese staged an improvised attack that included an old-style banzai charge and some stealth and deception as well. While many of the enemy soldiers screamed and charged, others used the terrain to creep toward the seam between the 23rd and 24th Marines. Some Japanese soldiers even dragged stretchers and yelled "Corpsman!" in an attempt to infiltrate the Marine line.

A mortar and artillery barrage preceded the attack, which was chewed up, leaving 650 dead Japanese soldiers littering the ground. The futile enemy assault simply broke the back of the Japanese defenses in the area, and the 4th Marine Division was able to reach the east coast of Iwo Jima within 48 hours.

As evening fell on March 10, the 4th Division's right flank had advanced about 3000ft (914m) with the 2nd and 3rd Battalions, 25th Marines, and the 2nd Battalion, 24th Marines, serving as a hinge for the closing of a great door. The remainder of the division, including the 1st and 3rd Battalions, 25th Marines, the 1st and 3rd Battalions, 24th Marines, and the 2nd Battalion, 23rd Marines, had fought their way northeast, east, and then southeast, squeezing the Japanese into a perimeter that was ever closer to the beach.

In the process, the Marines had fought through and around heavily defended hills and then the formidable defenses at Hill 382, the Amphitheater, Turkey Knob, and Minami village while pushing against the strong defenses northeast of Hill 382 quite nearly to the ocean. After days of hard fighting, General Cates formed a provisional battalion within the 4th Marine Division and charged its commander, Lieutenant Colonel Melvin Krulewitch, with cleaning out Japanese strongpoints that had been bypassed. The term "mopping up" hardly describes the severity of the combat that remained.

The general Marine advance northward on Iwo Jima gained impetus during the first week of March. The 3rd Marine Division battled in the center at Hills Peter and 199-Oboe and then moved on to Motoyama village, Hill 362-C, and a rock-strewn area that came to be known as Cushman's Pocket.

On March 2, east of Motoyama Airfield No.3, Lieutenant Colonel Robert E. Cushman and the

2nd Battalion, 9th Marines, got into a brawl with diehard Japanese forces, primarily of the 26th Tank Regiment. The Marines encircled the enemy stronghold, and after two weeks of brutal combat the area was clear of Japanese. Two of Cushman's companies, E and F, were decimated in the fighting, with only 10 survivors between them.

"The enemy position was a maze of caves, pillboxes, emplaced tanks, stone walls, and trenches", Cushman remembered. "We beat against this position for eight continuous days, using every supporting weapon. The core—main objective of the sector—still remained. The battalion was exhausted. Almost all leaders were gone and the battalion numbered about 400, including 350 replacements."

The 2nd Battalion, 21st Marines, hit Hill 362-C, located beyond Motoyama Airfield No.3, on March 6 in a resumption of five frustrating days of combat that had yielded little or no gain. It was another day of agonizingly slow progress as naval gunfire and artillery barrages failed to loosen the Japanese hold. Company G reached the top of neighboring Hill 357, but lost contact with the unit on its flank and was compelled to pull back. A company of Sherman tanks came to grief in the effort as two were disabled by mines and a third was hit by 47mm anti-tank fire, leaving three tankers dead and three wounded.

Below: Marine artillerymen pound distant targets on the island of Iwo Jima. These gunners of the 4th Marine Division worked closely with forward observers and showered Japanese positions with 105mm shells.

Finally, just after 2.00 p.m. on March 7, Company K, 3rd Battalion, 9th Marines, seized Hill 362-C, fulfilling its mission in an attack that had begun before daylight and with no initial artillery preparation in order to avoid tipping off the enemy defenders that another assault was underway.

Before dawn, as Company K Marines were clearing what they initially believed to be Hill 362-C, it was discovered that they were actually occupying Hill 331. Their objective for the day remained 750ft (229m) distant. The direction of the attack, however, was correct. As the sun rose, the Marines advanced at 7.15 a.m., following a 10-minute artillery barrage. Now alert, the Japanese poured fire into the Marines from their front and flanks, but the attack succeeded. The change of tactics to a predawn jump-off had provided a needed edge, and the Marines advanced more than 1200ft (366m).

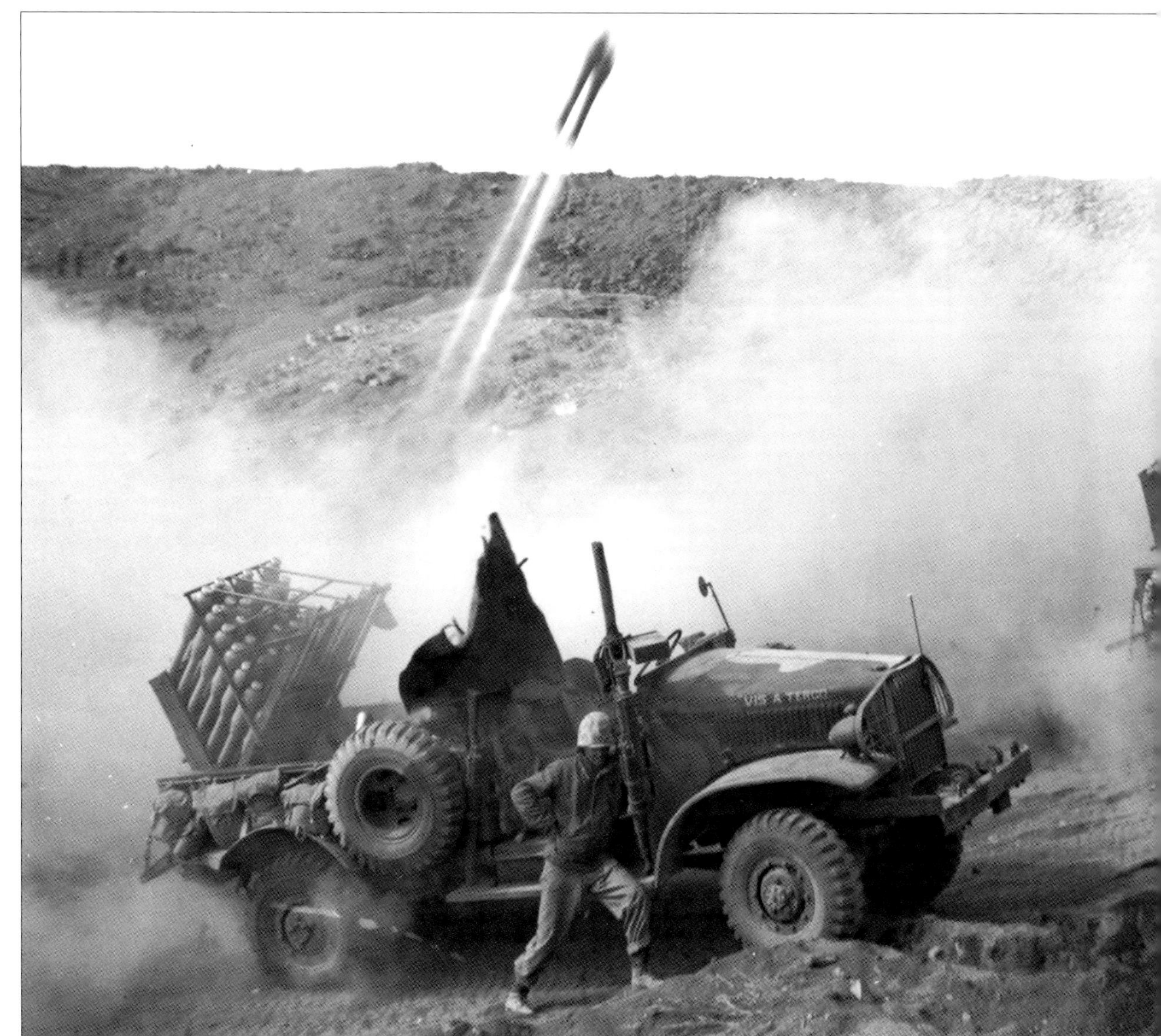

Lieutenant Colonel Harold C. Boehm, commander of the 3rd Battalion, 9th Marines, observed: "Most notable in the night attack was the fact that, although nearly all the basic dope was bad, the strategy proved very sound, since it turned out that the open ground taken under cover of darkness was the most heavily fortified of all terrain captured that day, and the enemy occupying this vital ground were taken completely by surprise (actually sleeping in their pillboxes and caves) ... It should be kept in mind, however, that a stroke of luck went a long way toward making the attack a success."

For three more days, the 3rd Marine Division fought to reach the northeastern beaches on Iwo Jima. Supported by naval gunfire and advancing across broken terrain, the Marines encountered resistance that was substantial at first, and then began to ebb. Elements of Company A, 1st Battalion, 21st Marines, reached the coast on March 10 and filled a canteen full of seawater, promptly sending it back to V Amphibious Corps headquarters with a note attached that read: "For inspection, not consumption".

That evening, General Erskine was able to report that organized resistance had ended in the 3rd Marine Division zone of operations. Scattered Japanese resistance, particularly along the cliffs overlooking the beach, continued for more than a week, and mopping-up operations were hotly contested at times.

During its two-week drive through the interior of Iwo Jima and then to the coast, the 3rd Marine Division lost 3563 casualties, including 827 dead and 2241 wounded.

Final Push

After the capture of Hill 362-B, the 5th Marine Division continued to advance to the north and east, eventually pushing the Japanese defenders into an area around Kitano Point in the extreme north. The division's final push on Iwo Jima began on March 11. Artillery and naval guns barked for nearly an hour, but the going was still rough for the two battalions in the lead. On March 14 and 15, the Marines gained roughly 3000ft (914m), and then on the 16th the 21st Marines, fresh out of a job in their previous location, came alongside the 26th Marines to grind out another 1200ft (366m).

Left: Fitted to light trucks, Marine launchers shoot a fusillade of rockets toward Japanese positions on Iwo Jima.

Marines struggle to unload ammunition and supplies that have been delivered along with vehicles to the beaches at Iwo Jima. The rough surf complicated logistical movement across the island, and as supplies began to arrive the invasion beaches were already choked with wrecked vehicles and debris.

201

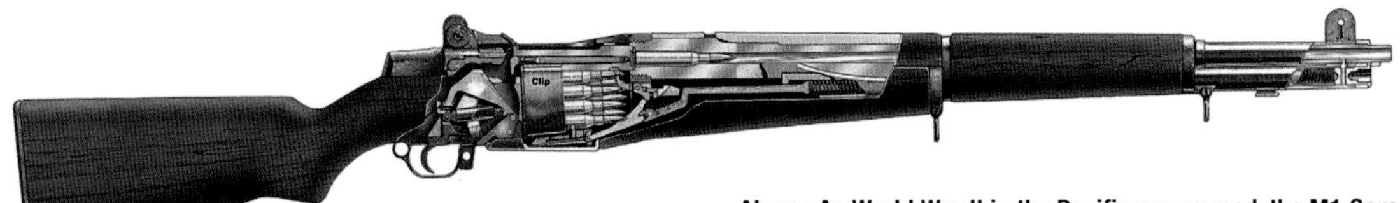

Above: As World War II in the Pacific progressed, the M1 Garand rifle became standard issue for the Marines. The semi-automatic M1 replaced the Springfield Model 1903 bolt-action rifle and proved to be one of the finest infantry weapons of the war. It fired the .30-06 Springfield round from an internal magazine fed by an eight-round clip.

During the heavy fighting on March 13, the 1st Battalion, 27th Marines, drove forward 900ft (274m), but was stopped cold by enemy fire coming from a draw in its immediate front. The battalion settled in for the night, but shortly after dark one of the few remaining heavy guns the Japanese had on Iwo Jima began to pound the Marines in their foxholes. The Japanese had previously abandoned the 8-inch gun, but crept back to open fire.

Carrying a bazooka, Pfc. Donald Schmille set out to silence the enemy weapon. When the Japanese soldiers saw movement, they opened up with rifles, machine guns, and a fusillade of hand grenades. Schmille was undeterred. When he reached an adequate vantage point, he stood up to acquire his target and blasted the position. Schmille undoubtedly saved many Marine lives. He was later awarded the Navy Cross.

By March 19, the 27th and 28th Marines had reached a reached a treacherous 2100ft (640m) box canyon on the northwest coast of Iwo Jima. The terrain was interspersed with crevices, draws, and jumbled rocky outcroppings. The Marines referred to it simply as the Gorge or Death Valley. It took more than a week of fighting to subdue the 500 Japanese troops holed up in the Gorge. M4 Sherman tanks equipped with bulldozer blades cut roads into the contested area, and tanks and halftracks leveled their 75mm guns at Japanese emplacements from point-blank range.

On March 20, Pfc. Daniel Albaugh of Company A, 1st Battalion, 27th Marines, earned a Navy Cross. When a Japanese pillbox blocked the advance of Albaugh's company and there was no way to flank it, he stepped directly in front of the enemy position and pumped three bazooka rounds into the structure before he was cut down. Enemy resistance in the Gorge finally came to a violent end on March 25, the 35th day of battle for Iwo Jima, as the 21st Marines defeated the last of the Japanese resistance in 12 hours of combat.

Demand for Surrender

For the Japanese, communications were a shambles. Kuribayashi was eventually able to exert command of only those troops within a few hundred yards of his command post. As the Marines closed in on the remaining enemy troop concentrations, surrender appeals were broadcast in Japanese. Two prisoners of war were actually given a message asking for surrender. They dutifully delivered it to Kuribayashi's headquarters and were allowed to return to the American lines.

Kuribayashi, though, was prepared to die. Although his actual fate is unclear, it is believed that he committed suicide on the night of March 25. Some accounts, however, suggest that he died leading a final, desperate attack by 300 soldiers against Marines of the 5th Pioneer Battalion and the 8th Field Depot along with personnel of the U.S. Army Air Forces VII Fighter Command positioned near Motoyama Airfield No.2.

Although the Japanese inflicted serious casualties, killing 100 Army pilots and Marines and wounding another 200, the attackers who survived to see the sunrise were systematically hunted down and wiped out. The Marines counted 223 dead Japanese soldiers when the melee was over.

Whatever his fate, Kuribayashi was resolute to the end and is remembered as the most formidable commander the Marines faced during their long, arduous trek across the Pacific. He may not have lived long enough to receive the news from Imperial Headquarters that he had been promoted to the rank of full general. On the night of March 25, he sent Tokyo one final forlorn communiqué: "We have not eaten or drunk for five days", it read, "but our fighting spirit is still running high. We are going to fight bravely to the last."

Below: This aerial view of Iwo Jima was taken after the island was declared secure in late March 1945. Mount Suribachi looms in the background. Iwo Jima provided a haven for thousands of crippled U.S. bombers returning from raids against the Japanese Home Islands.

The following day, although scattered pockets of resistance were still active across the island, Iwo Jima was declared secure.

As American military power crept closer to the Home Islands of Japan, one more great battle lay ahead. In less than a week, the III Amphibious Corps would assault Okinawa.

In total, 27 Medals of Honor were presented for gallantry above and beyond the call of duty at Iwo Jima—22 of these went to Marines, four to Navy Corpsmen, and one to the commander of a Navy landing craft. Of these, 14 Medals were posthumous, and more than one quarter of the 80 Medals of Honor awarded to Marines during World War II were earned at Iwo Jima. Summarizing the character of the great battle, Admiral Nimitz declared: "On Iwo island, uncommon valor was a common virtue."

Perhaps Nimitz came nearest to capturing the essence of Marine bravery and sacrifice at Iwo Jima, but even these stirring words resonate as something of an understatement.

CHAPTER 8

OKINAWA: TYPHOON OF STEEL

Only 340 miles (211km) from Japan's Home Island of Kyushu, Okinawa in the Ryukyu archipelago was the last objective of the American military surge across the Pacific during World War II—short of an invasion of Japan itself.

During four years of war, the U.S. Marine Corps had grown and developed into a massive, battle-hardened fighting force schooled in the art of amphibious warfare and tempered in the crucible of savage combat. Bitter fighting from Guadalcanal to Iwo Jima had served as proving grounds for landing operations on contested beaches, the improvement of air and naval fire support, supply and logistics enhancements, and coordination of tactical elements in the field.

Still, in several ways, the looming battle for Okinawa would provide the sternest test of the war for the Marines of the III Amphibious Corps and the XXIV Corps of the U.S. Army, which together comprised the Tenth Army under the unified command of Lieutenant General Simon Bolivar Buckner, a veteran Army officer and the son of a Confederate general who had fought in the American Civil War.

Opposite: A Marine springs to his feet to cross open ground on Okinawa. The Japanese made their defensive stand on the southern end of the island, fortifying hills, ridgelines, and draws with guns and automatic weapons with interlocking fields of fire.

By the spring of 1945, senior U.S. commanders were well aware of the ferocity of the Japanese defenders they had subdued across the expanse of the Pacific, and they were resigned to the belief that the bloodletting would continue until American fighting men occupied the Imperial Palace in Tokyo. Okinawa was simply another stepping stone to the invasion of Japan. Its harbors, airfields, and proximity to Kyushu would facilitate future operations.

At the direction of the Joint Chiefs of Staff, Admiral Chester Nimitz was charged with the seizure of Okinawa, and once again the Commander-in-Chief Pacific turned to the familiar team that included Admiral Raymond Spruance, commander of the Fifth Fleet, Admiral Richmond Kelly Turner, commander of the amphibious forces in the Pacific, and a cadre of planners who, by this time, knew their jobs in detail.

Operation Iceberg

Planning for the capture of Okinawa, codenamed Operation Iceberg, began in the autumn of 1944, and Love-Day (L-Day), so named to avoid confusion with the D-Day landings of Operation Overlord that had taken place in Western Europe on June 6, 1944, was set for April 1, 1945. The U.S. and British Royal navies marshaled 1300 warships, and supply and transport vessels of every description for Operation Iceberg, and 750,000 tons of supplies were available to sustain an anticipated lengthy campaign. The naval assemblage and troop buildup were actually larger those of Operation Overlord and the D-Day landings the previous year. Most who took note of the projected Okinawa invasion date were struck by the calendar's coincidental occurrence of Easter Sunday and April Fools' Day.

Below: The American assault on Okinawa was the largest amphibious assault of the Pacific War, involving up to a quarter of a million U.S. combat troops.

Buckner's powerful Tenth Army was comprised of more than 180,000 Marine and Army fighting men, and the commanding general took great pains to be inclusive with his staff structure. Among the 34 Marine staff officers of the Tenth Army that he brought to the shores of Okinawa was Deputy Chief of Staff Brigadier General Oliver P. Smith.

The III Amphibious Corps was led by Marine Major General Roy S. Geiger, an aviator who had commanded the 1st Marine Aircraft Wing at Guadalcanal, and included the veteran 1st Marine Division, known as the Old Breed, the fresh 6th Marine Division, and the 2nd Marine Division that would act as a reserve in the coming operation. Under the command of Major General John R. Hodge, the XXIV Army Corps included the 7th, 77th, and 96th Infantry

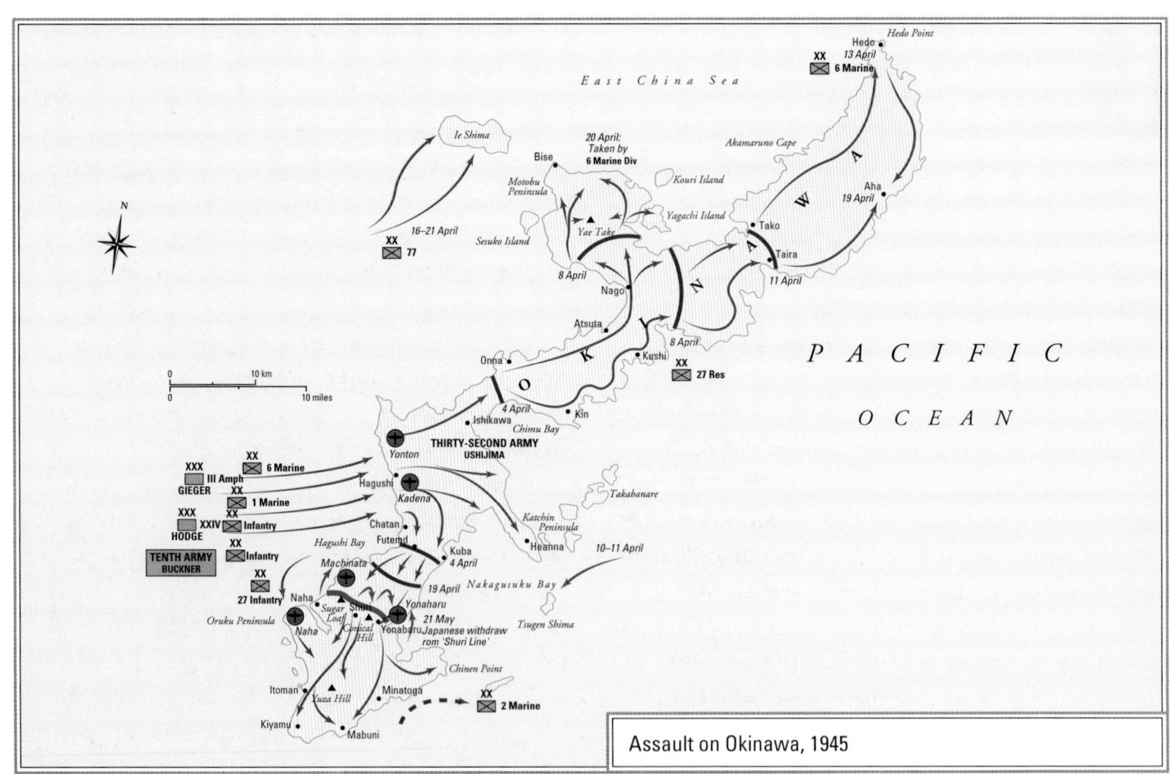

Assault on Okinawa, 1945

Divisions with the 27th Infantry Division in reserve.

Marines also held the senior command posts in Buckner's Tenth Army air complement. Brigadier General William J. Wallace led the fighter command, while Major General Francis P. Mulcahy, commander of the 2nd Marine Aircraft Wing, stepped up to lead the Tactical Air Force, Tenth Army. The 1st Marine Division, which had participated in the campaigns on Guadalcanal, Cape Gloucester, and Peleliu, was commanded by Major General Pedro A. del Valle, who had directed the III Amphibious Corps artillery at Guam during the Marianas Campaign. Formed on Guadalcanal in September 1944, the 6th Marine Division was the only Marine unit of its size that took shape overseas during World War II. Although Operation Iceberg would be its first campaign, its ranks were interspersed with veterans. Its commander, Major General Lemuel C. Shepherd, Jr., had led the 1st Marine Division at Cape Gloucester and the 1st Marine Provisional Brigade at Guam. Major General Leroy P. Hunt commanded the 2nd Marine Division, combat experienced at Guadalcanal, Tarawa, and the Marianas.

The invasion plan for Operation Iceberg included the capture of numerous small islands off the southwest coast of Okinawa prior to the main landings. Kerama Retto and the seven surrounding spits of land would serve as a principal supply and refueling point and a safe anchorage for ships damaged while supporting the landings.

Mine Clearance

Days of naval bombardment and preliminary air strikes were to soften up the Okinawan defenses. During the week prior to L-Day, Navy guns fired 13,000 rounds of heavy caliber ammunition, and carrier-based aircraft flew 3095 sorties. Underwater Demolition Teams (UDT) swam stealthily ashore, checking the depth of the water at various times of day and attaching explosives to mines and beach obstacles to clear the way for the coming invasion.

Despite recent experience at Iwo Jima, the Americans expected the beaches themselves to be heavily contested. The L-Day assault plan involved landings on the Hagushi beaches along the southwestern shore of Okinawa. In the north, the Marines of the 6th Division were to land with the 1st and 2nd Battalions of Colonel Merlin F. Schneider's 22nd Marines hitting Green Beaches 1 and 2. The 1st and 3rd Battalions of Colonel Alan Shapley's 4th Marines were to come ashore at Red Beaches 1, 2, and 3. Further south in the 1st Marine Division's sector, the 1st and 2nd Battalions of Colonel Edward W. Snedeker's 7th Marines were to land at Blue Beaches 1 and 2, while the 1st and 2nd Battalions of Colonel John H. Griebel's 5th Marines were to land on Yellow Beaches 1, 2, and 3. Still further south, elements of the Army's 7th and 96th Divisions were to come ashore on beaches designated Purple, Orange, White, and Brown. Once ashore, the Marines and Army troops were to strike eastward across the Ishikawa Isthmus, capture two key airfields, Yontan and Kadena, bisect the island, and then turn north and south to secure the length of Okinawa.

While the actual landings were taking place, the 2nd Marine Division was to execute a feint similar to the successful maneuver it performed off Tinian the previous year. The complicated movement involved loading the Marines aboard landing craft and approaching the Minatoga beaches on Okinawa's southeast coast simultaneously with the landings at the Hagushi beaches, distracting the Japanese defenders and then turning away.

The American planners were under no illusions. They expected heavy casualties, and they expected the initial landings to be hotly contested. Moreover, from Admiral Nimitz down to the lowliest sailor in the U.S. Navy,

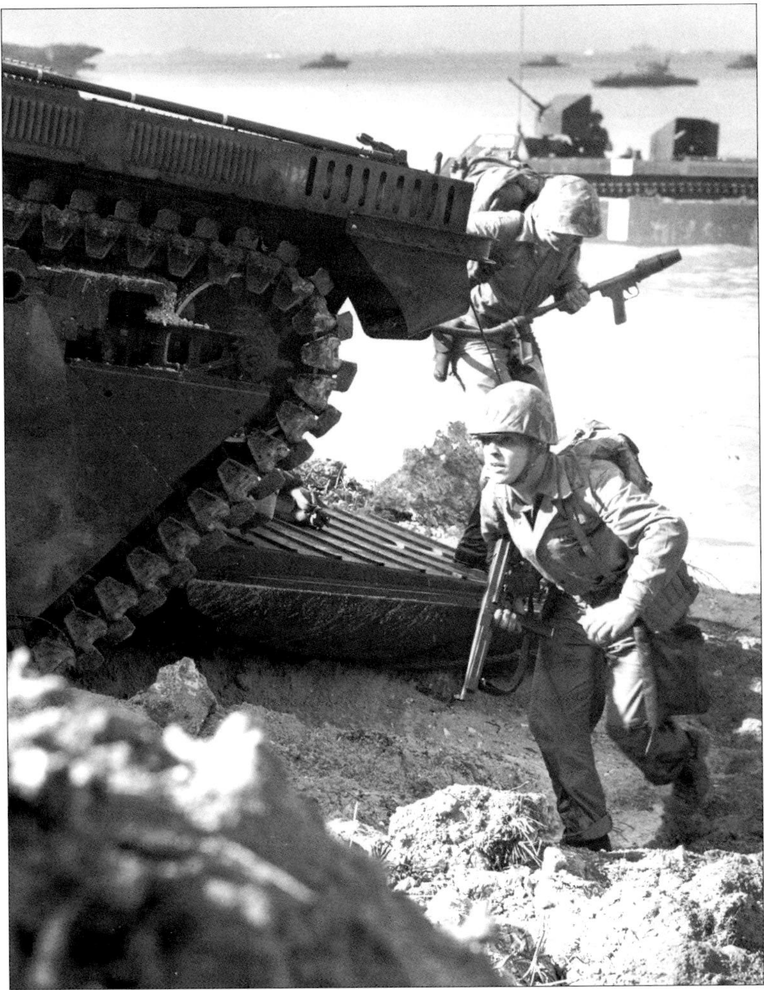

Home Islands was ever-present as well. By the time Okinawa was declared secure on June 22, 1945, that horror had been fully realized, and the prospects for even greater bloodshed were real enough to give even the most hardened veteran pause. The 82 days of fighting on Okinawa yielded an immense harvest of death and destruction.

American combat deaths on Okinawa totaled 7374, while 31,807 were wounded and 239 missing in action. Among the casualties were 19,500 Marines. At sea, the Navy suffered mightily—like never before or since—with 4907 killed or missing, 29 ships sunk, and 120 damaged. In total, 23 Medals of Honor were earned on Okinawa, and 13 of them were awarded to Marines and attached Navy corpsmen; 11 of these were posthumous. When victory was won, the Marine Corps, Army, and Navy rightly shared in the accolades that followed. Despite a glitch here and there, Okinawa was a model of interservice cooperation.

Above: Landing at Green Beach 1 on Okinawa, Marines of the 2nd Battalion, 22nd Marines, hustle from the personnel compartment of an armored LVT (Landing Vehicle, Tracked) while other landing craft may be seen just offshore.

there was concern for the safety of the fleet that was obliged to lie off Okinawa's shores for an extended period. The anxiety stemmed from the certainty that Japanese suicide aircraft, the dreaded Kamikaze, would assault the fleet in great numbers.

As bitter as the battle for Iwo Jima had been, the battle for Okinawa promised horrors of its own. The specter of a looming invasion of the

Japanese Casualties

The Japanese garrison, which numbered more than 100,000 including Okinawan conscripts, was decimated, and approximately 11,000 prisoners were taken. The others perished along with the pilots of 2373 Kamikaze aircraft and thousands of sailors who died during the last combat convulsion of the Imperial Navy, many of them aboard the super battleship *Yamato*. The death toll among Okinawan civilians was staggering at roughly 150,000 men, women, and children.

Under a blanket of air cover and pre-invasion shelling, the storming of Okinawa commenced on the morning of April 1, with landing craft engines roaring and churning a nearly unbroken string of white wakes that was 8 miles (13km) wide. Resistance was virtually nonexistent. American troops flooded ashore, and by the end of the first day 60,000 had been landed with only 28 fatalities, 104 wounded, and 27 missing in the entire Tenth Army. The beachhead was 8.5 miles (13.7km) wide and 2.8 miles (4.5km) deep.

The Marines could not believe their good fortune, and famed war correspondent Ernie Pyle noted: "Never before had I seen an invasion beach like Okinawa. There wasn't a dead or wounded man in our whole sector of it. Medical corpsmen were sitting among their sacks of bandages and plasma with nothing to do. There wasn't a single burning vehicle, nor a single boat lying wrecked on the reef or shoreline. The carnage that is almost inevitable on an invasion was wonderfully and beautifully not there."

Below: As the final run toward the invasion beaches of Okinawa commences, armoured LVT(A)-4s form into a line abreast. The LVT(A)-4 mounted a 75mm howitzer in a turret, clearly visible on the vehicle in the foreground.

Waiting Game

From his command post at Shuri Castle, Lieutenant General Mitsuru Ushijima, commander of the Japanese 32nd Army, watched the Americans put 16,000 combat troops ashore in an hour. The sight was awe inspiring and undoubtedly disconcerting, but it played into his defensive plan. Ushijima had arrived on Okinawa in August 1944, and was immediately resigned to a fight to the death. Like Kuribayashi at Iwo Jima, he understood the concept of defense in depth. While he would have to concede the Kadena and Yontan airfields to the Americans and allow them to establish a formidable force ashore, he would concentrate his resources in the rugged terrain of southwestern Okinawa, mount a resolute defense, and bleed the enemy white while waves of Kamikaze pilots would crash their

explosive-laden planes into the ships of the Fifth Fleet. The combined effort would exact fearful casualties and buy precious time for Imperial General Headquarters to continue preparations for the defense of the Home Islands.

Ushijima's forces included three infantry divisions—the veteran 9th, the 24th (well equipped but untested in battle), and the 62nd. The 44th Independent Mixed Brigade had lost 5600 of its combat troops on June 29, 1944, when the transport *Toyama Maru* was torpedoed and sunk by the submarine USS *Sturgeon* en route to Okinawa, and was eventually combined with the 15th Independent Mixed Regiment on the island. An array of artillery, mortar, engineer, and naval troops rounded out the sizable force allocated to Okinawa's defense.

Preparing Okinawa's Defenses

While the Americans continued to fight their way across the Pacific, Ushijima took full advantage of the time available to fortify the ridges, draws, hills, and ravines of southeastern Okinawa. The high ground was honeycombed with tunnels, bunkers, pillboxes, artillery emplacements, and machine-gun nests with interlocking fields of fire. Some of these were positioned in the mouths of multiple caves, connected to one another by a labyrinth of subterranean passages. The defenders even fortified the stone tombs of long deceased Okinawans, placing machine guns and riflemen inside these abodes of the dead.

Breaching the series of defensive lines that Ushijima constructed would prove to be agonizingly slow and costly for the Americans. The first line extended just below the Ishikawa Isthmus from Skyline Ridge in the east to Kakazu Ridge in the west. Three weeks of fighting were required to break through it. The second Japanese defense line stretched from Yonabaru near the east coast across Shuri Ridge and Shuri Castle, the ancient bastion of the kings who once ruled the Ryukyu Islands, to the port of Naha in the east. Ushijima intended to make his final stand at the third defensive line, strung along an arc of fortified hills that dominated the gentle slope of extreme southern Okinawa to the shores of the East China Sea.

Ushijima possessed a large number of heavy weapons, from the proven 47mm anti-tank gun that could penetrate the armor of the American M4 Sherman tank to 150mm howitzers and the powerful 320mm spigot mortars that threw huge shells nicknamed "ashcans" by the Marines. The general chose to bide his time, allowing the Marines and Army troops to overwhelm the meager forces he had committed to the northern portion of the island. The death struggle would come in the south.

For the American ground troops on Okinawa the opening hours of Operation Iceberg were exhilarating. Progress was swift and astonishing. In four days the invasion accomplished what senior commanders had expected to take three weeks. By 10.30 a.m. on L-Day, the 7th Infantry Division had Kadena airfield in hand, and then continued moving east and south with the 96th Division on its right. At 1.00 p.m., the 6th Marine Division was in possession of Yontan airfield. As darkness fell on April 3, the 1st Marine Division had crossed the Ishikawa Isthmus and captured the Katchin Peninsula. Okinawa had been cut in half. The Marines of the 1st and 6th Divisions then fanned out to the north and west. The greatest initial challenge was the lengthening supply line.

By April 4, the two captured airfields were operational, and Marine Air Groups 31 and 33 flew in from escort carriers offshore. Their versatile Vought F4U Corsairs served as both interdiction fighters flying combat air patrol

Opposite: Loaded with supplies and ammunition, Marines pass through a shattered Okinawan village, taking notice of the Japanese corpse lying nearby. Evidently the enemy soldier has been dead for some time as rigor mortis has stiffened the body.

(CAP) above the fleet and later as ground support aircraft during a transition of that responsibility from carrier-based Grumman F6F Hellcat fighters. Additional tactical air power reached Yontan and Kadena in the coming days. Night fighters, torpedo bombers, and observation planes arrived along with an Army Air Forces fighter wing.

Buckner intended to bludgeon his way straight through the stout Japanese fortifications.

The few Japanese troops that had been allocated to the defense of the center of Okinawa were soon the quarry of 1st Marine Division patrols that cleaned up pockets of resistance. Meanwhile, the 6th Marine Division raced northward, seizing the village of Nago, the largest settlement in northern Okinawa by April 7. In 13 days, the division advanced 55 miles (88km), and the 22nd Marines occupied the small thumb-shaped Hedo Misaki Peninsula at the extreme northern tip of the island.

Soon enough, however, the Marines were to experience stiff resistance—a foretaste of what awaited them elsewhere on Okinawa. Rising 1200ft (366m) above sea level near Hedo Misaki, Mount Yae Taki offered extremely favorable defensive ground. Here, Colonel Takesiko Udo and elements of the 44th Independent Mixed Brigade, known as the Udo Force, occupied prepared defenses in an area of six square miles (15 square km) and made a tough stand. Under Udo's command, two infantry battalions, an artillery company, and an anti-tank company—roughly 2000 troops altogether—stalled the Marines for five days.

Five battalions of the 4th and 29th Marines attacked Mount Yae Taki repeatedly from east and west, negotiating fields sewn thickly with mines and swept by accurate enemy gunfire that had been pre-registered on the approaches. Supporting fire from the 14-inch guns of the battleship USS *Tennessee* and the low-level bombing runs by Corsairs of Marine Fighter Squadron 322 (VMF-322) helped crack the tough nut of Mount Yae Take, and the Udo Force was annihilated. The Marines lost 207 killed in action and 757 wounded before the Motobu Peninsula was cleared of Japanese troops on April 20.

As the rapid conquest of northern Okinawa was being executed, Army and Marine riflemen completed the occupation of numerous small islands lying nearby. Commanded by Major James L. Jones, the Fleet Marine Force, Pacific, Force Reconnaissance Battalion, executed several landings in advance of Army assaults to seize these islands. On April 16, the Marines took Minna Shima, landing a battery of 105mm howitzers to support the 77th Infantry Division in its assault on Ie Shima, 3.4 miles (5.5km) away.

Tank Massacre

The Army troops of the 7th and 96th Divisions were the first to probe Ushijima's daunting prepared defenses in southern Okinawa. General Buckner came ashore on April 14 and soon committed the 27th Infantry Division to the effort to crack Ushijima's first defensive line. A major attack was launched on April 19 following a heavy preparatory artillery bombardment. Initial gains could not be consolidated, and the attack was thrown back. At Kakazu, advancing Sherman tanks got separated from their infantry support, and Japanese guns picked off 22 of the 30 armored vehicles committed to the battle.

With offensive momentum slowed considerably, Buckner rejected a suggestion from Major General Andrew Bruce, commander of the 77th Infantry Division, that a second amphibious landing could be mounted on the beaches of southern Okinawa to outflank the Japanese defenses. Buckner considered the operation too risky and the beaches unfavorable due to high cliffs from which the enemy might pour fire on the landing troops. Besides, it would exacerbate an already difficult supply situation. Instead, Buckner intended to bludgeon his way directly through the stout Japanese fortifications.

On April 23, Admiral Nimitz arrived at Yontan airfield from Guam, toured the area of Okinawa that belonged to American forces, and met with Buckner to discuss a revitalization of the effort to get the offensive moving. Nimitz was concerned about the safety of the Fifth Fleet offshore as the savage Kamikaze attacks were taking a fearful toll. He admonished Buckner to crank the offensive into high gear within five days. Otherwise, he rasped: "We'll get someone here to move it … I'm losing a ship and a half each day out here. You've got to get this thing moving."

General Alexander A. Vandegrift, the victor at Guadalcanal and current Commandant of the Marine Corps, was a member of Nimitz's entourage. Vandegrift brought up the topic of a second amphibious assault once again, offering the 2nd Marine Division for the job. He asserted that the division could be underway from Saipan within six hours. Again, Buckner declined. The available Army and Marine units were going to slug it out with Ushijima.

Kamikaze Sorties

Nimitz was uncharacteristically forceful in his discussion with Buckner, and his concern for the

Below: A Marine 105mm (4.13in) howitzer fires on Japanese positions from the Okinawan population center of Naha.

fleet was well founded. While fighting raged on Okinawa, the surrounding waters of the Pacific Ocean and the East China Sea were roiling in the midst of Operation Ten Go, the huge Japanese Kamikaze onslaught that called for 4500 aircraft to be hurled against the American ships.

Ten Go, or Heavenly Operation, included 10 massed Kamikaze sorties, known as Kikusui, or Floating Chrysanthemums, and each Kikusui might consist of more than 350 planes. These included bombers and fighters, old fixed-gear types, and even a few biplanes. Also among the aerial suicide weapons thrown at the Americans was a terrifying flying bomb called the Ohka, or Cherry Blossom, packed with more than 2600lb (1179kg) of explosives. An ancestor of the modern cruise missile, the Ohka was slung beneath the fuselage of a bomber, carried within range of the American fleet, and released. The pilot then engaged three solid fuel rockets and streaked toward his target at up to 650mph (1046km/h).

The Fifth Fleet remained on station and suffered terribly. When a pair of Kamikazes struck the USS *Bunker Hill* on May 11, the aircraft carrier had been in the combat zone for 58 days. Army, Navy, and Marine pilots did all that valor and devotion to duty could do in defense of the fleet. On April 22, for example, three Marine Corsairs of VMF-323 shot down 16 enemy planes in the short span of 20 minutes. Nevertheless, the Kamikazes were relentless. Inevitably, some suicide pilots managed to get through the curtain of CAP fighters and anti-aircraft fire. However, during one of the U.S. Navy's finest hours, the Fifth Fleet (redesignated the Third Fleet when Admiral William F. "Bull" Halsey relieved Admiral Spruance on May 27) was also known as "the fleet that came to stay".

Costly though they were, the gains made by the 7th and 96th Infantry Divisions and the grind of attritional combat prompted Ushijima to withdraw from his first line of defense under the cover an artillery barrage and thick fog. The retrograde movement was accomplished within hours of Admiral Nimitz's departure from Okinawa, and the 27th Infantry Division bore the brunt of the effort to clear the Japanese rearguard from the area between the forward fortifications and the Shuri Line.

Assaulting the Shuri Line

As April gave way to May, General Buckner ordered the 1st Marine Division to relieve the battered 27th Infantry Division on the right, and soon the 6th Marine Division was ordered to come up on the far right flank near the sea. General del Valle took charge in the western area on May 1. The 77th Infantry Division arrived from Ie Shima to relieve the 96th Division in the center. For 10 days, the 96th Division was to rest and regroup. Then it was ordered to relieve the bloodied 7th Infantry Division in the east. Thus, the line of the Tenth Army became four divisions abreast, assaulting the Shuri Line defenses across a compact front that extended only about 5.1 miles (8.2km) from east to west.

General del Valle ordered the 1st Marine Division to attack the Awacha Pocket on the morning of May 2. Moving forward in a steady rain, the 5th Marines seized elevated positions to its front but came under immediate fire from Japanese gunners. The high ground interlaced with draws and ravines channeled attacking Marines into deadly killing zones, and the day's results were less than had been hoped. After dark, the Marines spent hours fending off Japanese infiltrators, often in hand-to-hand combat. Incessant rain hampered the renewal of the attack on May 3, and another week of hard fighting was required to clear the enemy enclave.

Opposite: Lieutenant Colonel William Kuratich, the operations officer of a Marine air support control unit on Okinawa, briefs pilots before they take to their Grumman TBM Avenger bombers to deliver 500lb (226kg) bombs against Japanese positions.

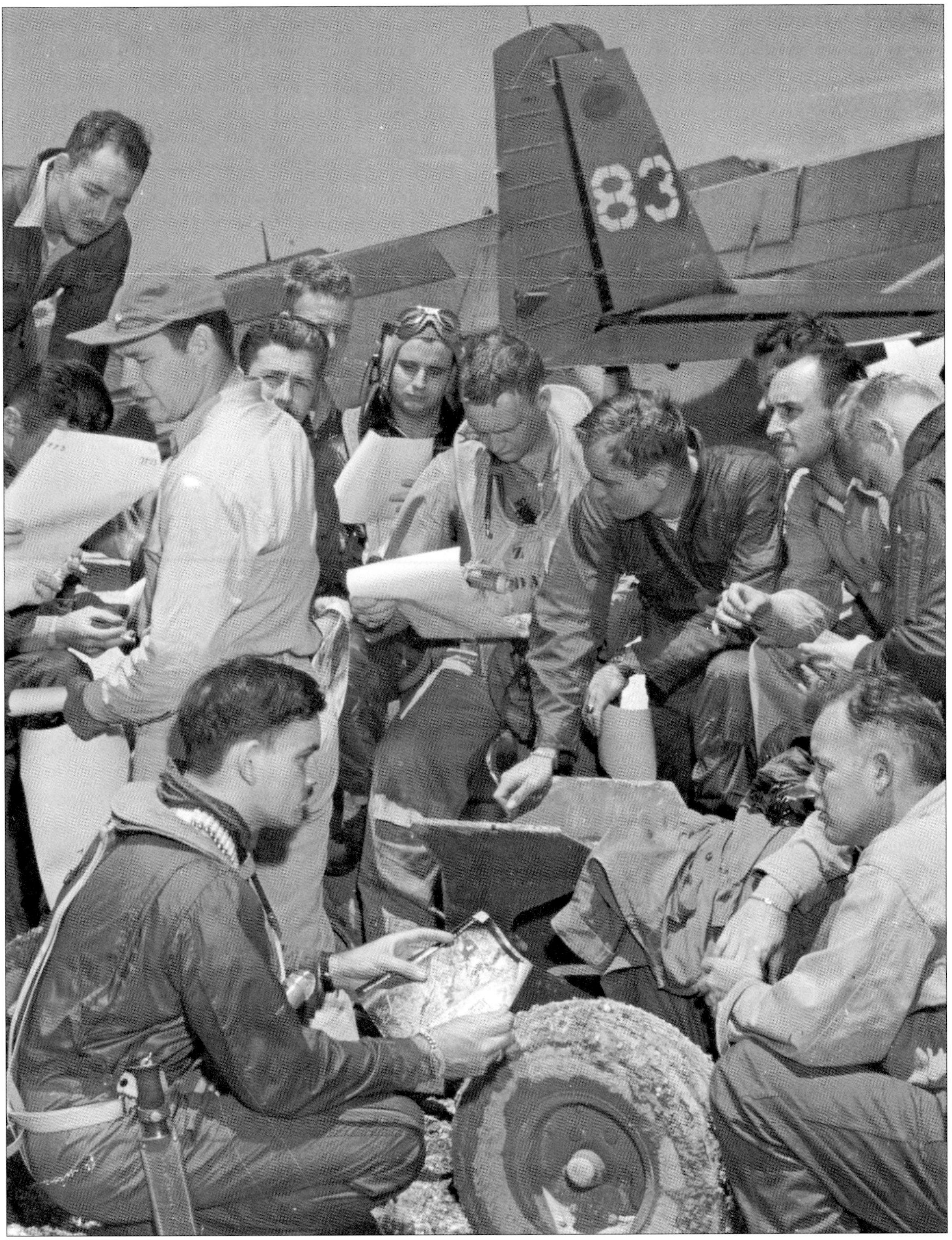
83

Japanese War Council

Just as General Buckner's reinforcement and realignment maneuvers were being completed, the Japanese briefly assumed the offensive. Ushijima was an affable fellow and appreciated the varied perspectives of his staff officers. He often allowed them to speak freely, and on the night of May 2 the discourse became heated during a war council at his headquarters in Shuri Castle.

Below: Flying in formation during a rocket attack against Japanese positions on Okinawa, Vought F4U Corsair fighters of the 2nd Marine Air Wing display the underwing hardpoints to which the rockets were affixed.

The 51-year-old Chief of Staff of the 32nd Army, Lieutenant General Isamu Cho was known as a nationalistic zealot. The impetuous officer had been involved in a conspiracy to establish a military dictatorship in Japan as early as 1931 and was, in fact, a war criminal who issued a horrific order to execute prisoners during the infamous Rape of Nanking in 1937. Cho refused to accept the notion of a defense in depth. He demanded a swift counterattack that would drive the Americans back.

Opposing Cho was 42-year-old Colonel Hiromichi Yahara, the 32nd Army senior staff officer responsible for planning. Yahara believed

that the idea of a counterattack, which no doubt would include a suicidal banzai charge, would result in high casualties and serve only to weaken the Japanese defenses. He asserted: "The army must continue its current operations, calmly recognizing its final destiny. Annihilation is inevitable no matter what is done."

Ushijima and every other staff officer present sided with Cho, and the counterattack was scheduled for the night of May 3, with a dual amphibious assault and the main thrust overland. The attack would be supported by every available artillery piece, exposing the guns to return fire as their heavy bombardment began at 10.00 p.m. and lasted until 4.30 a.m. on May 4. The 26th Shipping Engineer Regiment was among the leading elements of the counterattack that boarded barges and headed toward the beaches on the east coast of Okinawa near Skyline Ridge behind the forward American positions.

Moments after the Japanese troops embarked, patrolling U.S. Navy warships began to shadow them and then pounced, blasting many of the barges to bits. Those Japanese troops that made it ashore were greeted by withering fire from advance posts of the 7th Infantry Division and dispatched with ease.

The second amphibious landing occurred at Kusan on the west coast, where the 1st Battalion, 1st Marines, and the LVT-As of the 3rd Armored Amphibian Battalion shredded 700 Japanese troops. The 1st Reconnaissance Company and a War Dog platoon killed 75 more and hunted down the last 65 holdouts as the sun rose.

Ushijima ordered two battalions of the 24th Division to begin the land phase of the counterattack at 5.00 a.m. on May 4; however, they failed to reach their jump-off point at the scheduled time and were caught in the open. American artillery and mortar fire decimated their ranks. Then, after dark on the 4th, the last of the abortive Japanese offensive thrusts began with two infantry battalions assaulting 7th Division positions around the Tanaburu escarpment. Some penetrations were achieved, but these were isolated and destroyed throughout the following day. Only a few Japanese survivors were able to return to their lines as darkness fell on May 5.

Mutiny in the Ranks

The counterattack had been an utter disaster. The 32nd Army lost 6000 troops and 59 big guns. An angry group of junior officers drew their swords, surrounded Cho, and demanded an explanation for the failure. He was unable to speak. Yahara, the only senior Japanese officer to live through the battle for Okinawa, later described the

Above: Lieutenant General Simon Bolivar Buckner, Jr., commander of the U.S. Tenth Army on Okinawa, stands at left with binoculars. Buckner is accompanied by Major General Lemuel C. Shepherd (center), commander of the 6th Marine Division, who sports his pipe and bamboo cane, and Brigadier General William T. Clement, assistant commander of the 6th Marine Division.

abortive assaults collectively as "the decisive action of the campaign". On the mournful night of May 5, a tearful Ushijima summoned Yahara to his private quarters, apologized profusely, and swore that he would never again disregard the colonel's advice.

During the first week of May, the Tenth Army realignment was completed. The 1st Marine Division had already taken 1400 casualties in six days of fighting north of the Shuri Line, and Private Dale M. Hansen of the 2nd Battalion, 1st Marines, earned the Medal of Honor on May 7 when he destroyed a Japanese pillbox, picked up a rifle to replace his own that had been shattered in the attack, and proceeded to the crest of a nearby ridge. Confronted by six enemy soldiers, Hansen shot four of them before his rifle jammed. When the other two Japanese soldiers jumped him, Hansen beat them back with the rifle's butt and then scrambled for cover.

The 22-year-old from Nebraska was not finished. Rearmed with yet another rifle and a few grenades, Hansen went after the enemy again, killing eight and destroying a heavy mortar position. His one-man assault provided the catalyst for the Marines to claim an embattled ridgeline. Four days later, Hansen was killed by a Japanese sniper. His posthumous Medal of Honor was presented to his parents on May 30, 1946.

The 22nd Marines relieved the 7th Marines in early May as the 6th Marine Division anchored its right flank against the East China Sea on the extreme right of the Tenth Army. On May 9, the 1st Battalion, 1st Marines, assaulted Hill 60, and its commander, Lieutenant Colonel James C. Murray, Jr., was wounded by a sniper. During the night, the 1st Battalion, 5th Marines, fought hand-to-hand with scores of Japanese infiltrators.

On May 11, Buckner ordered an attack all along the Shuri Line. With Nimitz's words still ringing in his ears, the commanding general was doing his best to speed the battle along. However, the Japanese seemed to have fortified every cave, rock formation, and crevice on Okinawa, and progress was painful. Buckner was determined to grind it out against the Japanese, wearing them down. "We will take our time and kill the Japanese gradually", he told a group of reporters. The progress was marginal or nonexistent at times, but the killing was continual.

In two days of hard fighting, the 1st and 2nd Battalions, 7th Marines, captured Dakeshi Ridge. The battle was reminiscent of the fighting in the Umurbrogol on Peleliu, and each battalion commander in the 7th Marines was a veteran of that bloody engagement. The U-shaped ridge was studded with machine-gun emplacements and mortar positions, the defenders often firing from the reverse slopes and using the cover of the crest as protection from Marine return fire.

Sherman Advance

The 1st Battalion reached the top of Dakeshi Ridge at two points on May 11, but fell back under a hail of Japanese shells. One Marine recalled, "We did damned little attacking. Every time a man raised his head he was hit." The next morning, three Sherman tanks—one armed with a 75mm cannon and the others with flamethrowers—led the way up the slope. The tanks' .30- and .50-caliber machine guns chattered, and the flamethrowers belched streams of fiery jellied gasoline. The riflemen of the 2nd Battalion followed, cutting down the enemy troops that broke along the reverse slope.

When Ushijima learned that Dakeshi Ridge had fallen, he acknowledged: "The enemy's power lies in his tanks. It has become obvious that our battle against the Americans is a battle against their tanks." Although the American armored units took fearful losses on Okinawa, they were critical in achieving the eventual victory.

Dakeshi Ridge was only the first of numerous obstacles that studded the Shuri Line north of Ushijima's headquarters. Beyond lay the high ground of Wana Ridge and craggy Wana Draw

Below: On May 8, 1945, designated as VE Day (Victory in Europe) in the European Theater, the troops on Okinawa were still fighting to gain yards of ground against the stubborn Japanese enemy. This photograph was taken during the drive to capture the town of Naha, as the Marines awaited the order to advance.

that stretched southward from it. Wana Draw was a maze of caves, rocky outcroppings, and high cliffs—and it was defended stoutly by the 62nd Infantry Division. For nearly three weeks, the 1st Marine Division hurled itself against Wana Ridge and Wana Draw—the most difficult 3600ft (1097m) advance the Old Breed encountered during the entire Pacific War.

The bloody series of attacks against Wana Ridge and Wana Draw began on May 12. During earlier operations, the troops and tanks of the 1st Marine Division had perfected the tactics of infantry and armor cooperation. Tanks blasted and spewed flame, while riflemen stayed close to their covering armor and shot down any Japanese soldiers that ventured forward with satchel charges strapped to their bodies, intent on committing suicide by throwing themselves against the 33-ton Shermans.

In a single day's combat on May 16, the Marine Shermans and Army flamethrower tanks fired 5000 75mm shells and 175,000 rounds of .30-calibre ammunition and expended 600 gallons (2271l) of searing napalm against the enemy. On May 17, tanks working with the 2nd Battalion, 5th Marines, were hit by fire from twin 47mm anti-tank weapons. Coordinates were relayed to the USS *Colorado*, and the big battleship's guns silenced the enemy weapons with a well-placed salvo.

The fighting in Wana Draw was so severe that the 7th Marines lost 500 men in five days, depleting its strength substantially after 700 casualties had been absorbed in the fight for

Below: Men from Colonel Victor Bleasdale's 29th Marines catch a ride on a Sherman tank. American armor proved key in the victory at Okinawa.

Dakeshi Ridge. The 3rd Battalion, 7th Marines, lost a dozen officers in its rifle companies from May 16 to 19. Wana Draw was 1200ft (366m) wide as it spread southward from Wana Ridge, but it narrowed substantially in its approach to the high ground of Shuri Ridge and the village of Shuri, funneling the Marines into killing zones covered by machine-gun and rifle fire. Mortars and heavy guns pounded the advance.

The 1st Marines took in 500 replacements and reinvigorated the advance on May 20 after relieving the riddled and fatigued 7th Marines. Meanwhile, the 5th Marines captured Hill 55 on the western approaches to Wana Draw, finally silencing Japanese guns that had harassed the Americans for days. Progress was measured in yards—and tragically in the number of casualties. Through 19 days of hell, the Marines lost an average of 200 dead and wounded for every 100 yards gained. To add to the misery, much of the fighting took place in steady and at times drenching rain. During the last week of May, the 1st Marine Division was stalemated one ridgeline short of Shuri.

Sugar Loaf Hill

Early on May 10, the riflemen of the 6th Marine Division readied to move forward, crossing the Asa River near the western coast of Okinawa on a Bailey bridge hastily constructed by Marine engineers. During the next 36 hours, the Marines advanced roughly 3000ft (914m). By the morning of May 12, they were in front of a small hill that rose sharply just 230ft (70m) above them. Because of its distinctive topography, the Marines quickly settled on a nickname for the high ground: Sugar Loaf.

The otherwise unimpressive Sugar Loaf was flanked to the southeast and southwest by two more small hills. These were soon named Half Moon and Horseshoe respectively. One Marine described Sugar Loaf as "a pimple of a hill", and to the riflemen of the 22nd Marines it was obvious that the Japanese would put up a fight in defense of these mutually supporting positions.

However, the Marines did not realize that the complex of small hills was the command and control hub of the enemy's Shuri Line in the west. Sugar Loaf stood watch at the northern apex of the trio of hills, and the 2000 Japanese soldiers of the 15th Independent Mixed Regiment, commanded by Colonel Seiko Mita, were ordered to prevent an American breakthrough between the towns of Shuri and Naha. Another 3000 Japanese troops defended Half Moon and Horseshoe.

The battle for Sugar Loaf, Half Moon, and Horseshoe lasted an agonizing 10 days, and the ordeal of Captain Owen G. Stebbins' Company G, 2nd Battalion, 22nd Marines, was a harbinger of the bitter struggle that followed. Stebbins led a combined infantry-armor assault against Sugar Loaf, and within minutes two of his three platoons were pinned down by machine-gun and anti-tank fire. Charging ahead, Stebbins and his executive officer, Lieutenant Dale W. Bair, led the third platoon into a firestorm—28 of the 40 men in the platoon were hit within 300ft (91m) of their starting point, and machine-gun bullets smashed into both of Stebbins' legs.

Bair was shot in the left arm, and it flopped uselessly against his side. Undeterred, the lieutenant scraped together 25 Marines, some of them wounded, and charged back to the top of Sugar Loaf. A few of the Marines managed to run the gauntlet to the crest of the hill, but their position was untenable, and Bair ordered them to fall back. By nightfall, the blackened hulks of three Sherman tanks lay smoldering on the battlefield. Five assaults had failed to hold the bloody hill, and only 75 of the original complement of 200 Marines in Company G were unhurt.

The terrible contest continued into the evening of May 14 with elements of the 29th Marines fed into the fight alongside the two depleted

companies of the 22nd Marines that had already suffered mightily. A force of 44 Marines were marooned on the slope of Sugar Loaf, pinned down by Japanese fire with more than 100 of their original number killed or wounded and lying around them. Major Henry A. Courtney, Jr., executive officer of the 2nd Battalion, 22nd Marines, aroused the riflemen of Companies F and G to action.

Courtney concluded that his Marines could not defend their position indefinitely. Withdrawal would expose them further to murderous fire. The best option, he decided, was to attack. "Men, if we don't take the top of this hill tonight, the Japs will be down here to drive us away in the morning," Courtney yelled. "When we go up there, some of us are never going to come down again. You all know what hell it is on the top, but that hill's got to be taken, and we're going to do it. I'm going up to the top of Sugar Loaf Hill. Who's coming along?"

All 44 Marines responded to Courtney's plea for volunteers. The intrepid officer led his command to the crest of Sugar Loaf, and the Marines held into the night—until exhaustion and incessant mortar and small-arms fire had taken a fearful toll. The 15 surviving Marines filtered back down the hill with the approach of daylight. Courtney, however, suffered a fatal wound when a mortar fragment sliced into his neck. He received a posthumous Medal of Honor.

Among the courageous Marines who followed Courtney were the seven riflemen of Corporal James L. Day's squad from Company F, 2nd Battalion, 22nd Marines. Five squad members were soon lost to enemy fire, while Day and Pfc. Dale Bertoli became isolated on the western slope of Sugar Loaf. During a harrowing ordeal of four days and three nights, Day and Bertoli lobbed

Left: An M4 Sherman medium tank equipped with a flamethrower fires at an enemy position while Marine riflemen stand ready to pick off any Japanese troops that may exit the strongpoint.

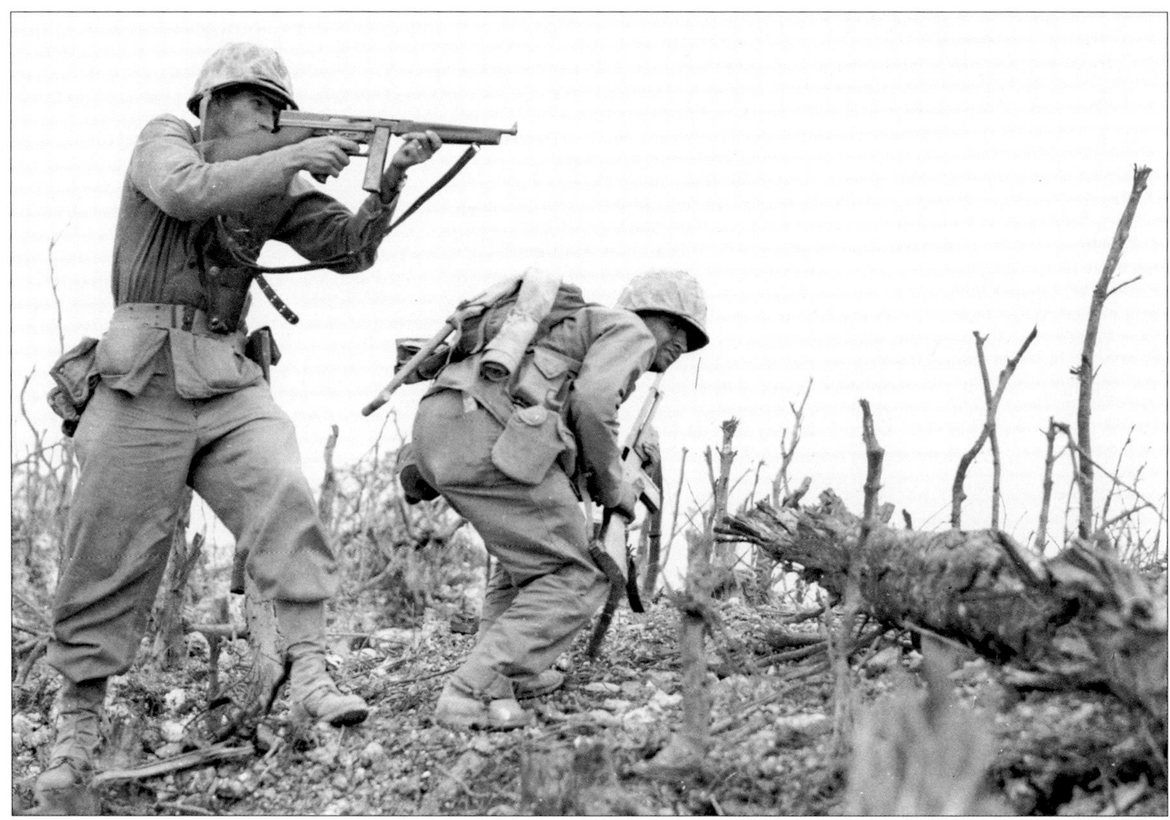

Above: During the heavy fighting at Wana Ridge and Wana Draw a Marine of the 1st Division stands erect to aim his M1928 Thompson submachine gun at a Japanese sniper.

grenades and emptied clips from their M1 Garand rifles into Japanese troops attempting to fight off successive Marine assaults against the little hill. Finally, the two were ordered to withdraw on May 17. Bertoli was killed in action a few days later, and Day was wounded. Some 40 years after the battle, Major General James L. Day returned to Okinawa to take command of Marine installations on the island.

Leading From the Front

In three days of fighting, the 22nd Marines had suffered nearly 50 percent casualties—400 killed and wounded. On May 15, a Japanese artillery shell struck the command post of the 1st Battalion, 22nd Marines, killing Major Thomas Myers, the battalion commander, and wounding the commander and executive officer of the tank company supporting the attacks on Sugar Loaf. Hit hard by the loss of one of his most valuable officers, General Shepherd issued a warning to other officers against exposing themselves to enemy fire. However, the directive was impractical—the officers had to lead, and to lead they had to face the peril head-on.

On May 16, the 29th Marines assumed center stage in the assault against the Japanese triple threat of Sugar Loaf, Horseshoe, and Half Moon. General Shepherd took a rather extraordinary step at the regimental command level, replacing the 29th's Colonel Victor F. Bleasdale and its executive officer with Colonel Harold C. Roberts and Lieutenant Colonel August C. Larson. The following day Company

E, 2nd Battalion, 29th Marines, charged Sugar Loaf four times, losing 160 men—although it inflicted many more casualties on the Japanese and held the hill for several hours before withdrawing at twilight.

At long last, on May 18 Company D, 2nd Battalion, 29th Marines took up the task. Captain Howard L. Mabie, the company commander, led the attack on Sugar Loaf while the Japanese positions on Half Moon and Horseshoe were kept under a blanket of suppressing fire from other units of the 29th Marines. Tanks supported the infantry, circling around both flanks of Sugar Loaf, proceeding south through minefields in the valley that had been so costly to cross, and raking the Japanese troops who emerged from their hiding places on the reverse slope of Sugar Loaf to confront the Marine infantry. Company D held Sugar Loaf through the night and never wavered.

General Shepherd fed the 4th Marines into the line to relieve the 29th, and by the end of the day on May 20 its 1st and 3rd Battalions had made substantial gains on both flanks of the 6th Division front. The 3rd Battalion seized most of Horseshoe, while the 2nd Battalion was in control of the majority of Half Moon.

Gunnery Sergeant Mike Goracoff of the 4th Marines assessed the long battle for Sugar Loaf and its environs: "We made 11 thrusts at that hill and fell back each time with most of our boys dead or missing. It wasn't uncommon to see a Pfc. commanding the platoon as it fell back from a push at the hill. It seemed that the lieutenants fell first, then the sergeants."

Below: Two miles (3.6km) north of the village of Naha, Marines prepare to assault a ridgeline. One of the Marines appears ready to fire a bazooka against a Japanese position. Although developed as an anti-tank weapon, the bazooka was also effective against bunkers and entrenched positions.

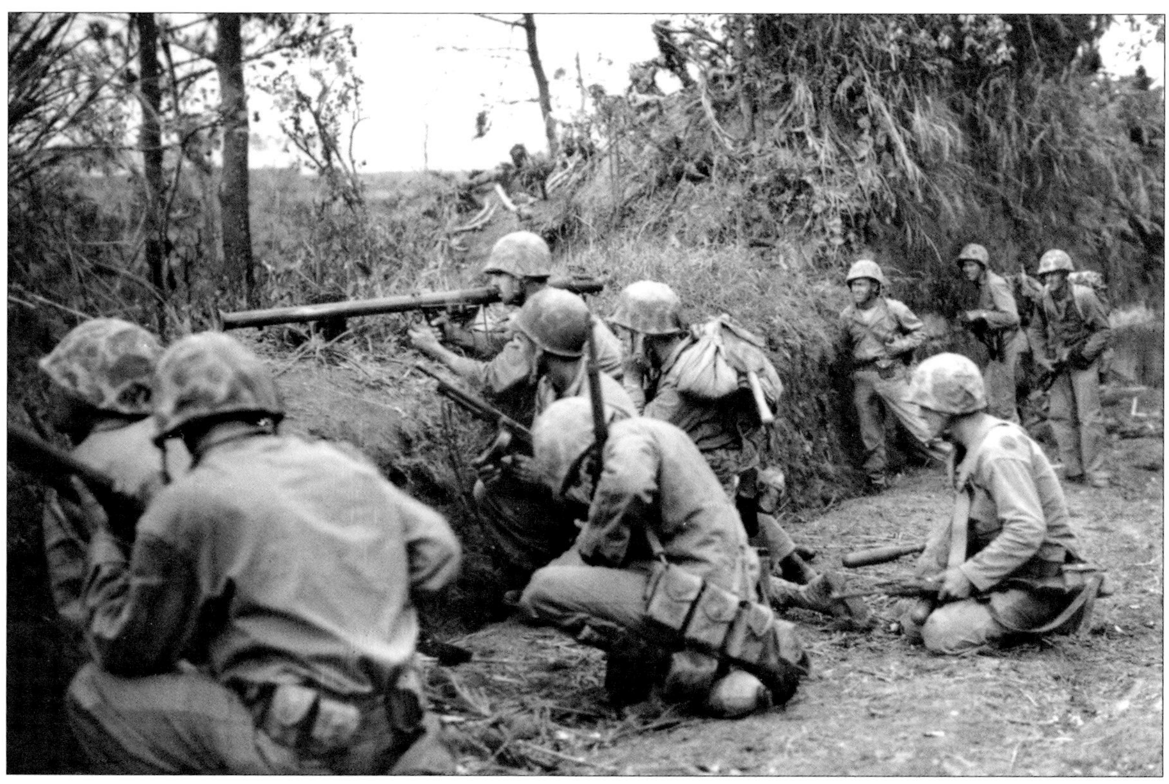

The battle for Sugar Loaf had cost the 6th Marine Division nearly 2700 killed and wounded. Another 1300 Marines were deemed casualties of combat fatigue—possibly forever affected by the nightmare of the intense combat.

While the Marines battled in the west, the 96th Infantry Division took Conical Hill and the 7th Infantry Division secured Yonabaru. Both flanks were vulnerable, and Ushijima deemed his positions at Shuri Ridge and Shuri Castle untenable. Colonel Yahara advised a withdrawal to the third and final defensive line across the Kiyamu Peninsula. Ushijima issued the order to withdraw, taking advantage of steady rain and fog to fall back.

Torrential rains slowed the ensuing American advance, turning roads into quagmires and restricting the movement of men and supplies. Nevertheless, tanks of the 6th Marine Division probed into the village of Naha on May 28, and patrols encountered only light resistance. By the next morning, Company A, 1st Battalion, 5th Marines, commanded by Captain Julian D. Dusenbury, moved out to attack Shuri Ridge. The Marines expected a fight, but they reached the crest of the ridge virtually without firing a shot.

Storming the Castle

Due to the surprising success of the Company A advance, Shuri Castle lay tantalizingly close. However, the prize was within the zone of operations of the neighboring 77th Infantry Division. Still, the opportunity to seize the objective was at hand. When his radio crackled with the news, General del Valle weighed the issue of antagonizing his Army counterpart, General Bruce, and decided that any ill will that resulted was worth it.

Company A moved swiftly, crossing into the 77th Division zone and taking Shuri Castle just after 10.00 a.m. Dusenbury was a South Carolinian and ordered a Confederate flag that he carried in his helmet liner run up the nearest pole. The senior commanders at Tenth Army headquarters were a bit disturbed when they saw the Stars and Bars flying above Shuri Castle, and two days later the Stars and Stripes was raised in its place. Marines of the 1st Division had previously raised the same flag on Peleliu.

General del Valle did in fact reach out to the 77th Division commander and the rest of his Army compatriots, trying to smooth over the most contentious instance of inter-service rivalry during the fight for Okinawa. "I don't think a single Army division commander would talk to me after that," he remembered. The hard feelings necessarily took a back seat to the business at hand, however.

Ushijima still controlled roughly eight square miles (21 square km) of southern Okinawa. Despite heavy American shelling and air attacks that took its toll on some exposed Japanese units during their retreat, the remnants of the 32nd

Below: The Browning Automatic Rifle (BAR) fired the Springfield .30-06 cartridge and brought automatic weapons capability to Marines at the squad level. It was capable of firing more than 500 rounds per minute from 20-round detachable box magazines.

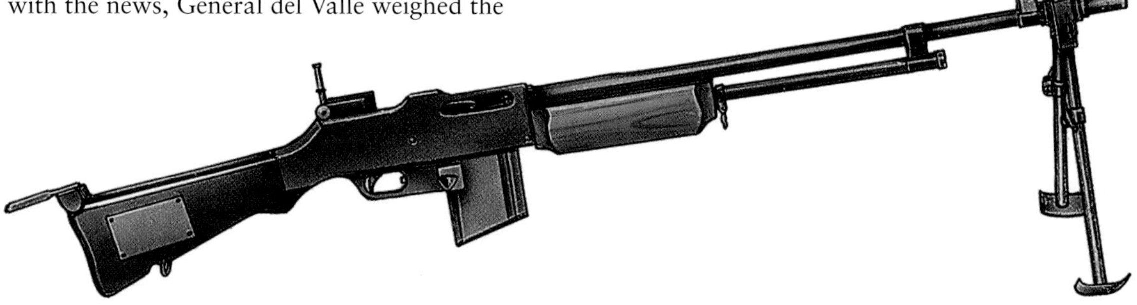

Above: Marine gunners crouch behind the gun shield of their towed 37mm (1.45in) cannon while taking aim at a Japanese position. The Japanese were so well entrenched on Okinawa that direct fire, explosive charges, flamethrowers, and hand grenades were the most effective means of eliminating resistance.

Army were not about to quit. The four-mile (6.4km) Japanese front stretched across Kunishi Ridge in the west to Hill 89, where Ushijima established his last command post, and then to Hill 95 on the east coast.

For several days General Buckner remained unconvinced that the Japanese were withdrawing from the Shuri Line, and once he realized that there was yet another strong defensive line to be cracked he realigned the Tenth Army front. From west to east, the 1st Marine Division, 96th Infantry Division, and 7th Infantry Division would continue the dirty work on Okinawa. The slog southward was renewed in heavy rain, and progress was painfully slow. Lieutenant Colonel Horatio C. Woodhouse, Jr., General Shepherd's younger cousin and commander of the 2nd Battalion, 22nd Marines, was killed by a sniper during the advance.

Meanwhile, the 6th Marine Division was tasked with securing Naha Airfield, and accomplishing the mission required control of the Oroku Peninsula. General Shepherd evaluated the situation. Rather than a protracted overland assault, he requested permission to mount an amphibious landing across the Kokuba estuary to hit the enemy flank. Overcoming the challenges of pulling together enough operational LVTs and a narrow 36-hour window to plan and execute the maneuver, Colonel Shapley's 4th Marines came ashore on the Oroku Peninsula on the morning of June 4. Elements of the 29th Marines followed while the 22nd Marines hammered the enemy from the landward side.

For nine more days the Marines battled nearly 5000 resolute defenders under the command of Rear Admiral Minoru Ota, one of the few remaining senior officers of the once powerful Special Naval Landing Force. Ota's assemblage of reserve and non-combat troops who were pressed into the line fought doggedly from the mouths of caves, the shells of wrecked planes along the edge of Naha airfield, and machine-gun nests. The defenders were decimated. Only 200 surrendered.

Ota sent a final message to the headquarters of the Imperial Navy in Tokyo and then committed suicide with his staff officers. "The troops under my command have fought gallantly, in the finest tradition of the Japanese Navy", he wrote. "Fierce bombardment may deform the mountains of Okinawa, but cannot alter the loyal spirit of our men."

The capture of the Oroku Peninsula and Naha airfield cost the Marines 1608 casualties.

Supported by tanks, the 7th Infantry Division's 32nd Regiment captured Hill 95 on June 12. On the same day, the 17th Regiment took possession of the eastern end of Yuza Dake escarpment, unhinging the right flank of Ushijima's defensive line. In the center, the 96th Division claimed the rest of the Yuza Dake by nightfall on the 13th.

In concert with the Army attacks, the 1st Marine Division began its assault on the western anchor of the Japanese line. With Colonel Snedeker's 7th Marines in the lead, its objective was Kunishi Ridge, and the prelude to that assault was completed when Hill 69 fell to the 2nd Battalion on June 10. Kunishi Ridge itself lay across open grassy fields and rice paddies, and from a topographical perspective it was much

Right: Below the forbidding walls of Shuri Castle, an anchor of the Japanese defenses in southern Okinawa, Marines encountered the ruins of a Christian church and were obliged to dislodge a Japanese sniper who had concealed himself there.

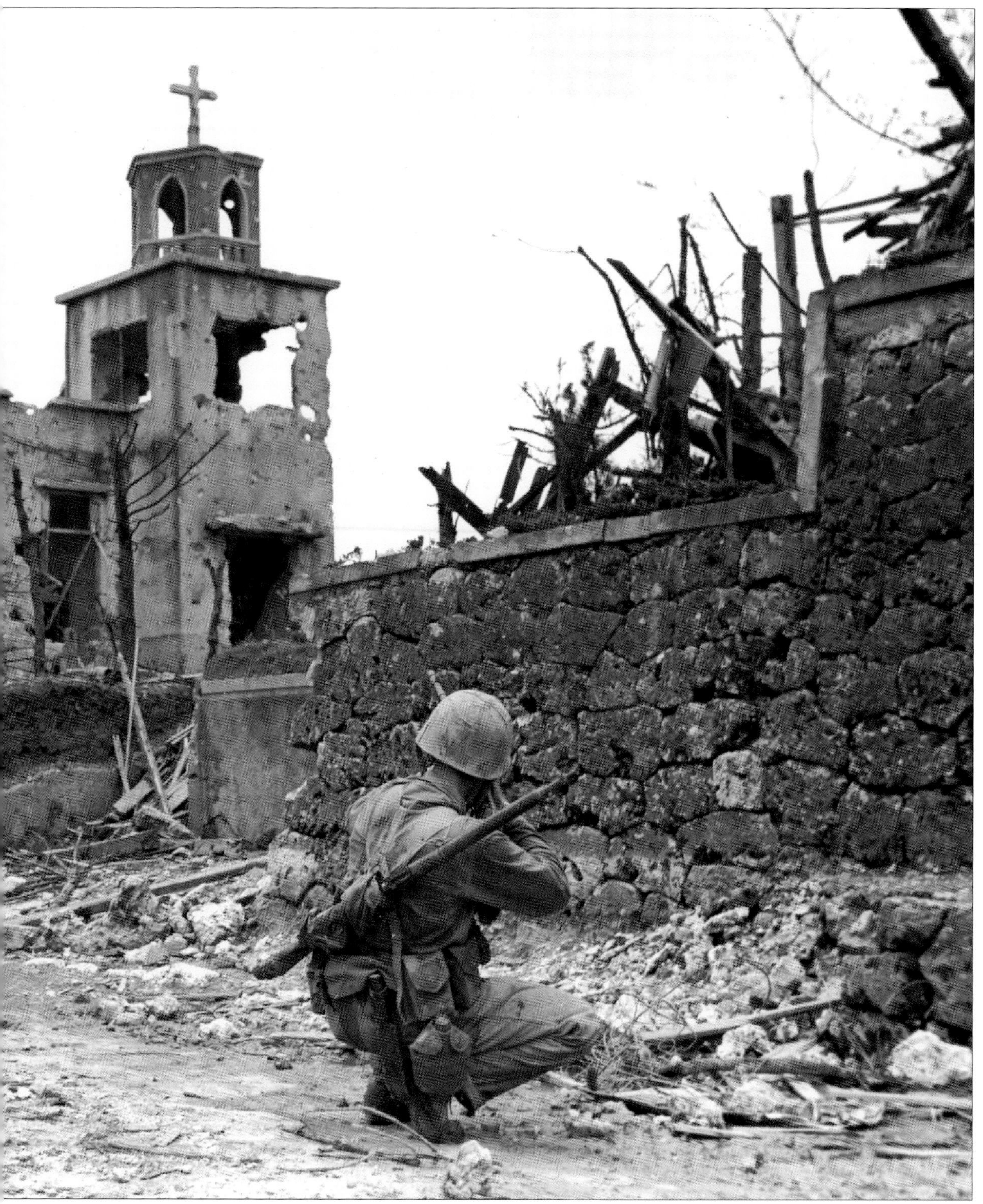

more imposing than Sugar Loaf. Although it lacked the concentrated covering firepower of the Sugar Loaf-Horseshoe-Half Moon complex, it was supported by artillery, mortars, and machine guns from neighboring high ground.

Night Attack

The 7th Marines launched its initial assaults on Kunishi Ridge on June 11, and these were repulsed with heavy losses. Snedeker then ordered a night attack, and by 5.00 a.m. two Marine companies were on the crest. They mowed down surprised Japanese troops who were cooking breakfast. Soon enough, the Japanese shook off the shock and mounted heavy counterattacks against the two Marine companies. Three attempts to reinforce the Marine contingent atop Kunishi Ridge were thrown back.

Innovation and courage then combined to implement a solution to the growing problem of reinforcing the beleaguered Marines on the high ground. Snedeker sent nine Sherman tanks across the valley, each of them loaded with six Marine riflemen. Once atop Kunishi Ridge, each tank disgorged its cargo through the escape hatch in the bottom of its hull and 22 wounded men were then loaded and evacuated.

Supplies and Reinforcements

As the grinding battle for Kunishi Ridge wore on, the 1st, 5th, and 7th Marines each contributed to the slow but continuing conquest of the strongpoint. The 2nd Battalion, 1st Marines, executed a second successful night attack on June 13, and after a dozen days in combat the 1st Marines was relieved by the 5th Marines. By the time the 7th Marines was relieved on June 18, the heroic 1st Tank Battalion had evacuated 1150 wounded men and delivered 90 tons of critical supplies and 550 reinforcements up the embattled slope. In five days of all-too-familiar fighting, the last heavily defended ridgeline on Okinawa was subdued.

When Colonel Snedeker's fatigued 7th Marines finally trudged rearward, it was relieved by the 8th Marines, a unit of the 2nd Marine Division that had initially been returned to Saipan. When fresh troops were needed to accelerate the land campaign, the 8th Marines was called back to Okinawa.

The Marines mowed down surprised Japanese troops who were having breakfast on Kunishi Ridge.

As the fresh Marine regiment went into the line on the 18th, General Buckner climbed the high ground of Mezado Ridge to observe the deployment. Japanese artillery spotters took note of the cluster of officers in an exposed position, and heavy guns on a nearby ridge opened fire. Five shells crashed down, fracturing the coral formations in a shower of rock shards and shrapnel. Buckner was struck in the chest by a splinter that was roughly the size of a dime. In 10 minutes he was dead, one of the highest-ranking American military officers killed in action in World War II.

General Geiger assumed temporary command of the Tenth Army after Buckner's death, and with the fall of Kunishi Ridge only a few pockets of resistance remained. Five days later, Army General Joseph Stilwell arrived to assume overall command.

Among the last bastions to fall, Hill 89 was occupied by elements of the 7th Infantry Division on June 20, while the 77th Division captured Hill 85. In conjunction with the fighting at Kunishi Ridge, the 6th Marine Division swung southward from the Oroku Peninsula, pounded the survivors of the Japanese 32nd Infantry Regiment, and reached Ara Saki, the southernmost point on Okinawa, where Company G, 2nd Battalion, 22nd Marines, raised the Stars and Stripes.

Interestingly, these Marines were repeating the feat they had accomplished in April at Hedo Misaki in the north.

On June 22, after a grueling campaign, General Geiger declared Okinawa secure. That same day, as the soldiers of the 7th Infantry Division swarmed above the entrance to his headquarters cave on Hill 89, General Ushijima committed ritual suicide along with General Ota. Both officers sliced their bellies open with daggers as a dutiful adjutant decapitated one and then the other. Prior to his death, Cho scrawled on a scrap of paper: "Our strategy, tactics, and techniques were all used to the utmost. We fought valiantly, but it was as nothing before the material strength of the enemy."

Ushijima ordered Yahara to make himself a prisoner of war. "If you die there will be no one left who knows the truth about the battle of Okinawa," he said to the colonel. "Bear the temporary shame, but endure it. This is an order from your Army commander."

The great battle of Okinawa, the climax of World War II in the Pacific, ended after nearly three months of agonizing combat. Both the Marines and the soldiers had fought with incredible valor and resolution to see the terrible campaign through to ultimate victory.

Below: During the long battle for Okinawa, supplies and reinforcements move sluggishly to the front line amid mud left by heavy rains.

IWO JIMA · OKINAWA · KOREA 1950
REVOLUTIONARY WAR 1775–1783 · FRENCH NAVAL WAR 1798–1801 · TRIPOLI 1801–1805 · WAR OF 1812–1815 · FLORIDA INDIAN WARS 1835–1842
UNCOMMON VALOR WAS A COMMON VIRTUE

CONCLUSION

During the dedication of the 3rd Marine Division Cemetery on Iwo Jima in March 1945, Major General Graves B. Erskine intoned: "… Let the world count our crosses! Let them count over and over …"

The United States Marine Corps came of age in World War II. From the Arctic Circle to the tropics, the Marines were true to their emblem of the eagle, globe, and anchor and their ringing motto, "Semper Fidelis". During the war years of 1941 to 1945, the Corps grew from a diminutive force to nearly half a million men on land, sea, and air. Of that number 19,733 were killed and 67,207 wounded, a casualty rate of approximately 17 per cent.

The Marine Corps became a steeled, hardened engine of war—particularly against the determined Japanese enemy in the Pacific. Honing the techniques of amphibious landings on hostile shores, prosecuting the lightning strike of 76 hours at Tarawa, the rigorous campaign warfare that marked extended confrontations on Guadalcanal, Peleliu, Saipan, Iwo Jima, and Okinawa, and achieving combat excellence as pilots locked in death-dealing battles with the pride of the enemy's air forces, Marines proved courageous, unflinching, and willing to give their lives for their comrades and their country.

Opposite: Set in the George Washington Memorial Parkway, the United States Marine Corps' War Memorial shows the raising of the U.S. flag over Mt. Surabachi, Iwo Jima, on February 21, 1945.

Through the course of World War II, 82 Marines exhibited valor beyond the call of duty that was worthy of the Medal of Honor. These examples of selfless sacrifice affirmed the commitment and initiative of the individual Marine to the final victory and ensured, as Secretary of the Navy James Forrestal said of the flag raising on Mount Suribachi, that there would be a Marine Corps for another 500 years.

In 1945, First Lady Eleanor Roosevelt remarked, "The Marines I have seen around the world have the cleanest bodies, the filthiest minds, the highest morale, and the lowest morals of any group of animals I have ever seen. Thank God for the United States Marine Corps!"

Such was high praise, and every Marine who heard these words took pride in them. Although the Corps was already considered an elite force, both internally and externally, that reputation was burnished to a high luster during World War II.

The Marine of World War II brought with him a terrible wrath, a highly trained and motivated mindset, and an unquenchable resolve to win. He left a legacy of personal bravery and established a record of combat achievement unsurpassed in the history of warfare.

Admiral Chester W. Nimitz, Commander-in-Chief Pacific, observed that only with the passage of time could the contribution of the Marines to final victory be fully measured. In some respects, more than 70 years later that contribution is still being assessed.

Marines in the European Theater

The hundreds of thousands of U.S. Marines who participated in World War II in the Pacific dwarfed the numbers of those who were involved in the European Theater of Operations. Fewer than 6000 Marines were committed to the fight against Nazi Germany and Fascist Italy. Nevertheless, they performed numerous functions from guard and gunnery duty aboard U.S. Navy vessels to covert operations under the auspices of the Office of Strategic Services (OSS), the forerunner of the modern Central Intelligence Agency.

Aside from their shipboard duties, the initial Marine presence in the European Theater involved the occupation of Iceland, an island situated along vital shipping lanes from continental Europe to Great Britain, and the site of air and naval facilities that could threaten Allied operations. On May 10, 1940, British Marines occupied Iceland. At the time, the British were strapped for manpower to fight the Germans in France. With the acquiescence of the Icelandic government, the "defense" of Iceland was then transferred to the still non-belligerent United States. On July 7, 1941, the 1st Provisional Marine Brigade, numbering 4100 troops, relieved the British forces on the island. In early 1942, the Marines were replaced by U.S. Army troops. Within two months, the bulk of these Marines were en route to fight in the Pacific.

Marine proficiency in amphibious warfare provided much-needed expertise in the planning of such operations in North Africa, the Mediterranean, and the D-Day landings in Normandy. The first such Marine contribution, however, involved Operation Jubilee, the dress rehearsal for the Normandy invasion that took place at the coastal town of Dieppe, France, on August 19, 1942. Brigadier General Harold D. Campbell, Marine Corps' liaison with the British Staff of Combined Operations, took part in the planning of the raid.

While Allied troops hit the five invasion beaches during the Normandy landings on June 6, 1944, Marine riflemen climbed to high vantage points aboard naval vessels, providing some security against potentially marauding German patrol boats. On August 29, at the French port of Marseilles, Marines from the cruisers *Augusta* and *Philadelphia* occupied German fortifications on neighboring islands and compelled 700 Germans to surrender.

Colonel Peter Ortiz and the Covert Marines

Among the most compelling and least known U.S. Marine exploits of World War II is the saga of 41 intrepid Marines who served with the Office of Strategic Services (OSS) in the European Theater. The covert Marines in Europe parachuted behind enemy lines or were landed on hostile shores, conducting raids and sabotage operations and training resistance fighters to disrupt Nazi logistics.

Although they are a relative few and their number is dwindling, the Marines of World War II who survive today have borne witness to the battle. They have seen the savagery of the struggle from Edson's Ridge to the Umurbrogol, from Turkey Knob to Suribachi to Sugar Loaf. They have brought the story of the U.S. Marine Corps in World War II forward, presenting it to free people everywhere as a reminder that the cost of freedom is substantial. Indeed, it is counted in crosses and remembered with stirring accounts of tremendous heroism.

The Marine Corps and its service in World War II epitomize the high ideals that were laudable then and now, the timeless tenets and values that are still worth defending today.

Among the most colorful OSS Marines was Colonel Peter Ortiz, who received two Navy Crosses for his work with the resistance in France. Ortiz, who spoke 10 languages, served from 1932 to 1937 with the French Foreign Legion and then returned to the United States, settling in Southern California and working in the film industry as a consultant on war films. With the outbreak of World War II, he reenlisted in the Foreign Legion and was captured in France by the Germans. Ortiz endured 18 months of captivity but managed to escape. Returning to the United States, he enlisted in the Marine Corps in June 1942. His combat experience was noted, and Ortiz received a commission as a 2nd lieutenant.

Ortiz conducted several covert operations in conjunction with the British Special Operations Executive and later under the auspices of the OSS. He was seriously wounded in North Africa, and during his recovery he was assigned to Operation Jedburgh, a coordinated British–American effort to lead resistance fighters across Europe in operations against the Nazis.

Accounts relate that Ortiz was fearless. One tale relates that he walked into a bar somewhere in occupied France wearing his Marine uniform beneath a raincoat. He ordered a round of drinks for a group of German officers, dropped the raincoat to reveal the Marine uniform, pulled two pistols, and ordered the Germans to drink toasts to President Roosevelt and the U.S. Marine Corps. Years later, Ortiz said that he escaped without killing the Germans, allowing them to spread the story of the event.

In August 1944, Ortiz and fellow operatives were inserted into southern France. They conducted sabotage operations for two weeks before being cornered and captured. Ortiz spent the rest of the war as a prisoner and was discharged from active duty in 1946. He remained in the Marine Corps Reserve and retired in 1955. He resumed his career in the film industry, working with the likes of actor John Wayne. Peter Ortiz died at the age of 74 on March 16, 1988. He was buried in Arlington National Cemetery, Virginia.

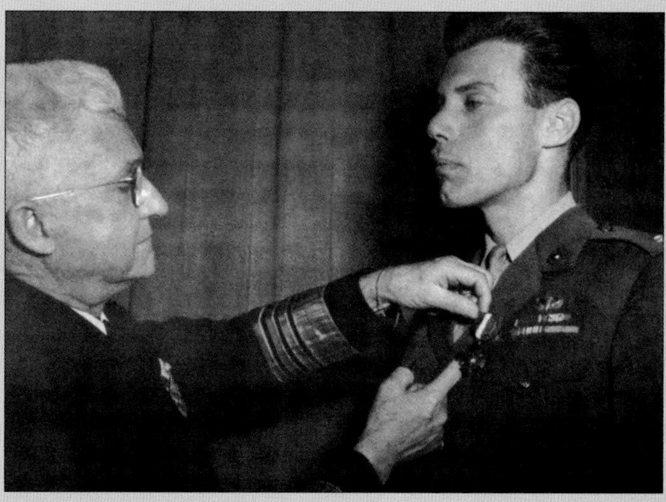

Right: Colonel Peter Ortiz receives his first Navy Cross from Admiral Harold R. Stark in London.

INDEX

Page numbers in *italics* indicate photograph or illustration

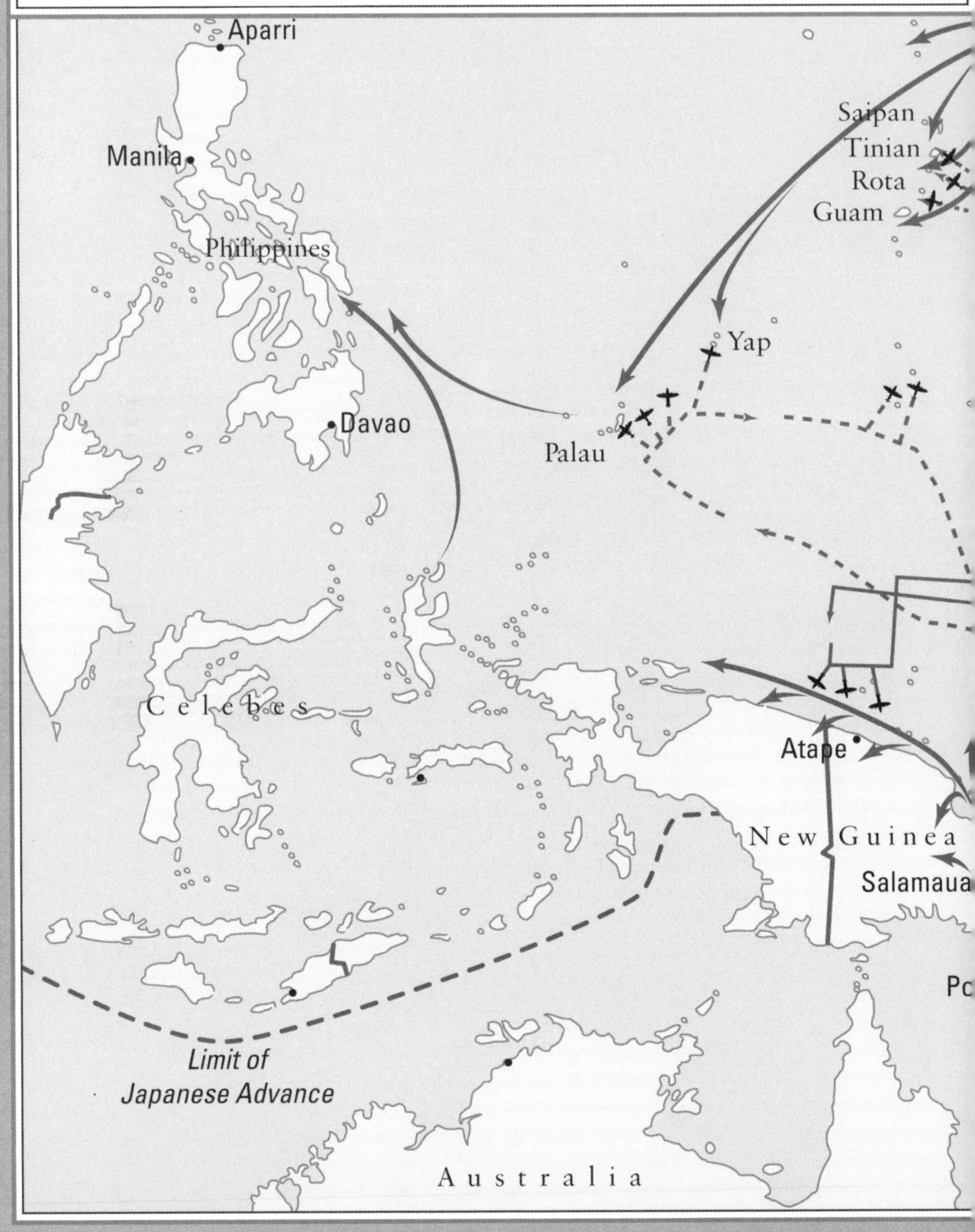
US Operations in the Pacific, 1944
Aparri
Manila
Philippines
Davao
Saipan
Tinian
Rota
Guam
Yap
Palau
Celebes
Atape
New Guinea
Salamaua
Limit of Japanese Advance
Australia